T

MACMILLAN MASTER SERIES

Accounting
Advanced English Language
Advanced Pure Mathematics
Arabic
Banking
Basic Management
Biology
British Politics
Business Administration
Business Communication
Business Law
C Programming
Catering Theory
Chemistry
COBOL Programming
Communication
Databases
Economic and Social History
Economics
Electrical Engineering
Electronic and Electrical Calculations
Electronics
English as a Foreign Language
English Grammar
English Language
English Literature
French
French 2
German

German 2
Global Information Systems
Human Biology
Internet
Italian
Italian 2
Japanese
Manufacturing
Marketing
Mathematics
Mathematics for Electrical and
    Electronic Engineering
Modern British History
Modern European History
Modern World History
Pascal Programming
Philosophy
Photography
Physics
Psychology
Science
Social Welfare
Sociology
Spanish
Spanish 2
Statistics
Study Skills
Visual Basic

Macmillan Master Series
Series Standing Order ISBN 0–333–69343–4
(outside North America only)

You can receive future titles in this series as they are published by placing a standing order.
Please contact your bookseller or, in case of difficulty, write to us at the address below with
your name and address, the title of the series and the ISBN quoted above.

Customer Services Department, Macmillan Distribution Ltd
Houndmills, Basingstoke, Hampshire RG21 6XS, England

Mastering

The Internet

William Buchanan, BSc, CEng, PhD
Senior Lecturer
Department of Electrical and Electronic Engineering
Napier University
Edinburgh

Series Editor
Timothy Davies
Computer Consultant

MACMILLAN

This book is dedicated to the memory of my Father.

First edition 1997

Published by
MACMILLAN PRESS LTD
Houndmills, Basingstoke, Hampshire RG21 6XS
and London
Companies and representatives
throughout the world

ISBN 0–333–69261–6

A catalogue record for this book is available
from the British Library.

This book is printed on paper suitable for recycling and
made from fully managed and sustained forest sources.

10   9   8   7   6   5   4   3   2   1
06   05   04   03   02   01   00   99   98   97

Printed in Great Britain by
Biddles Ltd
Guildford and King's Lynn

Contents

Preface

Data communications is now becoming one of the greatest industries in the world. The key to this growth is the use of the Internet which provides a global interconnection of networks and independently connected computers, using a standard communications standard known as TCP/IP.

Many people confuse the Internet with the World Wide Web (WWW), but the WWW is just one application of the Internet. Other uses include the transmission of electronic mail, remote computer login, transmission of remote data and control of remote devices.

This book covers the main technologies of the Internet, these are:

- Local area networks (Chapter 2).
- TCP/IP (Chapters 3 and 4).
- Electronic Mail (Chapter 5).
- WWW (Chapter 6).
- HTTP and Intranets (Chapter 7).
- HTML (Chapters 8 and 9).
- Javascript (Chapter 10).
- Java (Chapters 11 and 12).
- Windows NT/95 (Chapter 13).

One of the growth in the computing industry in the next few years will be in the development of Java programs. This book gives a basic introduction to Java programming, as well as an introduction to HTML programming.

Further information, from the author, on related subjects, such as emerging technologies and the diagrams from the text, is available on the WWW page:

```
http://www.eece.napier.ac.uk/~bill_b/mti.html
```

Help from the author can also be sought using the email address:

```
w.buchanan@napier.ac.uk
```

or, if unavailable, send an email to `bill_b@www.eece.napier.ac.uk`

Dr William J Buchanan, Napier University.

1 Introduction to the Internet

1.1 Introduction

The uses and the actual physical size of the Internet grows day-by-day. It is an area of technology that is immersed in jargon and ignorance. Many people often confuse the World Wide Web (WWW) with the Internet, but they have different purposes. The Internet, itself, is basically the global interconnection of networks and independently connected computers, whereas the WWW is a collection of computers which store digital information and, using standard transmission method, transmit it over the Internet. The WWW is thus one of the uses of the Internet, others include:

- Electronic mail.
- The connection of remote computers.
- Video conferencing.
- Remote control of remote equipment.
- Remote data acquisition.

The Internet basically exists as a global network. It is not owned by any one organisation or country and is thus not controlled by any political pressures. The data which is carried on the Internet is obviously governed by laws and regulations.

1.2 Standardised addressing

The Internet is an infrastructure of interconnected networks which communicate using the TCP/IP (Transport Control Protocol/Internet Protocol) standard. It can be viewed as a matrix of networks and independently connected computers.

Each node on the Internet has an associated IP address, in the form of W.X.Y.Z and, if they connect to a local area network, have a unique physical address of the form XX:XX:XX:XX (normally called the MAC address). If the node connects to telephone connection then its telephone number is equivalent to the MAC address, as illustrated in Figure 1.1. In general, the IP address is used to route data through the Internet and the MAC address is used to send data from one node to the next.

One way to imagine the relationship between the IP address and the MAC address is to relate it to the transport of a letter through the postal service. Most letters now have a postal (or zip) code along with the full address of the destination. The postal (or zip) code is then used to quickly route the letter through the postal system. Then when it arrives at the area sorting office the actual address of the letter is used to locate the destination of the recipient.

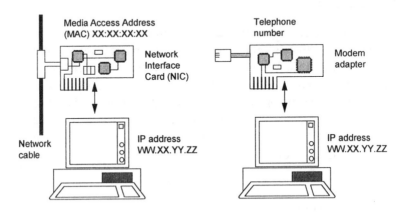

Figure 1.1   Node addresses

1.3 LANs, WANs and MANs

Computer systems operate on digital data and can communicate with other digital equipment over a network or through an independent connection. Networks are normally defined as either:

- Wide area networks (WANs), which normally connect networks over a large physical area, such as between different buildings, towns or even countries.
- Local area networks (LANs), which connect computers within a single office or building. They typically connect to a common electronic connection – commonly known as a network backbone. LANs can connect to other networks either directly or through a WAN.
- Metropolitan area networks (MANs), which normally connect networks around a town or city. An example of a MAN is the EaStMAN network which connects universities and colleges in Edinburgh and Stirling, UK.

The four main methods of connecting a network (or an independently connected computer) to another network are:

- Through a modem connection. A modem converts digital data into an analogue form that can be transmitted over a standard telephone line.
- Through an ISDN connection. An ISDN (integrated services digital network) connection uses the public telephone service. It differs from a modem connection in that the data sent is in a digital form.
- Through a gateway. A gateway connects one type of network to another type.
- Through a bridge or router. Bridges and routers normally connect one type of network to one of the same type.

Modems are used to connect a network (or independently attached computer) over the public switched telecommunications network (PSTN). Normally telephone-type connections are unsuitable for digital data as they have a limited bandwidth of between 400 to 3 400 Hz. The modem must then be used to convert the digital information into an analogue form which is transmittable over the telephones lines. Figure 1.2 illustrates the connection of computers to a PSTN. These computers can connect to the WAN through a service provider (such as CompuServe) or through another network which is connected by modem. The service provider has the required hardware to connect to the WAN.

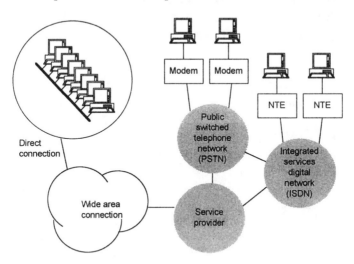

Figure 1.2 Connection of nodes to a PSTN

ISDN allows the transmission of many types of digital data into a truly global digital network. Transmittable data types include digitised video, digitised speech and computer data. Since the switching and transmission are digital, fast access times and relatively high bit-rates are possible. Typical base bit rates include 64 kbps. All connections to the ISDN require network termination equipment (NTE).

1.4 OSI model

A major problem in the electronics industry is the interconnection of equipment and the compatibility of software. Other problems can occur in the connection of electronic equipment in one part of the world to another in another part. For these reasons the International Standards Organisation (ISO) developed a model known as the OSI (open systems interconnection) model. Its main objects were to:

- Allow manufacturers of different systems to interconnect their equipment through standard interfaces.
- Allow software and hardware to integrate well and be portable on differing systems.
- Create a model which all the countries of the world use.

The OSI model is shown in Figure 1.3. Data passes from the top layer of the sender to the bottom and then up from the bottom layer to the top on the recipient. Each layer on the transmitter, though, communicates directly the recipient's corresponding layer. This creates a virtual data flow between layers.

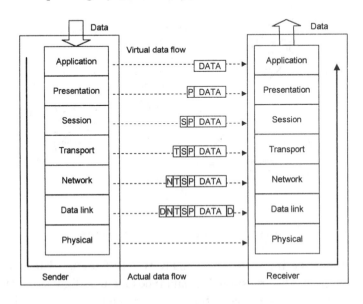

Figure 1.3 Seven-layer OSI model

The top layer (the application layer) initially gets data from an application and appends it with data that the recipients application layer will read. This appended data passes to the next layer (the presentation layer). Again it appends its own data, and so on, down to the physical layer. The physical layer is then responsible for transmitting the data to the recipient. The data sent can be termed a data packet or data frame.

Figure 1.4 shows the basic function of each of the layers.

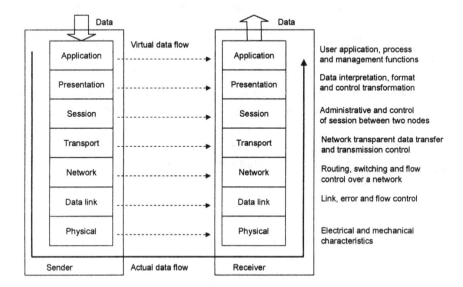

Figure 1.4 ISO open systems interconnection (OSI) model

The functions of the layers are:

1. **Physical**. Defines the electrical characteristics of the communications channel and the transmitted signals, such as voltage levels, connector types, cabling, and so on.
2. **Data link**. Ensures that the transmitted bits are received in a reliable way, such as adding extra bits to define the start and end of a data frame, adding extra error detection/ correction bits and ensuring that multiple nodes do not try to access a common communication channel at the same time.
3. **Network**. Routes data frames through a network. If data packets require to go out of a network then the transport layer routes it through interconnected networks. Its task may involve, for example, splitting up data for transmission and re-assembling it upon reception.
4. **Transport**. Provides an open communications path with the other system. It involves the setting up, maintaining and closing down a session. The communication channel and the internetworking of the data should be transparent to the session layer.

5. **Session**. Provides an open communications path with the other system. It involves the setting up, maintaining and closing down of a session. The communication channel and the internetworking of the data should be transparent to the session layer.
6. **Presentation**. Uses a set of translations that allows the data to be interpreted properly. It may have to carry out translations between two systems if they use different presentation standards such as different character sets or differing character codes. The presentation layer can also add data encryption for security purposes.
7. **Application**. Provides network services to application programs such as file transfer and electronic mail.

Figure 1.5 shows how typical networking systems fit into the OSI model. The data link and physical layers are covered by networking technologies such as Ethernet, Token Ring and FDDI. The networking layer is covered by IP (internet protocol) and transport by TCP (transport control protocol). The IP part routes data packets through a network and TCP routes packets between interconnected network.

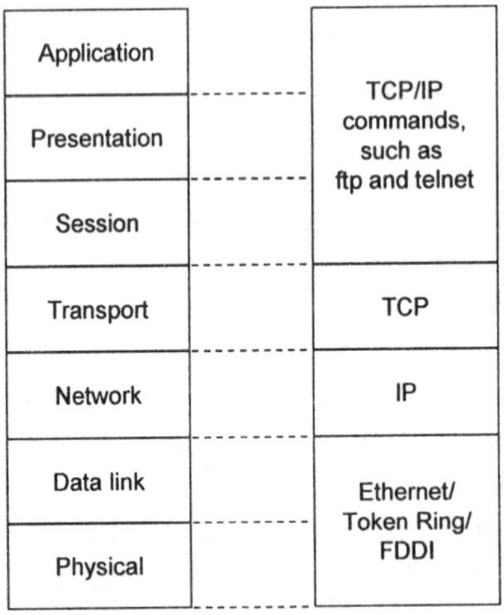

Application	TCP/IP commands, such as ftp and telnet
Presentation	
Session	
Transport	TCP
Network	IP
Data link	Ethernet/ Token Ring/ FDDI
Physical	

Figure 1.5   Typical technologies used in Internet communications

1.5 Network cable types

The cable type used on a network depends on several parameters, including:

- The data bit rate.
- The reliability of the cable.
- The maximum length between nodes.
- The possibility of electrical hazards.
- Power loss in the cables.
- Tolerance to harsh conditions.
- Expense and general availability of the cable.
- Ease of connection and maintenance.
- Ease of running cables, and so on.

The main types of cables used in networks are twisted-pair, coaxial and fibre optic, these are illustrated in Figure 1.6. Twisted-pair and coaxial cables transmit electric signals, whereas fibre optic cables transmit light pulses. Twisted-pair cables are not shielded and thus interfere with nearby cables. Public telephone lines generally use twisted-pair cables. In LANs they are generally used up to bit rates of 10 Mbps and with maximum lengths of 100 m.

Coaxial cable has a grounded metal sheath around the signal conductor. This limits the amount of interference between cables and thus allows higher data rates. Typically they are used at bit rates of 100 Mbps for maximum lengths of 1 km.

The highest specification of the three cables is fibre optic. This type of cable allows extremely high bit rates over long distances. Fibre optic cables do not interfere with nearby cables and give greater security, give more protection from electrical damage from by external equipment, are more resistance to harsh environments and are safer in hazardous environments.

A typical bit rate for a LAN using fibre optic cables is 100 Mbps, in other applications this can reach several gigabits/sec. The maximum length of the fibre optic cable depends on the transmitter and receiver electronics but a single length of 20 km is possible.

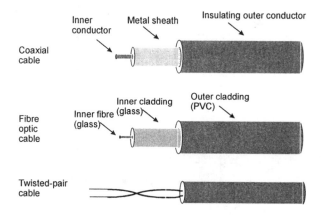

Figure 1.6 Typical network cable types

1.6 LAN Topology

Most computers in organisations connect to the Internet using a LAN. These networks normally consist of a backbone which is a common link to all the networks within the organisation. This backbone allows users on different network segments to communicate and also allows data into and out of the local network. Figure 1.7 shows a local area network which contains various segments: LAN A, LAN B, LAN C, LAN D, LAN E and LAN F. These are connected to the local network via the BACKBONE 1. Thus if LAN A talks to LAN E then the data must travel out of LAN A, onto BACKBONE1, then into LAN C and through onto LAN E.

Networks are partitioned from other networks with a bridge, a gateway or a router. A bridge links a network of one type to a identical type, such as Ethernet to Ethernet, or Token Ring to Token Ring. A gateway connects two dissimilar types of networks and routers operate in a similar way to gateways and can either connect to two similar or dissimilar networks. The key operation of a gateway, bridge or router is that they only allow data traffic through that is intended for another network, which is outside the connected network. This filters traffic and stops traffic, not indented for the network, from clogging-up the backbone. Most modern bridges, gateways and routers are intelligent and can automatically determine the topology of the network.

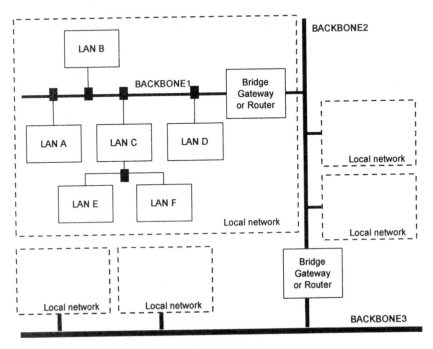

Figure 1.7 Interconnection of local networks

Spanning-tree bridges have built-in intelligence and can communicate with other bridges. They then can build up a picture of the interconnected networks. Then if more than one path exists between individual segments then the bridge automatically finds the alternate routes. This is useful when a fault develops on a route or a route becomes too heavily loaded. Conventional bridges can cause frames to loop around forever.

1.7 Network topologies

There are three basic topologies for LANs, which are shown in Figure 1.8, these are:

- A star network.
- A ring network.
- A bus network.

There are other topologies which are either a combination of two or more topologies or are derivatives of the main types. A typical topology is a tree topology which is essentially a star and a bus network combined, as illustrated in Figure 1.9. A concentrator is used to connect the nodes onto the network.

1.7.1 Star network

In a star topology, a central server switches data around the network. Data traffic between nodes and the server will thus be relatively low. Its main advantages are:

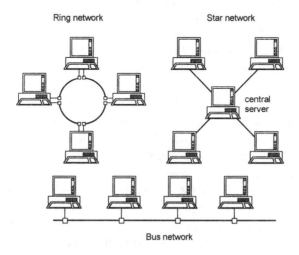

Figure 1.8 Network topologies

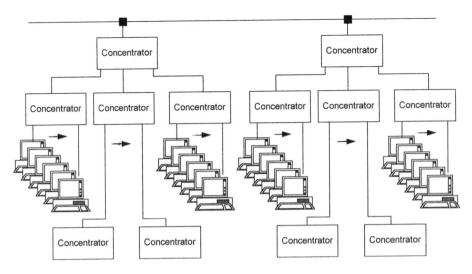

Figure 1.9 Tree topology

- Since the data rate is relatively low between central server and the node, a low-specification twisted-pair cable can be used connect the nodes to the server.
- A fault on one of the nodes will not affect the rest of the network. Typically, mainframe computers use a central server with terminals connected to it.

The main disadvantage of this type of topology is that the network is highly dependent upon the operation of the central server. If it were to slow down significantly then the network becomes slow. Also if it was to become unoperational then the complete network would shut down.

1.7.2 Ring network

In a ring network the computers link together to form a ring. To allow an orderly access to the ring a single electronic token is passed from one computer to the next around the ring, as illustrated in Figure 1.10. A computer can only transmit data when it captures a token. In a manner similar to the star network each link between nodes is basically a point-to-point link and allows almost any transmission medium to be used. Typically twisted-pair cables allow a bit rate of up to 16 Mbps, but coaxial and fibre optic cables are normally used for extra reliability and higher data rates.

A typical ring network is IBM Token Ring. The main advantage of token ring networks is that all nodes on the network have an equal chance of transmitting data. Unfortunately it suffers from several problems, the most severe is that if one of the nodes goes down then the whole network may go down.

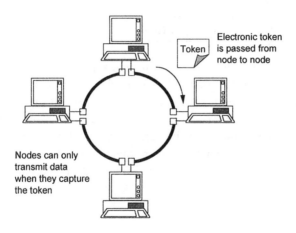

Figure 1.10 Token passing ring network

1.7.3 Bus network

A bus network uses a multi-drop transmission medium, as shown in Figure 1.11. All nodes on the network share a common bus and all share communications. This allows only one device to communicate at a time. A distributed medium access protocol determines which station is to transmit. As with the ring network, data packets contain source and destination addresses. Each station monitors the bus and copies frames addressed to itself.

Twisted-pair cables gives data rates up to 100 Mbps. Coaxial and fibre optic cables give higher bit rates and longer transmission distances. A bus network is a good compromise over the other two topologies as it allows relatively high data rates. Also, if a node goes down then it does not affect the rest of the network. The main disadvantage of this topology is that it requires a network protocol to detect when two nodes are transmitting at the same time. A typical bus network is Ethernet 2.0.

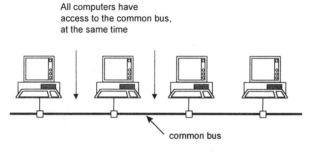

Figure 1.11 Bus topology

1.8 Routers, bridges and repeaters

Networks connect to other networks through repeaters, bridges or routers. A repeater corresponds to the physical layer of the OSI model and always routes data from one network segment to another. Bridges, on the other hand, route data using the data link layer (using the MAC address). Router direct data using the network layer (that is, using the network address, such as the IP address). Normally at the data link layer transmitted data is known as a data frame, while at the network layer it is referred to as a data packet. Figure 1.12 illustrates the 3 interconnection types.

1.8.1 Repeaters

All network connections suffer from a reduction in signal strength (attenuation) and digital pulse distortion. Thus, for a given cable specification and bit rate, each connection will have a maximum length of cable that can be used to transmit the data reliably. Repeaters can be used to increase the maximum interconnection length, and may do the following:

- Clean signal pulses.
- Pass all signals between attached segments.
- Boost signal power.
- Possibly translate between two different media types (such as fibre to twisted-pair cable).

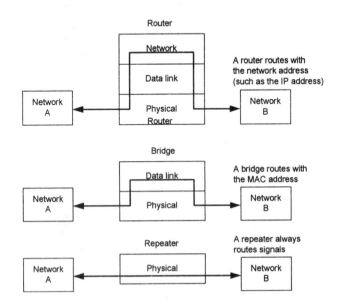

Figure 1.12 Repeaters, bridges and routers

1.8.2 Bridges

Bridges filter input and output traffic so that only data frames distended for a network are actually routed into that network and only data frames destined for the outside are allowed out of the network.

The performance of a bridge is governed by two main factors:

- **The filtering rate**. A bridge reads the MAC address of the Ethernet/ Token ring/ FDDI node and then decides if it should forward the packet into the network. Filter rates for bridges ranges from around 5000 to 70 000 pps (packets per second).
- **The forward rate**. Once the bridge has decided to route the frame into the internetwork then the bridge must forward the frame onto the Internet network media. Forwarding rates range from 500 to 140 000 pps and a typical forwarding rate is 90 000 pps.

A typical Ethernet bridge has the following specifications:

Bit rate: 10 Mbps
Filtering rate: 17 500 pps
Forwarding rate: 11 000 pps
Connectors: 2 DB15 AUI (female), 1 DB9 male console port, 2 BNC
                   (for 10BASE2) or 2 RJ-45 (for 10BASE-T).
Algorithm: Spanning tree protocol. It automatically learns the addresses of all devices on both interconnected networks and builds a separate table for each network.

Spanning tree architecture (STA) bridges

The spanning tree algorithm has been defined by the standard IEEE 802.1. It is normally implemented as software on STA-compliant bridges On power-up they automatically learn the addresses of all nodes on both interconnected networks and build up a separate table for each network.

They can also have two connections between two LANs so that when the primary path becomes disabled, the spanning tree algorithm can re-enable the previously disabled redundant link.

Source route bridging

With source route bridging a source device, not the bridge, is used to send special explorer packets which are then used to determine the best path to the destination. Explorer packets are sent out from the source routing bridges until they reach their destination workstation. Then each source routing bridge along the route enters its address in the routing information field (RIF) of the explorer packet. The destination node then sends back the completed RIF field to the source node. When the source device has determined the best path to the destination, it sends the data message along with the path instructions to the local bridge. It then forwards the data message according to the received path instructions.

1.8.3 Routers

Routers examine the network address field and determine the best route for the packet. They have the great advantage in that they normally support several different types of network layer protocols.

Routers need to communicate with other routers so that they can exchange routing information. Most network operating systems have associated routing protocols which support the transfer of routing information. Typical routing protocols using Internet communications are:

- BGP (border gateway protocol).
- EGP (exterior gateway protocol).
- OSPF (open shortest path first).
- RIP (routing information protocol).

Most routers support RIP and EGP. The main Internet-based protocols are discussed in the next section. In the past RIP was the most popular router protocol standard. Its widespread use is due to no small part to the fact that it was distributed along with the Berkeley Software Distribution (BSD) of UNIX (from which most commercial versions of UNIX are derived). It suffers from several disadvantages and has been largely replaced by OSFP and EGB. These protocols have the advantage over the RIP in that they can handle large internetworks as well reducing routing table update traffic.

RIP uses a distance vector algorithm which measures the number of network jumps (known as hops), up to a maximum of 16, to the destination router. This has the disadvantage that the smallest number of hops is to the best route from source to destination. The OSPF and EGB protocol uses a link state algorithm which can decide between multiple paths to the destination router. These are based, not only hops, but on other parameters such as delay capacity, reliability and throughput.

With distance vector routing each router maintains table by communicating with neighbouring routers. The number of hops in its own table are then computed as it knows the number of hops to local routers. Unfortunately the routing table can take some time to be updated when changes occur, because it takes time for all the routers to communicate with each other (known as slow convergence).

1.9 Exercises

The following questions are multiple choice. Please select from a–d.

1.9.1 The standard networking protocol used on the Internet is:

    (a)   Ethernet
    (b)   TCP/IP
    (c)   SPX/IPX
    (d)   Token Ring

1.9.2 What address is used by computers connecting to the Internet:

    (a)   IP address
    (b)   Node address
    (c)   Interrupt address
    (d)   Router address

1.9.3 What address is used by computers connecting to the Internet:

    (a)   IP address
    (b)   Node address
    (c)   Interrupt address
    (d)   Router address

1.9.4 A network which connects computers within a single building is normally defined as:

    (a)   local area network
    (b)   wide area network
    (c)   metropolitan area network
    (d)   enterprise area network

1.9.5 ISDN differs from a modem connect by the following:

    (a)   ISDN transmits data in an analogue form
    (b)   ISDN allows for a direct connection to a network
    (c)   ISDN does not use the public telephone network
    (d)   ISDN transmits data in a digital form

1.9.6 The three lower layers of the OSI model are:

(a)   Physical, data link and application
(b)   Physical, network and transport
(c)   Physical, data link and network
(d)   Physical, network and session

1.9.7   The function of the data link layer in the OSI model is:

(a)   To ensure that the transmitted bits are received in a reliable way
(b)   Routing, switching and flow control over a network
(c)   Network transparent data transfer and transmission control
(d)   Administrative and control of session between two nodes

1.9.8   The cable which offers the highest bit rate is:

(a)   Fibre optic cable
(b)   Twisted pair cable
(c)   Coaxial cable
(d)   Untwisted pair cable

1.9.9   Which of the following is the main disadvantage of a star network:

(a)   That the data transmitted between the central server and the node is relatively high compared to other network topologies
(b)   That the network is reliant on a central server
(c)   All nodes compete for the network
(d)   Nodes can only transmit data once they have a token

1.9.10   Which of the following is the main disadvantage of a ring network:

(a)   That the data transmitted between the central server and the node is relatively high compared to other network topologies
(b)   That the network is reliant on a central server
(c)   All nodes compete for the network
(d)   A break in the ring stops data from being transmitted

1.9.11   Which of the following is the main disadvantage of a bus network:

(a)   Nodes can only transmit data once they have a token
(b)   That the network is reliant on a central server
(c)   All nodes compete for the network
(d)   A break in the ring stops data from being transmitted

1.9.12 On an Internet-based network which address does a bridge route with:

    (a)   IP address
    (b)   Interrupt address
    (c)   MAC address
    (d)   Source address

1.9.13 On an Internet-based network which address does a router route with:

    (a)   IP address
    (b)   Interrupt address
    (c)   MAC address
    (d)   Source address

2 Local Area Networks (Ethernet)

2.1 Introduction

Most of the computers on the Internet connect through a LAN and the most commonly used LAN is Ethernet. DEC, Intel and the Xerox Corporation initially developed Ethernet and the IEEE 802 committee has since defined standards for it, the most common of which are Ethernet 2.0 and IEEE 802.3. This chapter discusses Ethernet technology and the different types of Ethernet.

In itself Ethernet cannot make a network and needs some other protocol such as TCP/IP to allow nodes to communicate. Unfortunately, Ethernet in its standard form does not cope well with heavy traffic, but this is overcome by the following:

- Ethernet networks are easy to plan and cheap to install.
- Ethernet network components, such as network cards and connectors, are cheap and well supported.
- It is well-proven technology which is fairly robust and reliable.
- It is simple to add and delete computers on the network.
- It is supported by most software and hardware systems.

A major problem with Ethernet is that, because computers must contend to get access to the network, there is no guarantee that they will get access within a given time. This contention also causes problems when two computers try to communicate at the same time then they must both back-off and no data can be transmitted. In its standard form it allows a bit rate of 10 Mbps, but new standards for fast Ethernet systems minimise the problems of contention and also increase the bit rate to 100 Mbps. Ethernet uses coaxial or twisted-pair cable.

Ethernet uses a shared-media, bus-type network topology where all nodes share a common bus. These nodes must then contend for access to the network as only one node can communicate at a time. Data is transmitted in frames which contain the MAC (media access control) source and destination addresses of the sending and receiving node, respectively. The local shared-media is known as a segment. Each node on the network monitors the segment and copies any frames addressed to itself.

Ethernet uses carrier sense, multiple access with collision detection

(CSMA/CD). On a CSMA/CD network, nodes monitor the bus (or Ether) to determine if it is busy. A node wishing to send data waits for an idle condition then transmits its message. Unfortunately collision can occur when two nodes transmit at the same time, thus nodes must monitor the cable when they transmit. When this happens both nodes stop transmitting frames and transmit a jamming signal. This informs all nodes on the network that a collision has occurred. Each of the nodes then waits a random period of time before attempting a re-transmission. As each node has a random delay time then there can be a prioritisation of the nodes on the network. Nodes thus contend for the network and are not guaranteed access to it. Collisions generally slow down the network. Each node on the network must be able to detect collisions and be capable of transmitting and receiving simultaneously. These nodes either connect onto a common Ethernet connection or can connect to an Ethernet hub, as illustrated in Figure 2.1.

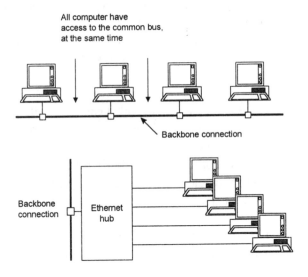

Figure 2.1 Connections to an Ethernet network

2.2 IEEE standards

The IEEE are the main standards organisation for LANs and they refer to the standard for Ethernet as CSMA/CD (carrier sense multiple access/ collision detect). Figure 2.2 shows how the IEEE standards for CSMA/CD fit into the OSI model. The two layers of the IEEE standards correspond to the physical and data link layers of the OSI model. On Ethernet networks, most hardware will comply with IEEE 802.3 standard. The object of the MAC layer is to allow many nodes to share a single communication channel. It also adds start and end frame delimiter, error detection bits, access control information and source and destination addresses. Each data Ethernet has an error detection scheme known as cyclic redundancy check (CRC).

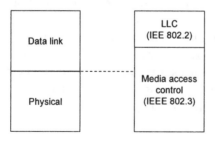

Figure 2.2 Standards for IEEE 802 LANs

2.3 Ethernet - media access control (MAC) layer

When sending data the MAC layer takes the information from the LLC link layer. Figure 2.2 shows the IEEE 802.3 frame format. It contains 2 or 6 bytes for the source and destination addresses (16 or 48 bits each), 4 bytes for the CRC (32 bits), 2 bytes for the LLC length (16 bits). The LLC part may be up to 1500 bytes long. The preamble and delay components define the start and end of the frame. The initial preamble and start delimiter are, in total, 8 bytes long and the delay component is a minimum of 96 bytes long.

A 7-byte preamble precedes the Ethernet 802.3 frame. Each byte of the preamble has a fixed binary pattern of 10101010 and each node on the network uses it to synchronise its clocks and transmission timings. It also informs nodes that a frame is to be sent and for them to check the destination address in the frame.

The end of the frame is a 96-byte delay period which provides the minimum delay between two frames. This slot time delay allows for the worst-case network propagation delay.

The start delimiter field (SDF) is a single byte (or octet) of 10101011. It follows the preamble and identifies that there is a valid frame being transmitted. Most Ethernet systems uses a 48-bit MAC address for the sending and receiving node. Each Ethernet node has a unique MAC address, which is normally defined as hexadecimal digits, such as:

```
        4C – 31 – 22 – 10  – F1 – 32
or      4C31 : 2210: F132.
```

A 48-bit address field allows 2^{48} different addresses (or approximately 281 474 976 710 000 different addresses).

The LLC length field defines whether the frame contains information or it can be used to define the number of bytes in the logical link field. The logical link field can contain up to 1500 bytes of information and has a minimum of 46 bytes, its format is given in Figure 2.3. If the information is greater than the upper limit then multiple frames are sent. Also, if the field is less than the lower limit then it is padded with extra redundant bits.

The 32-bit frame check sequence (or FCS) is an error detection scheme. It is used to determine transmission errors and is often referred to as a cyclic redundancy check (CRC) or simply as checksum.

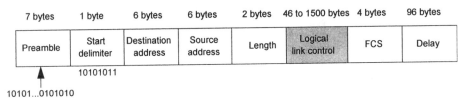

Figure 2.3 IEEE 802.3 frame format

2.4 Ethernet transceivers

Ethernet requires a minimal amount of hardware. The cables used to connect it are either unshielded twisted pair cable (UTP) or coaxial cables. These cables must be terminated with their characteristic impedance, which is $50\,\Omega$ for coaxial cables and $100\,\Omega$ for UTP cables.

Each node has transmission and reception hardware to control access to the cable and also to monitor network traffic. The transmission/ reception hardware is called a transceiver (short for *trans*mitter/re*ceiver*) and a controller builds up and strips down the frame. The transceiver builds the transmits bits at a rate of 10 Mbps – thus the time for one bit is $1/10\times10^{6}$, which is 0.1 µs.

The Ethernet transceiver transmits onto a single ether. When none of the nodes are transmitting then the voltage on the line is +0.7 V. This provides a carrier sense signal for all nodes on the network, it is also known as the heartbeat. If a node detects this voltage then it knows that the network is active and there are no nodes currently transmitting.

Thus when a node wishes to transmit a message it listens for a quiet period. Then if two or more transmitters transmit at the same time then a collision results. When they detect the signal then each node transmits a 'jam' signal. The nodes involved in the collision then wait for a random period of time (ranging from 10 to 90 ms) before attempting to transmit again. Each node on a network also awaits a retransmission. Thus collisions are inefficient in network as they stop nodes from transmitting. Transceivers normally detect collisions by monitoring the DC (or average) voltage on the line.

When transmitting, a transceiver unit transmits the preamble of consecutive 1s and 0s. The coding used is a Manchester code which represents a 0 as a high to a low voltage transition and a 1 as a low to high voltage transition. A low voltage is –0.7 V and a high is +0.7 V. Thus when the preamble is transmitted the voltage will change between +0.7 and –0.7 V, this is illustrated in Figure 2.4. If after the transmission of the preamble no collisions are detected then the rest of the frame is sent.

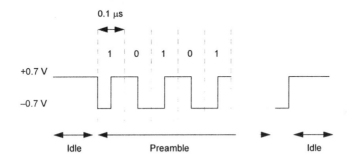

Figure 2.4 Ethernet digital signal

2.5 Ethernet types

The five main types of standard Ethernet are:

- Standard, or thick-wire, Ethernet (10BASE5).
- Thinnet, or thin-wire Ethernet, or Cheapernet (10BASE2).
- Twisted-pair Ethernet (10BASE-T).
- Optical fibre Ethernet (10BASE-FL).
- Fast Ethernet (100BASE-TX or 100VG-Any LAN).

The thin- and thick-wire types connect directly to an Ethernet segment, these are shown in Figure 2.5 and Figure 2.6. Standard Ethernet, 10BASE5, uses a high specification cable (RG-50) and N-type plugs to connect the transceiver to the Ethernet segment. A node connects to the transceiver using a 9-pin D-type connector. A vampire (or bee-sting) connector can be used to clamp the transceiver to the backbone cable.

Thin-wire, or Cheapernet, uses a lower specification cable (it has a lower inner conductor diameter). The cable connector required is also of a lower specification, that is, BNC rather than N-type connectors. In standard Ethernet the transceiver unit is connected directly onto the backbone tap. On a Cheapernet network the transceiver is integrated into the node.

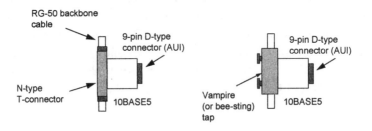

Figure 2.5 Ethernet connections for Thick Ethernet

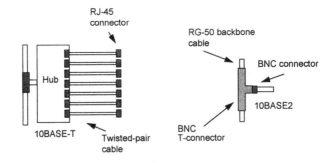

Figure 2.6 Ethernet connections for Thin Ethernet and 10BASE-T

Many modern Ethernet connections are to a 10BASE-T hub which connects UTP cables to the Ethernet segment. An RJ-45 connector is used for 10BASE-T. The fibre optic type, 10BASE-FL, allows long lengths of interconnected lines, typically up to 2 km. They use either SMA connectors or ST connectors. SMA connectors are screw-on types while ST connectors are push-on. Table 2.1 shows the basic specifications for the different types.

2.6 Twisted-pair hubs

Twisted-pair Ethernet (10BASE-T) nodes normally connect to the backbone using a hub, as illustrated in Figure 2.7. Connection to the twisted-pair cable is via an RJ-45 connector. The connection to the backbone can either be to thin- or thick-Ethernet. Hubs can also be stackable where one hub connects to another. This leads to concentrated area networks (CANs) and limits the amount of traffic on the backbone. Twisted-pair hubs normally improve network performance.

10BASE-T uses 2 twisted pairs cables, one for the transmit and one for the receive. A collision occurs when the node (or hub) detects that it is receiving data when it is currently transmitting data.

Table 2.1 Ethernet network parameters

Parameter	10BASE5	10BASE2	10BASE-T
Common name	Standard or thick-wire Ethernet	Thinnet or thin-wire Ethernet	Twisted-pair Ethernet
Data rate	10 Mbps	10 Mbps	10 Mbps
Maximum segment length	500 m	200 m	100 m
Maximum nodes on a segment	100	30	3
Maximum number of repeaters	2	4	4
Maximum nodes per network	1024	1024	
Minimum node spacing	2.5 m	0.5 m	No limit
Location of transceiver electronics	located at the cable connection	integrated within the node	in a hub
Typical cable type	RG-50 (0.5″ diameter)	RG-6 (0.25″ diameter)	UTP cables
Connectors	N-type	BNC	RJ-45/ Telco
Cable impedance	50 Ω	50 Ω	100 Ω

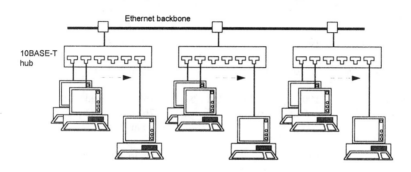

Figure 2.7 10BASE-T connection

2.7 100 Mbps Ethernet

Standard 10 Mbps Ethernet does not perform well when many users are running multi-media applications. Two improvements to the standard are Fast Ethernet (IEEE 802.3u) and 100VG-AnyLAN (IEEE 802.12). These give, at least, ten times the performance of standard Ethernet. New standards relating to 100 Mbps Ethernet are now becoming popular. The main types are:

- 100BASE-T (twisted-pair) – which uses 100 Mbps over two pairs of high quality twisted-pair cables (known as Cat-5 UTP cable).
- 100VG-AnyLAN (twisted-pair) – which uses 100 Mbps over two pairs of Cat-5 UTP cable.

2.7.1 100BASE-T

Fast Ethernet, or 100BASE-T, is simply 10BASE-T running at ten times the bit rate. It is a natural progression from standard Ethernet and thus allows existing Ethernet networks to be easily upgraded. Unfortunately, as with standard Ethernet, nodes contend for the network which reduces the network efficient when there are high traffic rates. Also, as it uses collision detect, the maximum segment length is limited by the amount of time for the farthest nodes on a network to properly detect collisions. On a Fast Ethernet network with twisted-pair copper cables this distance is 100 m and for a fibre optic link it is 400 m. Table 2.2 outlines the main network parameters for Fast Ethernet.

Since 100BASE-T standards are compatible with 10BASE-T networks then the network allows both 10 Mbps and 100 Mbps bit rates on the line. This makes upgrading simple as the only addition to the network is dual speed interface adapters. Nodes with the 100 Mbps capabilities can communicate at 100 Mbps, while they can also communicate with other, slower nodes, at 10 Mbps.

Table 2.2 Fast Ethernet network parameters

	100BASE-TX	100VG-AnyLAN
Standard	IEEE 802.3u	IEEE 802.12
Bit rate	100 Mbps	100 Mbps
Actual throughput	Up to 50 Mbps	Up to 96 Mbps
Maximum distance (hub to node)	100 m (twisted-pair, CAT-5) 400 m (fibre)	100 m (twisted-pair, CAT-3) 200 m (twisted-pair, CAT-5) 2 km (fibre)
Scaleability	None	Up to 400 Mbps
Advantages	Easy migration from 10BASE-T	Greater throughput, greater distance

2.7.2 100VG-AnyLAN

The 100VG-AnyLAN standard (IEEE 802.12) was developed mainly by Hewlett Packard and overcomes the contention problem by using a priority based, round robin arbitration method, known as Demand Priority Access Method (DPAM). Unlike Fast Ethernet, nodes always connect to a hub which regularly scans its input ports to determine if any nodes have requests pending.

100VG-AnyLAN has the great advantage that it supports both IEEE 802.3 (Ethernet) and IEEE 802.5 (Token ring) frames and can thus integrate well with existing 10BaseT and Token ring networks.

100VG-Any has an in-built priority mechanism with two priority levels: a high priority request and a normal priority request. A normal priority request is used for non-real time data, such as data files, and so on. High priority requests are used for real-time data, such as speech or video data. At present there is limited usage of this feature in hubs and there is no support mechanism for this facility once the data has left the hub.

100VG-AnyLAN allows up to seven level hubs (that is, one root and six cascaded hubs) with a maximum distance of 150 m between nodes. Unlike other forms of Ethernet it allows any number of nodes to be connected to a segment (for example 10BASE5 limits the number of nodes per segment to 100).

2.7.3 Migration to Fast Ethernet

If an existing network is based on standard Ethernet then, in most cases, the best network upgrade is either to Fast Ethernet or 100VG-AnyLAN. Since the protocols and access methods are the same there is no need to change any of network management software or application programs. The upgrade path for Fast Ethernet is simple and could be:

- Upgrade high data rate nodes, such as servers or high powered workstations to Fast Ethernet;
- Gradually upgrade NICs (Network Interface Cards) on Ethernet segments to cards which support both 10BASE-T and 100BASE-T. These cards automatically detect the transmission rate to give either 10 or 100 Mbps.

The upgrade path to 100VG-AnyLAN is less easy as it relies on hubs and, unlike Fast Ethernet, most NICs have different network connectors, one for 10BASE-T and the other for 100VG-AnyLAN (although it is likely that more NICs will have automatic detection). A possible path could be:

- Upgrade high data rate nodes, such as servers or high powered workstations to 100VG-AnyLAN.
- Install 100VG-AnyLAN hubs.

- Connect nodes to 100VG-AnyLAN hubs and change-over connectors.

It is difficult to assess the performance differences between Fast Ethernet and 100VG-AnyLAN. Fast Ethernet uses a well proven technology but suffers from network contention. 100VG-AnyLAN is a relatively new technology and the handshaking with the hub increases delay time. The maximum data throughput of a 100BASE-TX network is limited to around 50 Mbps, whereas 100VG-AnyLAN allows rates up to 96 Mbps.

The 100BASE-TX standard does not allow future upgrading of the bit rate, whereas 100VG-AnyLAN allows possible upgrades to 400 Mbps.

2.8 Exercises

2.8.1   The base bit rate of standard Ethernet is:

  (a)   1 kbps
  (b)   1 Mbps
  (c)   10 Mbps
  (d)   100 Mbps

2.8.2   The base bit rate of fast Ethernet is:

  (a)   1 kbps
  (b)   1 Mbps
  (c)   10 Mbps
  (d)   100 Mbps

2.8.3   Standard Ethernet (Thick-wire Ethernet) is also known as:

  (a)   10BASE2
  (b)   10BASE5
  (c)   10BASE-T
  (d)   10BASE-FL

2.8.4   Thin-wire Ethernet (Cheapernet) is also known as:

  (a)   10BASE2
  (b)   10BASE5
  (c)   10BASE-T
  (d)   10BASE-FL

2.8.5   Standard Ethernet (Thick-wire Ethernet) uses which type of cable:

    (a)   Twisted-pair cable
    (b)   Coaxial cable
    (c)   Fibre optic cable
    (d)   Radio link

2.8.6   Thin-wire Ethernet (Cheapernet) uses which type of cable:

    (a)   Twisted-pair cable
    (b)   Coaxial cable
    (c)   Fibre optic cable
    (d)   Radio link

2.8.7   The IEEE standard for Ethernet is:

    (a)   IEEE 802.1
    (b)   IEEE 802.2
    (c)   IEEE 802.3
    (d)   IEEE 802.4

2.8.8   The main disadvantage of Ethernet is that:

    (a)   Computer must contend for the network.
    (b)   It does not network well.
    (c)   It is unreliable.
    (d)   It is not secure.

2.8.9   A MAC address has how many bits:

    (a)   8 bits
    (b)   24 bits
    (c)   32 bits
    (d)   48 bits

2.8.10   Which bit pattern identifies the start of an Ethernet frame:

    (a)   11001100...1100
    (b)   00000000...0000
    (c)   11111111...1111
    (d)   10101010...1010

2.8.11 The main standards relating to Ethernet networks are:

    (a)   IEEE 802.2 and IEEE 802.3
    (b)   IEEE 802.3 and IEEE 802.4
    (c)   ANSI X3T9.5 and IEEE 802.5
    (d)   EIA RS-422 and IEEE 802.3

2.8.12 Which layer in the Ethernet standard communicates with the OSI network layer:

    (a)   the MAC layer
    (b)   the LLC layer
    (c)   the Physical layer
    (d)   the Protocol layer

2.8.13 Standard, or thick-wire, Ethernet is also known as:

    (a)   10BASE2
    (b)   10BASE5
    (c)   10BASE-T
    (d)   10BASE-F

2.8.14 Twisted-pair Ethernet is also known as:

    (a)   10BASE2
    (b)   10BASE5
    (c)   10BASE-T
    (d)   10BASE-F

2.8.15 Fibre optic Ethernet is also known as:

    (a)   10BASE2
    (b)   10BASE5
    (c)   10BASE-T
    (d)   10BASE-F

2.8.16 Which type of connector does twisted-pair Ethernet use when connecting to a network hub:

    (a)   N-type
    (b)   BNC
    (c)   RJ-45
    (d)   SMA

2.8.17   Which type of connector does Cheapernet, or thin-wire Ethernet, use
when connecting to the network backbone:

(a)   N-type
(b)   BNC
(c)   RJ-45
(d)   SMA

2.8.18   What is the function of a repeater in an Ethernet network:

(a)   it increases the bit rate
(b)   it isolates network segments
(c)   it prevents collisions
(d)   it boosts the electrical signal

2.8.19   Discuss the limitation of 10BASE5 and 10BASE2 Ethernet.

3 Transmission Control Protocol (TCP) and Internet Protocol (IP)

3.1 Introduction

Networking technologies, such as Ethernet, Token Ring and FDDI provide a data link layer function, that is, they allow a reliable connection between one computer and another on the same network. They do not provide inter-networking where data can be transferred from one network to another, or one network segment to another. For data to be transmitted across network requires an addressing structure which is read by a gateway or router. The interconnection of networks is known as internetworking (or internet for short) and each part of an internet is known as a subnetwork (or subnet).

TCP/IP are a pair of protocols which allow one subnet to communicate with another, where a protocol is defined as a set of rules which allow the orderly exchange of information. The IP protocol corresponds to the network layer of the OSI model and the TCP part to the transport layer. Their operation is thus transparent to the physical and data link layers and can thus be used on Ethernet, FDDI or Token Ring networks, as illustrated in Figure 3.1. The address of the data link layer corresponds to the physical address of the node, such as the MAC address (in Ethernet and Token Ring) or the telephone number (for a modem connection) and IP address is assigned to each node on the internet. It is used to identify the location of the network and any subnets.

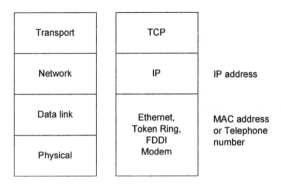

Figure 3.1 TCP/IP and the OSI model

TCP/IP was originally developed by the US Defense Advanced Research Projects Agency (DARPA) and their objective was to connect a number of universities and other research establishments to DARPA. The resulting internet is now known as the Internet and it has since outgrown this application with many commercial organisations now connecting to the Internet. The Internet uses TCP/IP to transfer data, where each node is assigned a unique network address, called an IP address. Note that any organisation can have its own internets, but if it is to connect to the Internet then the addresses must conform to the Internet addressing format.

The ISO have adopted TCP/IP as the basis for the standards relating to the network and transport layers of the OSI model. This standard is known as ISO-IP and the most currently available systems conform to the IP addressing standard.

Common applications which use TCP/IP communications are remote login and file transfer. Typical programs used in file transfer and login over TCP communication are `ftp` for file transfer program and `telnet` which allows remote log into another computer. Another useful program is `ping` which determines if a node is responding to TCP/IP communications.

3.2 TCP/IP gateways and hosts

TCP/IP hosts are nodes which communicate over interconnected networks using TCP/IP communications. A TCP/IP gateway node connects one type of network to another. It thus contains the required hardware to link the two different physical link connects between the different networks and also the hardware and software to convert frames from one network to the other. Typically, it converts a Token Ring MAC layer to an equivalent Ethernet MAC layer, and viceversa.

A router connects a network of a similar type to another of the same kind through a point-to-point link. The main operational difference between a gateway, a router, and a bridge, is that, for a Token Ring and Ethernet network, the bridge uses the 48-bit MAC address to route frames, whereas the gateway and router uses an IP network address. As an analogy to the public telephone system, the MAC address would be equivalent to a randomly assigned telephone number, whereas the IP address would contain the information on logically where the telephone is located, such as which country, area code, and so on.

Figure 3.2 shows how a gateway routes information. The gateway reads the frame from the computer on network A and it then reads the IP address contained in the frame. From this it makes a decision whether it is routed out of network A to network B. If it does then it relays the frame to network B.

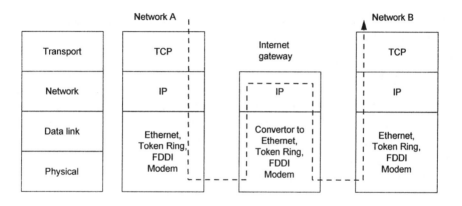

Figure 3.2 Internet gateway layers

3.3 Function of the IP protocol

The main functions of the IP protocol are to:

- Route IP data frames – which are called internet datagrams – around an internet. The IP protocol program running on each node knows the location of the gateway on the network. The gateway must then be able to locate the interconnected network. Data then passes from node to gateway through the internet.
- Fragment the data into smaller units if the data is greater than a given amount (64 kB).
- Report errors. When a datagram is being routed or is being reassembled an error can occur. If this happens then the node that detects the error reports back to the source node. Datagrams are deleted from the network if they travel through the network for more than a set time. Again, an error message is returned to the source node to inform it that the internet routing could not find a route for the datagram or that the destination node, or network, does not exist.

3.4 Internet datagram

The IP protocol is an implementation of the network layer of the OSI model. It adds a data header onto the information passed from the transport layer, the resultant data packet is known as an internet datagram. The header contains information such as the destination and source IP addresses, the version number of the IP protocol and so on. Figure 3.3 shows its format.

The datagram can contain up to 65 536 bytes (64 kB) of data. If the data to be transmitted is less than, or equal to, 64 kB, then it is sent as one datagram. If it is more than this then the sender splits the data into fragments and sends multiple datagrams. When transmitted from the source each datagram is routed separately through the internet and the received fragments are finally reassembled at the destination.

The fields in the IP datagram are:

- **Version**. The TCP/IP `version number` helps gateways and nodes interpret the data unit correctly. Differing versions may have a different format or the IP protocol interprets the header differently.
- **Type of service**. The `type of service` bit field is an 8-bit bit pattern in the form `PPPDTRXX`, where `PPP` defines the priority of the datagram (from 0 to 7), `D` sets a low delay service, `T` sets high throughput, `R` sets high reliability and `XX` are currently not used.
- **Header length**. The `header length` defines the size of the data unit in multiplies of 4 bytes (32 bits). The minimum length is 5 bytes and the maximum is 65 536 bytes. Padding bytes fill any unused spaces.
- **D and M bits**. A gateway may route a datagram and split it into smaller fragments. The `D` bit informs the gateway that it should not fragment the data and thus it signifies that a receiving node should receive the data as a single unit or not at all. The `M` bit is the more fragments bit and is used when data is split into fragments. The `fragment offset` contains the fragment number.
- **Time-to-live**. A datagram could propagate through the internet indefinitely. To prevent this, the 8-bit `time-to-live` value is set to the maximum transit time in seconds and is set initially by the source IP. Each gateway then decrements this value by a defined amount. When it becomes zero the datagram is discarded. It also defines the maximum amount of time that a destination IP node should wait for the next datagram fragment.
- **Protocol**. Different IP protocols can be used on the datagram. The 8-bit `protocol` field defines the type to be used.
- **Header checksum**. The `header checksum` contains a 16-bit pattern for error detection.
- **Source and destination IP addresses**. The `source` and `destination IP addresses` are stored in the 32-bit source and destination IP address fields.
- **Options**. The `options` field contains information such as debugging, error control and routing information.

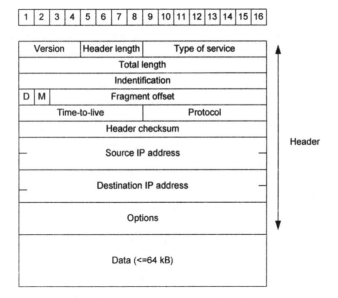

| 1 | 2 | 3 | 4 | 5 | 6 | 7 | 8 | 9 | 10 | 11 | 12 | 13 | 14 | 15 | 16 |

Figure 3.3   Internet datagram format and contents

3.5 ICMP

Messages, such as control data, information data and error recovery data, are carried between Internet hosts using the Internet Control Message Protocol (ICMP). These messages are sent with a standard IP header. Typical messages are:

- Destination unreachable (message type 3) – which is sent by a host on the network to say that a host is unreachable. The message can also include the reason the host cannot be reached.
- Echo request/echo reply (message type 8 or 0) – which is used to check the connectivity between two hosts. The ping command uses this message, where it sends an ICMP "echo request" message to the target host and waits for the destination host to reply with an "echo reply" message.
- Redirection (message type 5) – which is sent by a router to a host that is requesting its routing services. This helps to find the shortest path to a desired host.
- Source quench (message type 4) – which is used when a host cannot receive anymore IP packets at the present.

The ICMP message starts with three fields, as shown in Figure 3.4. The message type has 8 bits and identifies the type of message, these are identified in Table 3.1. The code field is also 8 bits long and a checksum field is 16 bits long. The information after this field depends on the type of message.

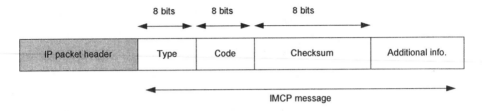

Figure 3.4 ICMP message format

The addition informational for the following message types are:

- For echo request and reply, the message header is followed by an 8-bit identifier, then an 8-bit sequence number followed by the original IP header.
- For destination unreachable, source quelch and time, the message header is followed by 32-bits which are used and then the original IP header.
- For timestamp request, the message header is followed by a 16-bit identifier, then by a 16-bit sequence number, followed by a 32-bit originating timestamp.

Table 3.1 Message type field value

Value	Message type	Value	Message type
0	Echo reply	12	Parameter problem
3	Destination unreachable	13	Timestamp request
4	Source quench	14	Timestamp reply
5	Redirect	17	Address mask request
8	Echo request	18	Address mask reply
11	Time-to-live exceeded		

3.6 TCP/IP internets

Figure 3.5 illustrates a sample TCP/IP implementation. A gateway MERCURY provides a link between a token ring network (NETWORK A) and the Ethernet network (ETHER C). Another gateway PLUTO connects NETWORK B to ETHER C. The TCP/IP protocol allows a host on NETWORK A to communicate with VAX01.

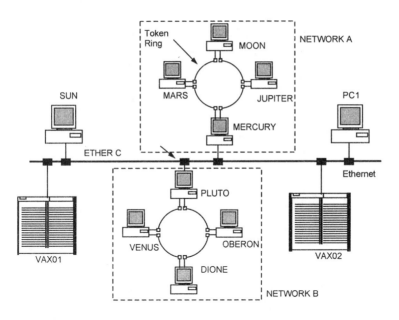

Figure 3.5 Example internet

3.6.1 Selecting internet addresses

Each node using TCP/IP communications requires a IP address which is then matched to its Token Ring or Ethernet MAC address. The MAC address allows nodes on the same segment to communicate with each other. In order for nodes on a different network to communicate, each must be configured with an IP address.

Nodes on a TCP/IP network are either hosts or gateways. Any nodes that run application software or are terminals are hosts. Any node which routes TCP/IP packets between networks is called a TCP/IP gateway node. This node must have the necessary network controller boards to physically interface to other networks it connects with.

3.6.2 Format of the IP address

A typical IP address consists of two fields: the left field (or the network number) which identifies the network, and the right number (or the host number) which identifies the particular host within that network. Figure 3.6 illustrates this.

The IP address is 32 bits long and can address over 4 million physical networks (2^{32} or 4 294 967 296 hosts). There are three different address formats, these are shown in Figure 3.7. Each of these types is applicable to certain types of networks. Class A allows up to 128 (2^{7}) different networks and up to 16 777 216 (2^{24}) hosts on each network. Class B allows up to 16 384 networks and up to 65 536 hosts on each network. Class C allows up to 2 097 152 networks each with up to 256 hosts.

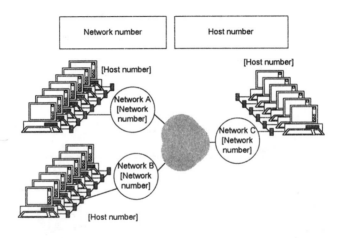

Figure 3.6 IP addressing over networks

The class A address is thus useful where there are a small number of networks with a large number of hosts connected to them. Class C is useful where there are many networks with a relatively small number of hosts connected to each network. Class B addressing gives a good compromise of networks and connected hosts.

When selecting internet addresses for the network, the address can be specified simply with decimal numbers within a specific range. The standard DARPA IP addressing format is of the form:

$$W.X.Y.Z$$

where W, X, Y and Z represent 1 byte of the IP address. As decimal numbers they range from 0 to 255. The 4 bytes together represent both the network and host address.

The valid range of the different IP addresses is given in Figure 3.7 and Table 3.2 defines the valid IP addresses. Thus for a class A type address there can be 127 networks and 16 711 680 (256×256×255) hosts. Class B can have 16 320 (64×255) networks and class C can have 2 088 960 (32×256×255) networks and 255 hosts.

Addresses above 223.255.254 are reserved, as are addresses with groups of zeros.

Table 3.2 Ranges of addresses for type A, B and C internet address

Type	Network portion	Host portion
A	1 - 126	0.0.1 - 255.255.254
B	128.1 - 191.254	0.1 - 255.254
C	192.0.1 - 223.255.254	1 - 254

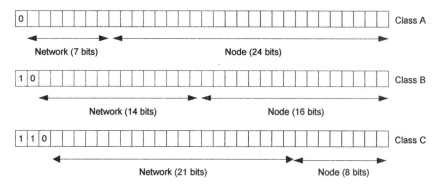

Figure 3.7 Type A, B and C IP address classes

3.6.3 Creating IP addresses with subnet numbers

Besides selecting IP addresses of internets and host numbers, it is also possible to designate an intermediate number called a subnet number. Subnets extend the network field of the IP address beyond the limit defined by the type A, B, C scheme. They allow a hierarchy of internets within a network. For example, it is possible to have one network number for a network attached to the internet, and various subnet numbers for each subnet within the network. This is illustrated in Figure 3.8.

For an address X.Y.Z.W and type for a type A address X specifies the network and Y the subnet. For type B the Z field specifies the subnet, as illustrated in Figure 3.9.

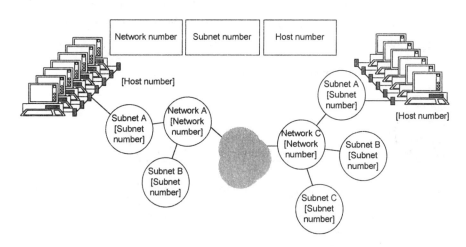

Figure 3.8 IP addresses with subnets

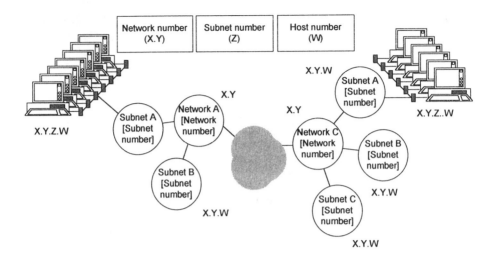

Figure 3.9 Internet addresses with subnets

To connect to a global network a number is normally assigned by a central authority. For the Internet network it is assigned by the Network Information Centre (NIC). Typically, on the Internet an organisation is assigned a type B network address. The first two fields of the address specify the organisation network, the third specifies the subnet within the organisation and the final specifies the host.

3.6.4 Specifying subnet masks

If a subnet is used then a bit mask, or subnet mask, must be specified to show which part of the address is the network part and which is the host.

The subnet mask is a 32-bit number which has 1s for bit positions specifying the network and subnet parts and 0s for the host part. A text file called `hosts` is normally used to set up the subnet mask. Table 3.3 shows example subnet masks.

Table 3.3 Default subnet mask for type A, B and C IP addresses

Address Type	Default mask
Class A	255.0.0.0
Class B	255.255.0.0
Class C and Class B with a subnet	255.255.255.0

To set up the default mask the following line is added to the `hosts` file.

```
📄 Hosts file
255.255.255.0  defaultmask
```

3.7 Domain name system

An IP address can be defined in the form WWW.XXX.YYY.ZZZ, where XXX, YYY, ZZZ and WWW are integer values in the range 0 to 255. On the Internet the WWW.YYY.YYY part normally defines the subnet and the ZZZ the host. Such names may be difficult to remember and a better method is to use symbolic names rather than IP addresses.

Users and application programs can then use symbolic names rather than IP addresses. The directory network services on the Internet determines the IP address of the named destination user or application program. This has the advantage that users and application program can move around the Internet and are not fixed to an IP address.

An analogy relates to the public telephone service. A phone directory contains a list of subscribers and their associated telephone numbers. If someone looks for a telephone number, first the user's name is looked-up and their associated phone number found. The telephone directory listing maps a user's name (symbolic name) to an actual telephone number (the actual address).

Table 3.4 lists some example Internet domain assignments for World Wide Web (WWW) servers. Note that domain assignments are not fixed and can change their corresponding IP addresses, if required. The binding between the symbolic name and its address can thus change at any time.

Table 3.4 Example Internet network addresses

Web server	Internet domain names	Internet IP address
NEC	web.nec.com	143.101.112.6
Sony	www.sony.com	198.83.178.11
Intel	www.intel.com	134.134.214.1
IEEE	www.ieee.com	140.98.1.1
University of Bath	www.bath.ac.uk	136.38.32.1
University of Edinburgh	www.ed.ac.uk	129.218.128.43
IEE	www.iee.org.uk	193.130.181.10
University of Manchester	www.man.ac.uk	130.88.203.16

3.8 Internet naming structure

The Internet naming structure uses labels separated by periods, an example is eece.napier.ac.uk. It uses a hierarchical structure where organisations are grouped into primary domain names. These are com (for commercial organisations), edu (for educational organisations), gov (for government organisations), `mil` (for military organisations), `net` (Internet network support centres) or `org` (other organisations). The primary domain name may also define which country the host is located, such as `uk` (United Kingdom), `fr` (France), and so on. All hosts on the Internet must be registered to one of these primary domain names.

The labels after the primary field relate the subnets within the network. For example in the address `eece.napier.ac.uk`, the `ac` label relates to an academic institution within the `uk`, `napier` to the name of the institution and `eece` the subnet with that organisation. An example structure is illustrated in Figure 3.10.

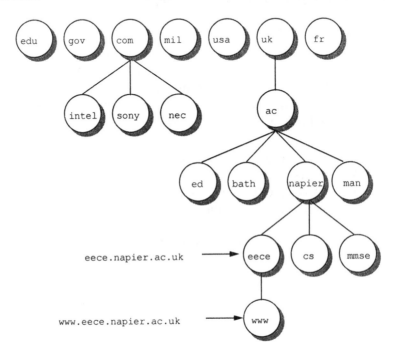

Figure 3.10   Example domain naming

3.9 Domain name server

Each institution on the Internet has a host which runs a process called the domain name server (DNS). The DNS maintains a database called the directory information base (DIB) which contains directory information for that institution. When a new host is added, the system manager adds its name and its IP address. It can then access the Internet.

A computer which wishes to communicate with another node will communicate with the DNS in order to determine its MAC address (that is the physical address of the remote computer).

3.10 Example network

A university network is shown in Figure 3.11. The connection to the outside global Internet network is via the Janet gateway node, its IP address is 146.176.1.3. Three subnets 146.176.160, 146.176.129 and 146.176.151 connect the gateway to departmental bridges. The Computer Studies bridge address is 146.176.160.1 and the Electrical department bridge has an address 146.176.151.254.

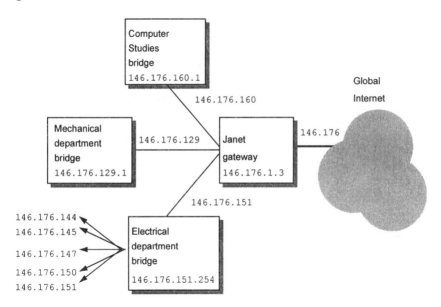

Figure 3.11 Example network

The Electrical department bridge links, through other bridges, to the subnets 146.176.144, 146.176.145, 146.176.147, 146.176.150 and 146.176.151.

The topology of the Electrical department network is shown in Figure 3.12. The main bridge into the department connects to two Ethernet network of PCs (subnets 146.176.150 and 146.176.151) and to another bridge (Bridge 1). Bridge 1 connects to the subnet 146.176.144. Subnet 146.176.144 connects to workstations and X-terminals. It also connects to the gateway moon which links the token ring subnet 146.176.145 with the Ethernet subnet 146.176.144. The gateway Oberone, on the

146.176.145 subnet, connects to an Ethernet link 146.176.146. This then connects to the gateway Dione which is also connected to the token ring subnet 146.176.147.

Each node on the network is assigned with an IP address. The *hosts* file for the set up in Figure 3.12 is shown next. For example the IP address of mimas is 146.176.145.21 and for miranda it is 146.176.144.14. It should be noticed that the gateway nodes: oberon, moon and dione all have two IP addresses.

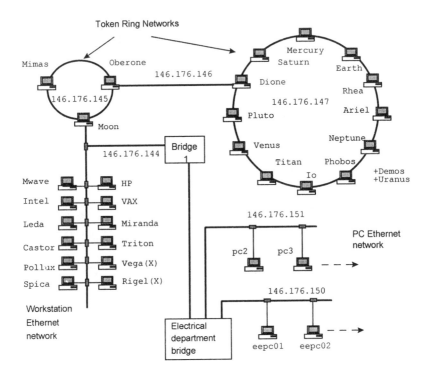

Figure 3.12   Example network

🖹 Contents of host file

```
146.176.1.3          janet
146.176.144.10       hp
146.176.145.21       mimas
146.176.144.11       mwave
146.176.144.13       vax
146.176.144.14       miranda
146.176.144.20       triton
146.176.146.23       oberon
146.176.145.23       oberon
146.176.145.24       moon
146.176.144.24       moon
146.176.147.25       uranus
146.176.146.30       dione
```

```
146.176.147.30      dione
146.176.147.31      saturn
146.176.147.32      mercury
146.176.147.33      earth
146.176.147.34      deimos
146.176.147.35      ariel
146.176.147.36      neptune
146.176.147.37      phobos
146.176.147.39      io
146.176.147.40      titan
146.176.147.41      venus
146.176.147.42      pluto
146.176.147.43      mars
146.176.147.44      rhea
146.176.147.22      jupiter
146.176.144.54      leda
146.176.144.55      castor
146.176.144.56      pollux
146.176.144.57      rigel
146.176.144.58      spica
146.176.151.254     cubridge
146.176.151.99      bridge_1
146.176.151.98      pc2
146.176.151.97      pc3
        :::::
146.176.151.71      pc29
146.176.151.70      pc30
146.176.151.99      ees99
146.176.150.61      eepc01
146.176.150.62      eepc02
255.255.255.0       defaultmask
```

3.11 Exercises

The following questions are multiple choice. Please select a–d.

3.11.1 Which of the following best describes a gateway:

- (a) it speeds the routing frames on a network
- (b) it connects a network to a telephone line
- (c) it echoes all frames from one network to another
- (d) it connects dissimilar networks

3.11.2 The ping program is used to:

- (a) determine if a node is responding to TCP/IP communications
- (b) determine IP addresses
- (c) remotely log-in to a node
- (d) transfer files from a remote node

3.11.3   The `telnet` program is used to:

  (a)   determine if a node is responding to TCP/IP
         communications
  (b)   remotely log-in to a node
  (c)   transfer files from a remote node
  (d)   determine IP addresses

3.11.4   The `ftp` program is used to:

  (a)   determine if a node is responding to TCP/IP
         communications
  (b)   remotely log-in to a node
  (c)   transfer files from a remote node
  (d)   determine IP addresses

3.12 Tutorial

3.12.5   Determine the IP addresses, and their type, of the following 32-bit
             addresses:

  (a)   `10001100.01110001.00000001.00001001`
  (b)   `01000000.01111101.01000001.11101001`
  (c)   `10101110.01110001.00011101.00111001`

3.12.6   If possible, determine some IP addresses and their corresponding
             Internet domain names.

3.12.7   Determine the countries which use the following primary domain
             names:

  (a) de   (b) nl   (c) it   (d) se   (e) dk   (f) sg
  (g) ca   (h) ch   (i) tr   (j) jp   (k) au

  Determine some other domain names.

④ TCP/IP II

4.1 Introduction

TCP and IP are extremely important protocols as they allow hosts to communicate over the Internet in a reliable way. TCP provides a connection between two hosts and supports error handling. This chapter discusses the following:

- **TCP.** The IP part allows data to be routed through a network, whereas TCP establishes and maintains a connection.
- **Ports and sockets.** An important concept of TCP/IP communications is the usage of ports and sockets. A port identifies the process type (such as FTP, TELNET, and so on) and the socket identifies a unique connection number. In this way TCP/IP can support multiple simultaneous connections of applications over a network.
- **IP Ver6.** The IP header contains the 32-bit IP address of the source and destination node. Unfortunately, the standard 32-bit IP address is not large enough to support the growth in nodes connecting to the Internet. Thus a new standard, IP Version 6 (IP Ver6), has been develop to support a 128-bit address, as well as additional enhancements.
- **TCP/IP programs.** These programs can be used to connect to other hosts and also to determine routing information.

4.2 IP Ver6

The IP Ver4 standard has proved so popular that it is has outgrown its purpose. Its main weakness is that it only supports a 32-bit IP address, which is not enough to cover the growth in Internet nodes. To overcome this, IP Version 6 (IP Ver6) is currently under discussion, the main techniques being investigated are:

- TUBA (TCP and UDP with Bigger Addresses).
- CATNIP (Common Architecture for the Internet).
- SIPP (Simple Internet Protocol Plus).

It is likely that none of these will provide the complete standard and the resulting standard will be a mixture of the three. The main features of IP Ver6 are likely to be a 128-bit IP network address and support for authentication and data encryption.

4.2.1 IPv6 datagram

Figure 4.1 shows the basic format of the IPv6 header. The main change to the IP packet is the support of a 128-bit network address, of which the main fields are:

- Version number (4 bits) – which contains the version number, such as 6 for IPv6 and is thus used to differentiate between IPv4 and IPv6.
- Priority (4 bits) – which is a 4-bit value indicating the priority of the datagram. For example:
  - ◆ 0 defines no priority.
  - ◆ 1 defines background traffic.
  - ◆ 2 defines unattended transfer.
  - ◆ 4 defines attended bulk transfer.
  - ◆ 6 defines interactive traffic.
  - ◆ 7 defines control traffic.
- Flow label (24 bits) – which is still experimental, but will be used to identify different data flow characteristics.
- Payload length (16 bits) – which defines the total size of the IP datagram (and includes the IP header attached data).

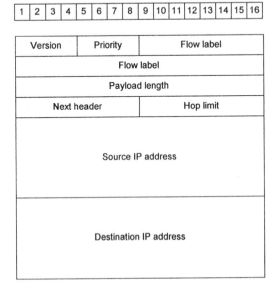

Figure 4.1 IPv6 header format

- Next header – which indicates which is the type of header that follows the IP header. For example:
  - ◆ 0 defines IP information.
  - ◆ 6 defines TCP information.
  - ◆ 43 defines routing information.
  - ◆ 58 defines ICMP information.
- Hop limit – which defines the maximum number of hops (jumps between gateways) that the datagram will take as it transverses over the network. Each router decrements this value by 1 and when it reaches 0 it will be deleted.
- IP addresses (128 bits) – which contains the 128-bit IP address. There will be three main groups of IP addresses, these are unicast, multicast and anycast. A unicast address identifies a particular host, a multicast address enables all hosts with a particular group to receive the same datagram and the anycast address will be addressed to a number of interfaces on a single multicast address.

4.3 Transmission control protocol

TCP fits into the OSI transport layer and IP fits into the network layer. TCP thus sits above IP which means that the IP header is added onto the higher-level information (such as transport, session, presentation and application). The main function of TCP is to provide a robust and reliable transport protocol. It is characterised as a reliable, connection-oriented, acknowledged and data stream-oriented server. IP, in itself, cannot support the connection of two nodes, whereas TCP does. With TCP, the connection is initially established and then is maintained for the length of the connection.

The TCP information contains simple acknowledgment messages and a set of sequential numbers. It also supports multiple simultaneous connections using destination and source port numbers, and manages these for both transmission and reception. As with IP, it supports data fragmentation and reassembly, and data multiplexing/demultiplexing.

The setup and operation of TCP is as follows:

1. When a host wishes to make a connection, TCP sends out a request message to the destination machine which contains a unique number called a socket number and a port number. The port number has a value which is associated with the application (for example, a TELNET connection has the port number of 23 and an FTP connection has a port number of 21). This message is then passed to the IP layer which then assembles a

datagram and is then transmitted to the destination.

2. When the destination host receives the connection request it returns a message containing its own unique socket number and a port number. The source and destination socket and port numbers thus identify the virtual connection between the two hosts.

3. After the connection has been made then data can flow between the two hosts (called a data stream).

After TCP receives the stream of data, it assembles the data into packets, called TCP segments. After the segment has been constructed, TCP adds a header (called the Protocol Data Unit) to the front of the segment. This header contains information such as a checksum, port number, destination and source socket numbers and segment sequence numbers The TCP layer then sends the packaged segment down to the IP layer, which encapsulates it and sends it over the network as a datagram.

4.3.1 Ports and sockets

As previously mentioned TCP adds a port number and socket number for each host. The port number identifies the required service, whereas the socket number is a unique number for that connection. Thus a node can have several TELNET connections with the same port number, but each connection will have a different socket number. A port number can be of any value but there is a standard convention which most systems work with. Table 4.1 defines some of the most widely used values, these are defined from 0 to 255. Port numbers above 255 can be used for non-specified applications.

Table 4.1 Typical TCP port numbers

Port	Process name	Notes
20	FTP-DATA	File Transfer Protocol- DATA
21	FTP	File Transfer Protocol-Control
23	TELNET	Telnet
25	SMTP	Simple Mail Transfer Protocol
49	LOGIN	Login protocol
53	DOMAIN	Domain name server
79	FINGER	Finger
161	SNMP	SNMP

4.3.2 TCP header format

The sender's TCP layer communicates with the receiver's TCP layer using the TCP protocol data unit. It defines parameters such as the source port, destination port, and so on, and is illustrated in Figure 4.2. The fields are:

- Source and destination port number – which are 16-bit values which identify the local port number (source) and remote port number (destination).

- Sequence number – which identifies the current sequence number of the data segment. This allows the receiver to keep track of data segments received, thus any which are missing can be easily identified.
- Data Offset – which is a 32-bit value and identifies the start of the data.
- Flags – The flag field is defined as UAPRSF, where U is the urgent flag, A the acknowledgment flag, P the push function, R the reset flag, S the sequence synchronise flag and F the end-of-transmission flag.
- Window – which is a 16-bit value and gives the number of data blocks that the receiving host can accept at a time.
- Checksum – which is a 16-bit checksum for the data and header.
- UrgPtr – which is the urgent pointer and is used to identify an important area of data (most systems do not support this facility).

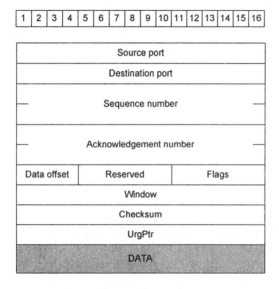

Figure 4.2 TCP header format

4.4 TCP/IP commands

There are several standard programs available over TCP/IP links. The example sessions is this section relate to the network outlined in Figure 3.12. These applications must include:

- FTP (file transfer protocol) – which is used to send files from one computer system to another.

- HTTP (hypertext transfer protocol) – which is the protocol used in the world wide web (WWW) and can be used for client-server applications involving hypertext (*this will be discussed in more detail in Chapter 7*).
- MIME (Multi-purpose Internet Mail Extension) – which gives enhanced electronic mail facilities over TCP/IP (*this will be discussed in more detail in Chapter 5*).
- SMTP (Simple Mail Management Protocol) – which gives simple electronic mail facilities over TCP/IP (*this will be discussed in more detail in Chapter 5*).
- TELNET – which allows remote login using TCP/IP.
- PING – which determines if a node is responding to TCP/IP communications.

4.4.1 ping

The ping (Packet INternet Gopher) program determines if a host is responding to TCP/IP communication. It is typically used to trace problems in networks and uses the Internet Control Message Protocol (ICMP) to send a request for a response from the target host. Sample run 4.1 shows that miranda is active and ariel isn't.

🖥 Sample run 4.1: Using PING command

```
C:\WINDOWS>ping miranda
miranda (146.176.144.14) is alive

C:\WINDOWS>ping ariel
no reply from ariel (146.176.147.35)
```

The ping program can also be used to determine the delay between one host and another, and also if there are any IP datagram losses. In Test run 4.2 the local host is pc419.eece.napier.ac.uk, (which is on the 146.176.151 segment) and the host miranda is tested (which is on the 146.176.144 segment). It can be seen that the delay is, on average, only 1 ms and that there is no loss of datagram (data packets).

🖥 Sample run 4.2: Using PING command

```
225 % ping miranda
PING miranda.eece.napier.ac.uk: 64 byte packets
64 bytes from 146.176.144.14: icmp_seq=0. time=1. ms
64 bytes from 146.176.144.14: icmp_seq=1. time=1. ms
64 bytes from 146.176.144.14: icmp_seq=2. time=1. ms

----miranda.eece.napier.ac.uk PING Statistics----
3 packets transmitted, 3 packets received, 0% packet loss
round-trip (ms)  min/avg/max = 1/1/1
```

In Test run 4.3 the destination node (www.napier.ac.uk) is located within the same building but is on a different IP segment (147.176.2). It is also routed through a bridge. It can be seen that the packet delay has increased to between 9 and 10 ms. Again there is no packet loss.

🖳 Sample run 4.3: Using PING command

```
226 % ping www.napier.ac.uk
PING central.napier.ac.uk: 64 byte packets
64 bytes from 146.176.2.3: icmp_seq=0. time=9. ms
64 bytes from 146.176.2.3: icmp_seq=1. time=9. ms
64 bytes from 146.176.2.3: icmp_seq=2. time=10. ms
----central.napier.ac.uk PING Statistics----
3 packets transmitted, 3 packets received, 0% packet loss
round-trip (ms)  min/avg/max = 9/9/10
```

Sample run 4.4 shows a connection between Edinburgh, UK to Bath, UK (www.bath.ac.uk, which has an IP address of 138.38.32.5). This is a distance of approximately 400 miles and it can be seen that the delay is now between 30 and 49 ms. This time there is 25 % packet loss.

🖳 Sample run 4.4: Using PING command

```
222 % ping www.bath.ac.uk
PING jess.bath.ac.uk: 64 byte packets
64 bytes from 138.38.32.5: icmp_seq=0. time=49. ms
64 bytes from 138.38.32.5: icmp_seq=2. time=35. ms
64 bytes from 138.38.32.5: icmp_seq=3. time=30. ms
----jess.bath.ac.uk PING Statistics----
4 packets transmitted, 3 packets received, 25% packet loss
round-trip (ms)  min/avg/max = 30/38/49
```

Finally, in Test 4.5 the ping program tests a link between Edinburgh, UK and a WWW server in the USA (home.microsoft.com, which has the IP address of 207.68.137.51). It can be seen that, in this case, the delay is between 447 and 468 ms, and that the loss is 60 %.

```
224 % ping home.microsoft.com
PING home.microsoft.com: 64 byte packets
64 bytes from 207.68.137.51: icmp_seq=2. time=447. ms
64 bytes from 207.68.137.51: icmp_seq=3. time=468. ms
----home.microsoft.com PING Statistics----
5 packets transmitted, 2 packets received, 60% packet loss
```

4.4.2 ftp (file transfer protocol)

The ftp program uses the TCP/IP protocol to transfer files to and from remote nodes. Initially the user logs into the remote computer and then the commands that can be used are similar to DOS commands such as cd (change directory), dir (list directory), open (open node), close (close node), pwd (present working directory). The get command copies a file from the remote node and the put command to copy it to the remote node.

The type of file to be transferred must be specified. This file can be ASCII text (the command used is `ascii`) or binary (the command used is `binary`).

Sample run 4.5 shows a session with the remote VAX computer (Internet name VAX, address `146.176.144.13`). The `get` command is used to get the file *TEMP.DOC* from VAX and transfer it to the calling PC.

🖥 Sample run 4.5

```
C:\NET> ftp vax
Connected to vax.
Name (vax:nobody): bill_b
Password (vax:bill_b):
331 Password required for bill_b.
230 User logged in, default directory DUA2:[STAFF.BILL_B]
ftp> dir
200 PORT Command OK.
125 File transfer started correctly
docs.dir;1           MAY  4 13:31 1993       512 (,RWE,RWE,RE)
fortran.dir;1        MAY 10 11:00 1990       512 (,RWE,RWE,RE)
temp.doc;1           MAY  5 07:33 1993        46 (,RWE,RE,)
226 File transfer completed ok
754 bytes received in 2.012100 seconds (0.37 Kbytes/s)
ftp>
ftp> get temp.doc
200 PORT Command OK.
125 File transfer started correctly
226 File transfer completed ok
45 bytes received in 0.005000 seconds (8.79 Kbytes/s)
ftp> quit
221 Goodbye.

C:\NET>dir *.doc
 Volume in drive C is MS-DOS_5
 Volume Serial Number is 3B33-13D3
 Directory of C:\NET

ASKME     DOC      3369 03/07/92    1:25
TEMP      DOC        45 24/05/94   14:47
        2 file(s)        3414 bytes
                      2093056 bytes free
C:\NET>
```

Sample run 4.6 shows a session of sending a file from the local node (in this case the PC) and to a remote node (in this case VAX). The `put` command is used for this purpose.

🖥 Sample run 4.6

```
C:\NET>ftp vax
Connected to vax.
Name (vax:nobody): bill_b
Password (vax:bill_b):
331 Password required for bill_b.
230 User logged in, default directory DUA2:[STAFF.BILL_B]
ftp> put askme.doc
200 PORT Command OK.
125 File transfer started correctly
226 File transfer completed ok
```

```
3369 bytes sent in 0.011000 seconds (299.09 Kbytes/s)
ftp> dir *.doc
200 PORT Command OK.
125 File transfer started correctly
askme.doc;1     MAY 24 14:53 1994      3396 (,RW,R,R)
temp.doc;1      MAY  5 07:33 1993        46 (,RWE,RE,)
226 File transfer completed ok
215 bytes received in 1.019100 seconds (0.21 Kbytes/s)
ftp>
```

4.4.3 telnet

The `telnet` program uses TCP/IP to remotely log into a remote node.
Sample run 4.7 shows an example of login into the node `miranda`.

🖥 Sample run 4.7: Using TELNET for remote login
```
C:\NFS>telnet miranda
        HP-UX miranda A.09.01 A 9000/720 (ttys5)
login: bill_b
Password:
(c)Copyright 1983-1992 Hewlett-Packard Co.,  All Rights Reserved.
                :::::::
          (c)Copyright 1988 Carnegie Mellon
[51:miranda :/net/castor_win/local_user/bill_b ] %
```

4.4.4 nslookup

The `nslookup` program interrogates the local `hosts` file or a DNS server to
determine the IP address of an Internet node. If it cannot find it in the local
file then it communicates with DNS servers outside its own network to see if
they know the address. Sample run 4.8 shows that the IP address of
`www.intel.com` is `134.134.214.1`.

🖥 Sample run 4.8: Example of nslookup
```
C:\> nslookup
Default Server:  ees99.eece.napier.ac.uk
Address:   146.176.151.99
> www.intel.com
Server:  ees99.eece.napier.ac.uk
Address:   146.176.151.99
Name:    web.jf.intel.com
Address:   134.134.214.1
Aliases:   www.intel.com

230 % nslookup home.microsoft.com
Non-authoritative answer:
Name:    home.microsoft.com
Addresses:   207.68.137.69, 207.68.156.11, 207.68.156.14, 207.68.156.56
207.68.137.48, 207.68.137.51
```

4.4.5 netstat (network statistics)

On a Unix system the command `netstat` can be used to determine the status of the network. The −r option shown in Sample run 4.9 shows that this node uses moon as a gateway to another network.

⌨ Sample run 4.9: Using Unix netstat command

```
[54:miranda :/net/castor_win/local_user/bill_b ] % netstat -r
Routing tables
Destination     Gateway          Flags    Refs       Use  Interface
localhost       localhost        UH          0     27306  lo0
default         moon             UG          0   1453856  lan0
146.176.144     miranda          U           8   6080432  lan0
146.176.1       146.176.144.252  UGD         0        51  lan0
146.176.151     146.176.144.252  UGD        11      5491  lan0
[55:miranda :/net/castor_win/local_user/bill_b ] %
```

4.4.6 traceroute

The traceroute program can be used to trace the route of an IP packet through the Internet. It uses the IP protocol time-to-live field and attempts to get a response from each of the gateways along the path to a defined host. The default probe datagram length is 38 bytes (although the test runs uses 40 byte packets by default). Sample run 4.10 shows an example of traceroute from a PC (pc419.eece.napier.ac.uk). It can be seen that initially it goes though a bridge (pcbridge.eece.napier.ac.uk) and then to the destination (miranda.eece.napier.ac.uk).

⌨ Sample run 4.10: Example traceroute

```
www:~/www$ traceroute miranda
traceroute to miranda.eece.napier.ac.uk (146.176.144.14), 30 hops max,
    40 byte packets
1 pcbridge.eece.napier.ac.uk (146.176.151.252) 2.684 ms 1.762 ms 1.725 ms
2 miranda.eece.napier.ac.uk (146.176.144.14) 2.451 ms   2.554 ms   2.357 ms
```

Sample run 4.11 shows the route from a PC (pc419.eece.napier.ac.uk) to a destination node (www.bath.ac.uk). Initially from the originator the route goes through a gateway (146.176.151.254) and then goes through a routing switch (146.176.1.27) and onto the EaStMAN ring via 146.176.3.1. The route then goes round the EaStMAN to a gateway at the University of Edinburgh (smds-gw.ed.ja.net). It is then routed onto the SuperJanet network and reaches a gateway at the University of Bath (smds-gw.bath.ja.net). It then goes to another gateway (jips-gw.bath.ac.uk) and finally to its destination (jess.bath.ac.uk). Figure 4.3 shows the route the packet takes.

Note that the gateways 4 and 8 hops away either don't send the required message or send them with a Time-to-Live value which is too small to be returned to the originator.

Sample run 4.11: Example traceroute

```
www:~/www$ traceroute www.bath.ac.uk
traceroute to jess.bath.ac.uk (138.38.32.5), 30 hops max, 40 byte packets
 1   146.176.151.254 (146.176.151.254)  2.806 ms   2.76 ms   2.491 ms
 2   sil-switch.napier.ac.uk (146.176.1.27)  19.315 ms  11.29 ms   6.285 ms
 3   sil-cisco.napier.ac.uk (146.176.3.1)  6.427 ms   8.407 ms   8.872 ms
 4   * * *
 5   smds-gw.ed.ja.net (193.63.106.129)  8.98 ms   30.308 ms   398.623 ms
 6   smds-gw.bath.ja.net (193.63.203.68)  39.104 ms  46.833 ms  38.036 ms
 7   jips-gw.bath.ac.uk (146.97.104.2)  32.908 ms  41.336 ms  42.429 ms
 8   * * *
 9   jess.bath.ac.uk (138.38.32.5)  41.045 ms  *  41.93 ms
```

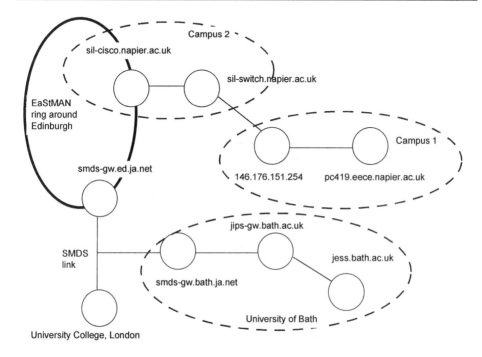

Figure 4.3   Route between local host and the University of Bath

Test run 4.12 shows an example route from a local host at Napier University, UK to the US. As before it goes through the local gateway (146.176.151.254) and then goes through three other gateways to get onto the SMDS Super JANET connection. The data packet then travels down this connection to University College, London (gw5.ulcc.ja.net). It then goes onto high speed connects to the US and arrives at a US gateway (mcinet-2.sprintnap.net). Next it travels to core2-hssi2-0.WestOrange.mci.net before reaching the Microsoft corporation gateway in Seattle (microsoft.Seattle.mci.net). It finally finds it way to the destination (207.68.145.53). The total journey time is just less than half a second.

🖳 Sample run 4.12: Example traceroute

```
> traceroute home.microsoft.com
 1 146.176.151.254 (146.176.151.254)   2.931 ms   2.68 ms   2.658 ms
 2 sil-switch.napier.ac.uk (146.176.1.27)   6.216 ms   8.818 ms   5.885 ms
 3 sil-cisco.napier.ac.uk (146.176.3.1)   6.502 ms   6.638 ms   10.218 ms
 4 * * *
 5 smds-gw.ed.ja.net (193.63.106.129)   18.367 ms   9.242 ms   15.145 ms
 6 smds-gw.ulcc.ja.net (193.63.203.33)   42.644 ms   36.794 ms   34.555 ms
 7 gw5.ulcc.ja.net (128.86.1.80)   31.906 ms   30.053 ms   39.151 ms
 8 icm-london-1.icp.net (193.63.175.53)   29.368 ms   25.42 ms   31.347 ms
 9 198.67.131.193 (198.67.131.193)   119.195 ms   120.482 ms   67.479 ms
10 icm-pen-1-H2/0-T3.icp.net (198.67.131.25) 115.3 ms 126.1 ms 149.9 ms
11 icm-pen-10-P4/0-OC3C.icp.net (198.67.142.69) 139.2ms 197.9ms 195.7ms
12 mcinet-2.sprintnap.net (192.157.69.48)   199.2 ms 267.4 ms 287.8 ms
13 core2-hssi2-0.WestOrange.mci.net (204.70.1.49) 216 ms 688ms 228ms
14 microsoft.Seattle.mci.net (166.48.209.250) 310.4ms   282ms 313.6ms
15 * microsoft.Seattle.mci.net (166.48.209.250)   324.797 ms 309.518 ms
16 * 207.68.145.53 (207.68.145.53)   435.195 ms *
```

4.4.7 arp

The arp utility program displays the IP to Ethernet MAC address mapping. It can also be used to delete or manually change any included address table entries. Within a network a router forwards data packets depending on the destination IP address of the packet. Each connection must also specify a MAC address to transport the packet over the network, thus the router must maintain a list of MAC addresses. The arp protocol maintains this mapping and adds address within this table on an as-needed basis. When a MAC address is required an arp message is sent to the node with an arp REQUEST packet which contains the IP address of the requested node. It will then reply with an arp RESPONSE packet which contains its MAC address and its IP address.

4.5 Exercises

The following questions are multiple choice. Please select a–d.

4.5.1   What is the function of a TCP/IP socket:

    (a)   It defines the type of connection.
    (b)   It defines a unique connection number for the application.
    (c)   It defines the type of connection and also a unique connection number for the application.
    (d)   It defines a unique hardware address.

4.5.2   What is the function of a TCP/IP port:

(a) It defines the type of connection.
(b) It defines a unique connection number for the application.
(c) It defines the type of connection and also a unique connection number for the application.
(d) It defines a unique hardware address.

4.5.3 Which TCP/IP program is used to log into a remote host:

    (a)   `telnet`
    (b)   `ftp`
    (c)   `nslookup`
    (d)   `traceroute`

4.5.4 Which TCP/IP program is used to determine the IP address of a host:

    (a)   `telnet`
    (b)   `ftp`
    (c)   `nslookup`
    (d)   `traceroute`

4.5.5 Which TCP/IP program is used to transfer files from a remote host:

    (a)   `telnet`
    (b)   `ftp`
    (c)   `nslookup`
    (d)   `traceroute`

4.6 Tutorial

4.6.1 Using the `ping` program determine if the following nodes are responding:

    (i)   `www.eece.napier.ac.uk`
    (ii)   `home.microsoft.com`
    (iii)   `www.intel.com`

4.6.2 Using the `traceroute` program determine the route from your local host to the following destinations:

    (i)   `www.napier.ac.uk`

(ii)   `home.microsoft.com`
(iii) `www.intel.com`

Identify each part of the route and note the timing information.

5 Electronic Mail

5.1 Introduction

One use of the Internet which almost every business agrees improves productivity is electronic mail. Traditional methods of sending mail within an office environment are inefficient and normally involve::

- Requesting a secretary to type the letter.
- Printing it.
- Proof-reading it.
- Re-printing it.
- Sending it through the internal/external mail system.

This, of course, is relatively slow and can be open to security breaches.

A faster method and more secure method of sending information is to use electronic mail where messages are sent almost in an instant. For example, a memo with 100 words will be sent in a fraction of a second. It is also simple to send to specific groups, various individuals, company-wide, and so on. Other types of data can also be sent with the mail message such as images, sound, and so on. The main advantages of electronic mail are:

- It is normally much cheaper than using the telephone (although, as time equates to money for most companies, the relative saving/cost relates mainly to a user's typing speed).
- Many different types of data can be transmitted, such as images, documents, speech, and so on.
- It is much faster than the postal service.
- Users can filter incoming messages easier than they can with the telephone.
- It normally cuts out the need for work to be typed, edited and then printed by a secretary.
- It reduces the burden on mailroom.
- It is normally more secure than traditional methods.
- It is relatively easy to send to groups of people (traditionally, either a circulation list was required or a copy to everyone in the group was required).

- In many cases it is possible to determine if the recipient has actually read the message (that is, the electronic mail system sends back an acknowledgment message).

The main disadvantages are:

- It stops people using the telephone (telephone communications tend to be more personal).
- It cannot be used as a legal document.
- Electronic mail messages can be sent on the 'spur of the moment' and are then later regretted (sending by traditional methods normally allows for a re-think). In extreme cases, messages can be sent to the wrong person (typically when replying to an email message, where a message is sent to the mailing list rather than the originator).
- It may be difficult to send electronic mail to some remote sites. Many organisations have either no electronic mail or have a totally internal mail system. Large companies are particularly wary of external Internet connections and limit the amount of external traffic.
- Not everyone reads their electronic mail on a regular basis (although this is changing as more organisations adopt email as the standard inter-personnel communications media).

The main standards which relate to the protocol of the transmission and reception of electronic mail are:

- Simple Mail Transfer Protocol (SMTP) – which is used with the TCP/IP protocol suite. It has traditionally been limited to the text-based electronic messages.
- Multi-Purpose Internet Mail Extension (MIME) – which allows the transmission and reception of mail which contains various types of data, such as speech, images and motion video. It is a newer standard than SMTP and uses much of its basic protocol.

5.2 Shared-file versus client/server approach

An email system can either use a shared-file approach or can be client/server based. In a shared file system the source mail client sends the mail message to the local post office. This post office then transfers control to a message transfer agent which then stores the message for a short time before sending it to the destination post office. The destination mail client periodically checks its own post office to determine if it has mail for it. This arrangement is often known as store and forward and the process is illustrated in Figure 5.1. Most PC-based email systems use this type of mechanism.

A client/server approach involves the source client setting up a real-time remote connection with the local post office, which then sets up a real-time connection with the destination, which in turn sets up a remote connection with the destination client. The message will thus arrive at the destination when all the connections are complete.

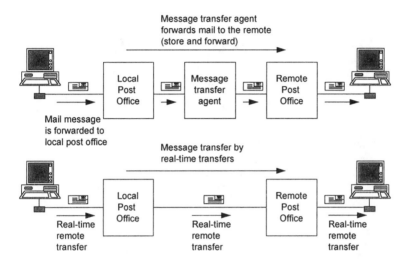

Figure 5.1 Shared-file versus client/server

5.3 Electronic mail overview

Figure 5.2 shows a typical email architecture. It contains four main elements:

1. Post offices – where outgoing messages are temporally buffered (stored) before transmission and where incoming messages are stored. The post office runs the server software capable of routing messages (a message transfer agent) and maintaining the post office database.
2. Message transfer agents – for forwarding messages between post offices and to the destination clients. This software can either reside on the local post office or on a physically separate server.
3. Gateways – which provide part of the message transfer agent functionality. They translate between different email systems, different email addressing schemes and messaging protocols.
4. Email clients – which is normally the computer which connects to the post office. It contains three parts:

- Email Application Program Interface (API), such as MAPI, VIM, MHS and CMC.
- Messaging protocol. The main messaging protocols are SMTP or X.400. SMTP is defined in RFC 822 and RFC 821. X.400 is an OSI-defined email message delivery standard.
- Network transport protocol, such as Ethernet, FDDI, and so on.

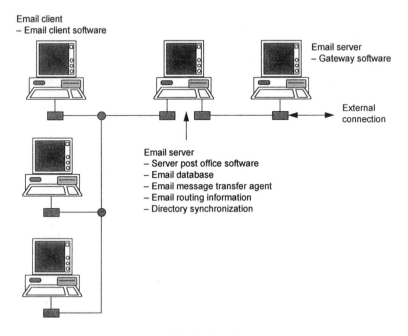

Figure 5.2 Email architecture

The main APIs are:

- MAP (messaging API) – Microsoft part of Windows Operation Services Architecture.
- VIM (vendor-independent messaging) – Lotus, Apple, Novell and Borland derived email API.
- MHS (message handling service) – Novell Network interface which is often used as an email gateway protocol.
- CMC (common mail call) – Email API associated with the X.400 native messaging protocol.

Gateways translate the email message from one system to another, such as from Lotus cc:Mail to MS Mail. Typical gateway protocols are:

- MHS (used with Novell Netware).

- SMTP.MIME (used with Internet environment).
- X.400 (used with X.400).
- MS Mail (used with Microsoft Mail).
- cc:Mail (used with Lotus cc:Mail).

An example PC-based email package is Lotus cc:Mail. Figure 5.3 shows a sample screen.

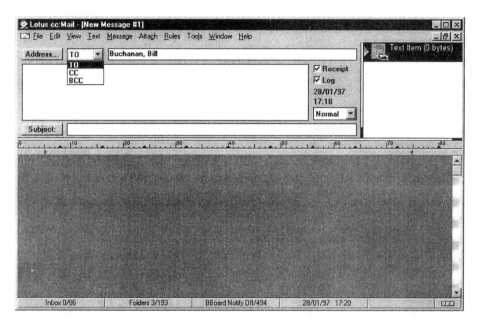

Figure 5.3 Sample Lotus cc:Mail screen

5.4 Internet email address

The Internet email address is in the form of a name (such as f.bloggs), followed by an '@' and then the domain name (such as anytown.ac.uk). For example:

```
f.bloggs@anytown.ac.uk
```

No spaces are allowed in the address as these are replaced by a period character ('.'). Figure 5.4 shows an example Internet address builder from Lotus cc:Mail.

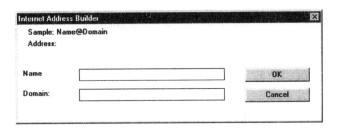

Figure 5.4 Internet address format

5.5 SMTP

The Internet Advisory Board (IAB) have defined the protocol SMTP in RFC 821 (Refer to Appendix B for a list of RFC standards). This section discusses the protocol for transferring mail between hosts using the TCP/IP protocol.

As SMTP is a transmission and reception protocol it does not actually define the format or contents of the transmitted message except that the data has 7-bit ASCII characters and that extra log information is added to the start of the delivered message to indicate the path the message took. The protocol itself is only concerned in reading the address header of the message.

5.5.1 SMTP operation

SMTP defines the conversation that takes place between an SMTP sender and an SMTP receiver. Its main functions are the transfer of messages and to provide ancillary functions for mail destination verification and handling.

Initially the message is created by the user and a header is added which includes the recipient's email address and other information. This message is then queued by the mail server and when it has time it will attempt to transmit it.

Each mail may have the following requirements:

- Each email can have a list of destinations, the email program then makes copies of the messages and passes them onto the mail server.
- The user may maintain a mailing list, and the email program must remove duplicates and replace mnemonic names with actual email addresses.
- Allows for normal message provision, such as blind carbon copies (BCC).

An SMTP mail server processes email messages from an outgoing mail queue and then transmits them using one or more TCP connections with the destination. If the mail message is transmitted to the required host then the SMTP sender deletes the destination from the message's destination list. After all the destinations have been sent, the sender then deletes the message from the queue.

If there are several recipients for a message on the same host then the SMTP protocol allows a single message to be sent with the recipients specified. Also, if there are several messages to be sent to a single host then the server can simply open a single TCP connection and all the messages can be transmitted in a single transfer (there is thus no need to set up a connection for each message).

SMTP also allows for efficient transfer with error messages. Typical errors include:

- Destination host is unreachable. A likely cause is that the destination host address is incorrect. For example, `f.bloggs@toy.ac.uk` might actually be `f.bloggs@toytown.ac.uk`.
- Destination host is out of operation. A likely cause is that the destination host has developed a fault or has been shut-down.
- Mail recipient is not available on the host. A likely cause are that the recipient does not exist on that host, the recipient name is incorrect or the recipient has moved. For example, `fred.bloggs@toytown.ac.uk` might actually be `f.bloggs@toytown.ac.uk`. To overcome the problem of user names which are similar to the defined user's name then some systems allow for certain aliases for recipients, such as `f.bloggs`, `fred.bloggs` and `freddy.bloggs`, but there is a limit to the number of aliases that a user can have. If a user has moved then some systems allow for a redirection of the email address. UNIX systems use the `.forward` file in the users home directory for redirection. For example on a UNIX system, if the user has moved to `fred.bloggs@toytown.com` then this address is simply added to the `.forward` file.
- TCP connection failed on the transfer of the mail. A likely cause is that there was a time-out error on the connection (maybe due to the receiver or sender being busy or there was a fault in the connection).

SMTP senders have the responsibility for a message up to the point where the SMTP receiver indicates that the transfer is complete. It should be noted that this only indicates that the message has arrived at the SMTP receiver and thus does not indicate:

- That the message has been delivered to the recipient's mailbox.
- That the recipient has read the message.

Thus, SMTP does not guarantee to recover from lost messages and gives no end-to-end acknowledgment on success receipt (normally this is achieved by an acknowledgment message being returned). Error indications are also not guaranteed. However, TCP connections are normally fairly reliable.

Normally if an error occurs in the reception then a message will be sent back to the sender to explain the problem. The user can then try and determine the problem with the message.

SMTP receivers accept an arriving message and either places it in a user's mailbox or if that user is located at another host, it copies it to the local outgoing mail queue for forwarding.

Most transmitted messages go from the sender's machine to the host over a single TCP connection. Sometimes, though, the connection will be made over multiple TCP connections over multiple hosts. This can be achieved by the sender specifying a route to the destination in the form of a sequence of servers.

5.5.2 SMTP overview

An SMTP sender initially initiates a TCP connection. When this is successful then the sender sends a series of commands to the receiver, who then replies with a single reply for each command. All command and responses are sent with ASCII characters and are terminated with the carriage return (CR) and line feed (LF) characters (often known as CRLF).

Each command consists of a single line of text, beginning with a four-letter command code followed by in some cases an argument field. Most replies are a single line, although multiple-line replies are possible. Table 5.1 gives some sample commands.

Table 5.1 SMTP commands

Command	Description
HELO *domain*	Sends an identification of the domain
MAIL FROM: *sender-address*	Sends identification of the originator (sender-address)
RCPT FROM: *receiver-address*	Sends identification of the recipient (receiver-address)
DATA	Transfer text message
RSEY	Abort current mail transfer
QUIT	Shut down TCP connection
EXPN *mailing-list*	Send back membership of mailing list
SEND FROM: *sender-address*	Send mail message to the terminal
SOML FROM: *sender-address*	If possible, send mail message to the terminal, otherwise send to mailbox
VRFY username	Verify user name (username).

SMTP replies with a three-digit code and possibly other information. Some of the responses are listed in Table 5.2. The first digit gives the category of the reply, such as 2xx (a positive completion reply), 3xx (a positive intermediate reply), 4xx (a transient negative completion reply) and 5xx (a permanent negative completion reply). A positive reply indicates that the requested action has been accepted, and a negative reply indicates that the action was not accepted.

Positive completion reply indicates that the action has been successful and a positive intermediate reply indicates that the action has been accepted but the receiver is waiting for some other action before it can give a positive completion reply. A transient negative completion reply indicates that there is a temporary error condition which can be cleared by other actions and a permanent negative completion reply indicates that the action was not accepted and no action was taken.

Table 5.2 SMTP responses

Command	Description
211	System status
214	Help message
220	Service ready
221	Service closing transmission channel
250	Request mail action completed successfully
251	Addressed user does not exist on system but will forward to *receiver-address*
354	Indicate to the sender that the mail message can now be sent. The end of the message is identified by two CR, LF characters
421	Service is not available
450	Mailbox unavailable and the requested mail action was not taken.
451	Local processing error, requested action aborted
452	Insufficient storage, requested action not taken
500	Command unrecognised due to a syntax error
501	Invalid parameters or arguments
502	Command not currently implemented
503	Bad sequence of commands
504	Command parameter not currently implemented
550	Mail box unavailable, request action not taken
551	The addressed user is not local, please try *receiver-address*
552	Exceeded storage allocation, requested mail action aborted
553	Mailbox name not allowed, requested action not taken
554	Transaction failed

5.5.3 SMTP transfer

Figure 5.4 shows a sample successful email transmission. For example if:

```
f.bloggs@toytown.ac.uk
```

is sending a mail message to:

```
a.person@place.ac.de
```

Then a possible sequence of events:

- Setup TCP connection with receiver host.
- If the connection is successful then the receiver replies back with a 220 code (server ready). If it is unsuccessful then it returns back with a 421 code)
- Sender sends a HELO command to the hostname (such as HELO toytown.ac.uk).
- If the sender accepts the incoming mail message then the receiver returns a 250 OK code. If it is unsuccessful then it returns back with a 421, 451, 452, 500, 501 or 552 code.
- Sender sends a MAIL FROM: sender command (such as MAIL FROM: f.bloggs@toytown.ac.uk).
- If the receiver accepts the incoming mail message from the sender then it returns a 250 OK code. If it is unsuccessful then it returns back codes such as 251, 450, 451, 452, 500, 501, 503, 550, 551, 552 or 553 code.
- Sender sends a RCPT TO: receiver command (such as RCPT TO: a.person@place.ac.de).
- If the receiver accepts the incoming mail message from the sender then it returns a 250 OK code.
- Sender sends a DATA command.
- If the receiver accepts the incoming mail message from the sender then it returns a 354 code (start transmission of mail message).
- The sender then transmits the email message.
- The end of the email message is sent as two LF, CR characters.
- If the reception has been successful then the receiver sends back a 250 OK code. If it is unsuccessful then it returns back with a 451, 452, 552 or 554.
- Sender starts the connection shutdown by sending a QUIT command.
- Finally the sender closes the TCP connection.

5.5.4 RFC 822

SMTP uses RFC 822 which defines the format of the transmitted message. RFC 822 contains two main parts:

- A header – which is basically the mail header and contains information for the successful transmission and delivery of a message. This typically contains the sender and receiver's email address, the time the message was sent and received. Any computer involved in the transmission can be added to the header.
- The contents.

Normally the email reading program will read the header and format the information to the screen to show the sender's email address, and displays the contents of the message separately from the header.

An RFC 822 message contains a number of lines of text in the form of a memo (such as To:, From:, Bcc:, and so on). A header line usually has a keyword followed by a colon and then followed by keyword arguments. The specification also allows for a long line to be broken up into several lines.

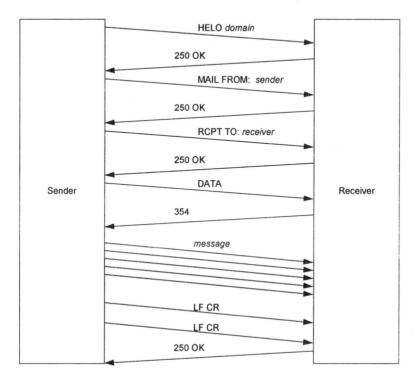

Figure 5.5 Sample SMTP email transmission

The following is an example RFC 822 message with the header shown in italics and the message body in bold. Table 5.3 explains some of RFC 822 contents of the header.

```
From FREDB@ACOMP.CO.UK Wed Jul  5 12:36:49 1995
Received: from ACOMP.CO.UK ([154.220.12.27]) by cen-
tral.napier.ac.uk (8.6.10/8.6.10) with SMTP id MAA16064 for
<w.buchanan@central.napier.ac.uk>; Wed, 5 Jul 1995 12:36:43 +0100
Received: from WPOAWUK-Message_Server by ACOMP.CO.UK
    with Novell_GroupWise; Wed, 05 Jul 1995 12.35:51 +0000
Message-Id: <sffa8725.082@ACOMP.CO.UK >
X-Mailer: Novell GroupWise 4.1
Date: Wed, 05 Jul 1995 12:35:07 +0000
From: Fred Bloggs <FREDB@ACOMP.CO.UK>
To: w.buchanan@central.napier.ac.uk
Subject:  Technical Question
Status: REO

Dear Bill
```

I have a big problem. Please help.

Fred

Table 5.3 Header line descriptions

Header line	Description
From FREDB@ACOMP.CO.UK Wed Jul 5 12:36:49 1995	Sender of the email is FREDB@ ACOM.CO.UK
Received: from ACOMP.CO.UK ([154.220.12.27]) by central.napier.ac.uk (8.6.10/8.6.10) with SMTP id MAA16064 for <w.buchanan@central.napier.ac.uk>; Wed, 5 Jul 1995 12:36:43 +0100	It was received by CENTRAL.NAPIER.AC.UK at 12:36 on 5 July 1995
Message-Id: <sffa8725.082@ACOMP.CO.UK >	Unique message ID
X-Mailer: Novell GroupWise 4.1	Gateway system
Date: Wed, 05 Jul 1995 12:35:07 +0000	Date of original message
From: Fred Bloggs <FREDB@ACOMP.CO.UK>	Sender' email address and full name
To: w.buchanan@central.napier.ac.uk	Recipient' email address
Subject: Technical Question	Mail subject

5.6 X.400

RFC 821 (the transmission protocol) and RFC 822 (the message format) have now become the defacto standards for email systems. The CCITT, in 1984, defined a new recommendations for email called X.400. The RFC821/822 systems is simple, and works relatively well, whereas X.400 is complex and is poorly designed. These points have helped RFC 821/822 to become a defacto standards, whereas X.400 is now almost extinct (see Figure 5.6 for the basic X.400 addressing builder and Figure 5.7 for the extended address builder).

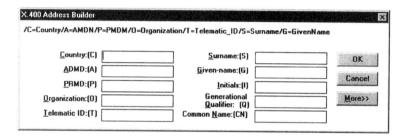

Figure 5.6 X.400 basic addressing

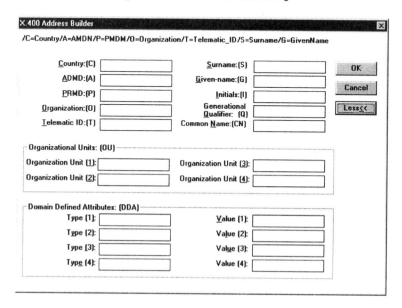

Figure 5.7 X.400 extended addressing

5.7 MIME

SMTP suffers from several drawback, such as:

- SMTP can only transmit ASCII characters and thus cannot transmit executable files or other binary objects.
- SMTP does not allow the attachment of files, such as images, audio and so on.
- SMTP can only transmit 7-bit ASCII characters and thus does support extended ASCII character set.

For this purpose a new standard, Multipurpose Internet Mail Extension

(MIME), has been defined which is compatible with existing RFC 822 implementations. It is defined in the specifications RFC 1521 and 1522. Its enhancements include the following:

- Five new message header fields in the RFC 822 header which provide extra information about the body of the message.
- Use of various content formats for the support multimedia electronic mail.
- Define transfer encodings to transform attached files.

The five new header fields defined in MIME are:

- MIME-version – A message that conforms to RFC 1521 and 1522 has a MIME-version of 1.0.
- Content-type – This field defines the type of data attached.
- Content-transfer-encoding – This field indicates the type of transformation necessary to represent the body in a format which can be transmitted as a message.
- Content-id – This field is used to uniquely identify MIME multiple attachments in the email message.
- Content-description – This field is a plain-text description of the object with the body. It can be used by the user to determine the data type.

These fields can appear in a normal RFC 822 header. Figure 5.8 shows an example email message. It can be seen in the right-hand corner that the API has split the message into two parts: the message part and the RFC 822 part. The RFC 822 part is shown in Figure 5.9. It can be seen that, in this case, that the extra MIME messages are:

```
MIME-Version: 1.0
Content-Type: text/plain; charset=us-ascii
Content-Transfer-Encoding: 7bit
```

which defines that it is MIME Version 1.0, the content-type is text/plain (standard ASCII) and uses the US ASCII character set, and the content-transfer-encoding is 7-bit ASCII.

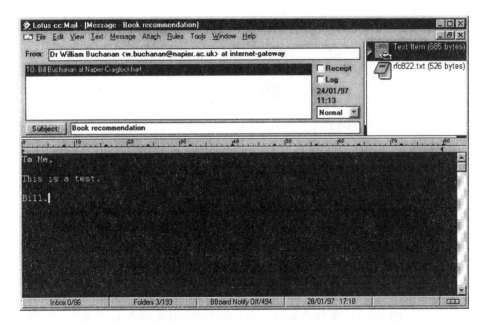

Figure 5.8   Sample email message showing message and RFC822 part

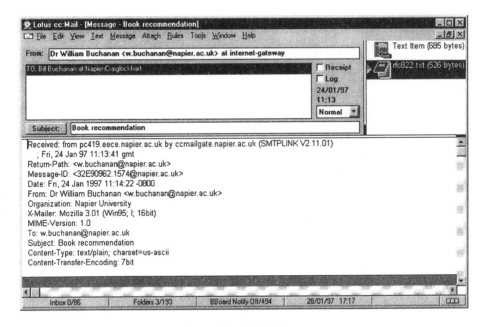

Figure 5.9   RFC 822 part

📖 *RFC 822 example file listing (refer to Figure 5.9)*

```
Received: from pc419.eece.napier.ac.uk by ccmailgate.napier.ac.uk
(SMTPLINK V2.11.01)
```

```
        ; Fri, 24 Jan 97 11:13:41 gmt
Return-Path: <w.buchanan@napier.ac.uk>
Message-ID: <32E90962.1574@napier.ac.uk>
Date: Fri, 24 Jan 1997 11:14:22 -0800
From: Dr William Buchanan <w.buchanan@napier.ac.uk>
Organization: Napier University
X-Mailer: Mozilla 3.01 (Win95; I; 16bit)
MIME-Version: 1.0
To: w.buchanan@napier.ac.uk
Subject: Book recommendation
Content-Type: text/plain; charset=us-ascii
Content-Transfer-Encoding: 7bit
```

5.7.1 MIME content types

Content types define the format of the attached files. There are a total of 16 different content types in 7 major content groups. If the text body is pure text then no special transformation is required. RFC 1521 defines only one sub-type, which is text/plain which gives a standard ASCII character set.

An MIME encoded email can contain multiple attachments. The content-type header field includes a boundary which defines the delimiter between multiple attachments. A boundary always starts on a new line and has the format:

```
-- boundary name
```

The final boundary is:

```
-- boundary name --
```

For example, the following message contains two parts:

📖 **Example MIME file with 2 parts**
```
From: Dr William Buchanan <w.buchanan@napier.ac.uk>
MIME-Version: 1.0
To: w.buchanan@napier.ac.uk
Subject: Any subject
Content-Type: multipart/mixed; boundary="boundary name"

This part of the message will be ignored.

-- boundary name
Content-Type: multipart/mixed; boundary="boundary name"

This is the first mail message part.

-- boundary name

And this is the second mail message part.

-- boundary name --
```

Table 5.4 MIME content-types

Content type	Description
text/plain	Unformated text, such as ASCII
text/richtext	Rich text format which is similar to HTML
multipart/mixed	Each attachment is independent from the rest and should be presented to the user in the order they were initially ordered in.
multipart/parallel	Each attachment is independent from the rest but they are in no specific order
multipart/alternative	Each attachment is a different version of the original data
multipart/digest	This is similar to multipart/mixed but each part is message/rfc822
message/rfc822	Contains the RFC 822 text
message/partial	Used in fragmented mail messages
message/external-body	Used to define a pointer to an external object (such as an ftp link)
image/jpeg	Defines a JPEG image using JFIF file format
image/gif	Defines GIF image
video/mpeg	Defines MPEG format
audio/basic	Defines 8-bit μ-Law encoding at 8 kHz sampling rate
application/postscript	Defines postscript format
application/octet-stream	Define binary format which consists of 8-bit bytes

The part of the message after the initial header and before the first boundary can be used to add a comment. This is typically used to inform users who do not have a MIME-compatible program about the method used to encode the received file. A typical method used to convert binary data into ASCII characters are the programs UUENCODE (to encode a binary file into text) or UUDECODE (to decode a uuencoded file).

The four types of subtypes of multipart type can be used to sequence the attachments, the main subtypes are:

- multipart/mixed subtype, which is used when attachments are independent but need to be arranged in a particular order.
- multipart/parallel subtype, which is used when the attachments should be present at the same. A typical example is to present an animated file along with an audio attachment.
- multipart/alternative subtype, which is used to represent an attachment in a number of different format.

5.7.2 Example MIME

The following file listing shows the message part of a MIME encoded email message (that is, it excludes the RFC 822 header part). It can be seen that the sending email system has added the comment about the MIME encoding. In this case the MIME boundaries have been defined by:

```
--  IMA.Boundary.760275638
```

📖 *Example MIME file*

This is a Mime message, which your current mail reader
may not understand. Parts of the message will appear as
text. To process the remainder, you will need to use a Mime
compatible mail reader. Contact your vendor for details.

--IMA.Boundary.760275638

Content-Type: text/plain; charset=US-ASCII
Content-Transfer-Encoding: 7bit
Content-Description: cc:Mail note part

This is the original message .....

--IMA.Boundary.760275638--

5.7.3 Mail fragments

A mail message can be fragmented using the content-type field of message/partial and then reassembled back at the source. The standard format is:

```
Content-type: message/partial;
    id="idname"; number=x; total=y
```

where *idname* is the message identification (such as xyz@hostname, *x* is the number of the fragment out of a total of *y* fragments. For example, if a message has three fragments then these could be sent as:

📖 *Example MIME file with 3 fragments (first part)*
From: Fred Bloggs <f.bloggs@toytown.ac.uk>
MIME-Version: 1.0
To: a.body@anytown.ac.uk
Subject: Any subject
Content-Type: message/partial;
    id="xyz@toytown.ac.uk"; number=1; total=3
Content=type: video/mpeg

First part of MPEG file

📖 *Example MIME file with 3 fragments (second part)*
From: Fred Bloggs <f.bloggs@toytown.ac.uk>
MIME-Version: 1.0
To: a.body@anytown.ac.uk
Subject: Any subject
Content-Type: message/partial;

```
id="xyz@toytown.ac.uk"; number=2; total=3
Content=type: video/mpeg
```

Second part of MPEG file

📖 *Example MIME file with 3 fragments (third part)*
```
From: Fred Bloggs <f.bloggs@toytown.ac.uk>
MIME-Version: 1.0
To: a.body@anytown.ac.uk
Subject: Any subject
Content-Type: message/partial;
    id="xyz@toytown.ac.uk"; number=3; total=3
Content=type: video/mpeg
```

Third part of MPEG file

The receiver would then build these 3 fragments back into a single file.

5.7.4 Transfer encodings

MIME allows for different transfer encodings within the message body. The main transfer encoding are:

- 7bit – No encoding, and all of the characters are 7-bit ASCII characters.
- 8bit – No encoding, and extended 8-bit ASCII characters are used.
- quoted-printable – Encodes the data so that non-printing ASCII characters (such as line feeds and carriage returns) are displayed in a readable form.
- base64 – Encodes by mapping 6-bit blocks of input to 8-bit blocks of output, all of which are printable ASCII characters.
- x-token – Another non-standard encoding method.

When the transfer encoding is:

`Content-transfer-encoding: quoted-printable`

then the message has been encoded so that all non-printing characters have been converted to printable characters. A typical transform is to insert a $=xx$ where xx is the hexadecimal equivalent for the ASCII character. For example:

A form feed (FF) would be encoded with '=0C',

A transfer encoding of base64 is used to map 6-bit characters to a printable character. It is a useful method in disguising text in an encrypted form and also for converting binary data into a text format. It takes the input bit stream and reads it with 6 bits at a time, and then maps this to an 8-bit printable character. Table 5.5 shows the mapping.

Table 5.5 MIME base64 encoding

Bit value	Encoded character	Bit value	Encoded character	Bit value	Encoded character	Bit value	Encoded character
0	A	16	Q	32	g	48	w
1	B	17	R	33	h	49	x
2	C	18	S	34	i	50	y
3	D	19	T	35	j	51	z
4	E	20	U	36	k	52	0
5	F	21	V	37	l	53	1
6	G	22	W	38	m	54	2
7	H	23	X	39	n	55	3
8	I	24	Y	40	o	56	4
9	J	25	Z	41	p	57	5
10	K	26	a	42	q	58	6
11	L	27	b	43	r	59	7
12	M	28	c	44	s	60	8
13	N	29	d	45	t	61	9
14	O	30	e	46	u	62	+
15	P	31	f	47	v	63	/

Thus if a binary file had the bit sequence of:

```
101000101010100010101010
```

It would first be split into groups of 6 bits, as follows:

```
101000   101010   100010   101010   000000
```
this would thus be converted into the ASCII sequence of:

```
YsSqA
```

which is in a transmittable form.

Thus the 7-bit ASCII sequence of "FRED" would use the bit pattern:

```
1000110 1010010 1000101 1000100
```

which would be split into groups of 6 bits as:

```
100011 010100 101000 101100 010000
```

which would be encoded as:

```
jUosQ
```

5.8 Exercises

5.8.1   The main drawback of SMTP is:

    (a)   It is incompatible with most email systems
    (b)   It can only be used for text-based email
    (c)   It is slow when transferring an email
    (d)   It is only used on UNIX systems

5.8.2   The advantage that MIME has over SMTP is:

    (a)   That it allows the attachment of other data types (such as speech and images).
    (b)   It is faster when transferring
    (c)   It is compatible with more systems
    (d)   It is only used on UNIX systems

5.8.3   The share-file (store and forward) email approach involves:

    (a)   Sending the mail message to multiple sites
    (b)   Sending the mail message in fragments
    (c)   Using real-time remote transfer
    (d)   Using a message transfer agent

5.8.4   The client/server email approach involves:

    (a)   Sending the mail message to multiple sites
    (b)   Sending the mail message in fragments
    (c)   Using real-time remote transfer
    (d)   Using a message transfer agent

5.8.5   The main function of an email post office is to:

    (a)   Forward messages to clients
    (b)   Store incoming messages and temporally store outgoing messages
    (c)   Translate messages between different systems
    (d)   Provide the user interface program

5.8.6   The main function of an email gateways is to:

    (a)   Forward messages to clients
    (b)   Store incoming messages and temporally store outgoing

messages

(c)   Translate messages between different systems

(d)   Provide the user interface program

5.8.7   The main function of an email message transfer agent is to:

(a)   Forward messages to clients

(b)   Store incoming messages and temporally store outgoing messages

(c)   Translate messages between different systems

(d)   Provide the user interface program

5.8.8   The standard text format used for email messages is:

(a)   ISO characters

(b)   ANSI characters

(c)   EBCDIC characters

(d)   7-bit ASCII characters

5.8.9   The SMTP transmission protocol has been defined in which IAB standard:

(a)   RFC 822

(b)   RFC 821

(c)   IEEE 802.2

(d)   RFC 802

5.8.10   The SMTP message format has been defined in which IAB standard:

(a)   RFC 822

(b)   RFC 821

(c)   IEEE 802.2

(d)   RFC 802

5.8.11   How is routing information added to an SMTP message

(a)   It is encoded with special codes

(b)   It is added to the end of the message

(c)   It is sent as a separate file

(d)   It is added to the header of the message

5.8.12   The likely reason that the X.400 standard has never been universally accepted is:

(a)   It is too complex
(b)   It is too simple
(c)   It is difficult to incorporate into email systems
(d)   It is not an international standard

5.8.13   The main disadvantage of SMTP is:

(a)   It is not suited to client/server applications
(b)   It does not support file attachments
(c)   It is too slow
(d)   It is incompatible with many systems

5.8.14   How are attachments delimited in MIME encoded messages:

(a)   `++ boundary name`
(b)   `-- boundary name`
(c)   `<< boundary name`
(d)   `>> boundary name`

5.8.15   A typical format used to convert binary files into ASCII text is:

(a)   LHA
(b)   PKZIP
(c)   UUENCODE
(d)   ZIP

5.8.16   How is the type of attachment defined:

(a)   It is defined in the address field
(b)   It is sent as separate message
(c)   Automatically with the type of encoding
(d)   With the content type

5.9 Tutorial

5.9.1   Identify the main functional differences between SMTP and MIME.

5.9.2   Contrast shared-file and client/server approach for electronic mail.

5.9.3   Give an example set of messages between the sender and a recipient for a succesful SMTP transfer.

5.9.4   Give an example set of messages between the sender and a recipient for an unsuccesful SMTP transfer.

5.9.5   If you have access to email read an email and identify each part of the header.

5.9.6   Explain how base64 encoding can be used to attach binary information.

5.9.7   Encode the following bit stream with base64 encoding:

(i)   0111000000000101011010100000001111110111110

(ii)   111110001110110101110010011110011010111111

6 | The World Wide Web

6.1 Introduction

The World Wide Web (WWW) is a collection of information sources which are available over the Internet. It was initially conceived, in 1989, by CERN, the European Particle Physics Research Laboratory in Geneva, Switzerland, and its main objective was to interlink a number of different systems to exchange various types of information. This information can be in the form of text, images, audio and video.

One of its main characteristics is that stored information tends to be distributed over a geographically wide area. The result of the project has been the world-wide acceptance of the protocols and specifications used. A major part of its success was due to the full support of the National Center for Supercomputing Applications (NCSA) who developed a family of user interface systems known collectively as Mosaic.

The WWW, or Web, is basically an infrastructure of information. This information is stored on the WWW on Web servers and it uses the Internet to transmit data around the world. These servers run special programs which allow information to be transmitted to remote computers which are running a Web browser, as illustrated in Figure 6.1.

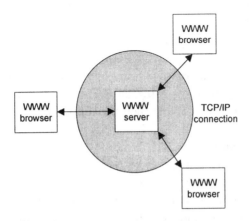

Figure 6.1 Web servers and browsers

Information is generally distributed on the Web and is stored on Web servers. This information is accessed by means of pages which can contain text and links to multimedia applications such as graphic images, digitised sound files and video animation. The Web encourages the use of standardised file formats and especially compressed file formations. The standard media files used on the Web (with typical file extensions) are:

- **Images**. GIF (GIF) or JPEG (JPG) compressed image files.
- **Video**. Compressed video such as QuickTime movies for video (QT or MOV), MS video (AVI) and MPEG files (MPG).
- **Printer files**. Postscript files (PS or EPS).
- **Audio**. Compressed audio (AU, SND or WAV).
- **Generally compressed files**. (ZIP, Z or GZ).
- **Java script**. Java script (JAV, JS or MOCHA).
- **Text files**. Text files (TEX or TXT).

6.2 WWW topology

The Web topology allows for the distribution of information and thus information does not have to be stored locally. Figure 6.2 illustrates an example distribution of information, where the information on subject A is stored on sources 2 and 3, and information on subject B is stored on information sources 3, 4 and 5. The information sources are then binded together with a number of links. The distribution of information in this way has several advantages including:

- Each new source of information does not have to be replicated to all sources of information.
- New additional sources of information can be added by simply adding new links.
- Links to information can be easily broken and, if necessary, replaced.
- Several sources of the same information can be stored. Thus if one of the sources were to be unavailable then the information can still be retrieved from other sources.
- Each source of information builds into a larger information source. Thus local sources only have to hold the information for the local site and thus the processing and storage capability needed to process the information only requires to be enough to service the demand for local information.
- Information from one source can be used for several subjects. For example, in Figure 6.2 the information source 3 is used for subject A and subject B.

An example of this could be in the map of an area where many subjects, such as a tourist map, hotel guides, sports grounds, and so on, could refer to the same map.

The main disadvantages of this distributed method are:

- If the one source of the required information is not available then no-one can access that information.
- Information can be fragmented and disjointed.
- Links can fossilise where sources of information are not updated on a regular basis.
- Information sources can be lost, where either a source of information has moved or has been deleted.

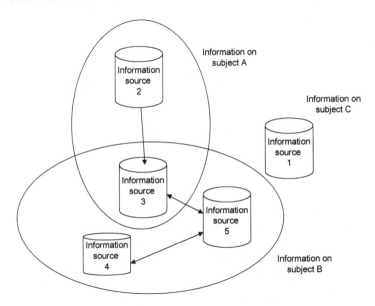

Figure 6.2 Distributed information

The user either traces information by either following a link which then leads to another and finally to the relevant information or uses a search program. The two method of finding information are thus:

- **Searching.** There are many search programs (engines) on the Web, such as Yahoo (as shown in Figure 6.3). These allow the user to enter one or more keywords and the search engine produces a list of relevant pages. This is equivalent to a reader finding information in a book, where a reader normally refers to the index and from there the actual page number(s) is found.

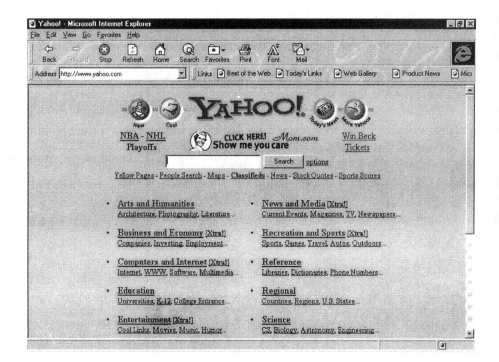

Figure 6.3 Yahoo search

- **Following links**. The search method is fine when the user knows the exact word to search for but it is no good when the user does not know the key search words, or if the search word is not a key search word in the search engine. When this happens the user normally searches for the subject by following related link until the relevant information is found. A typical example is when the user is searching for an individual's home page. For example, if a user wants to find the home page of a Lecturer within a College then the user may go through the following steps:

1. Locate the college.
2. Locate the facility within the college.
3. Locate the department within the facility.
4. Locate the group within the department.
5. Locate the Lecturer within the group.

Typically a user may go back to a previous link and trace the route that was taken. This may be to locate an interesting source of information or to try another route. This type of tracing is supported by most Web browsers with the Back and Forward option.

Figure 6.4 shows an example of linked Web connections. The user initially accesses a page on a German Web server, this then contains a link to a Japanese server. This server contains links to UK and USA servers. This type of arrangement leads to the topology that resembles a spider's web, where information is linked from one place to another. It differs from a spider's web in that is it not symmetrical and can be viewed as an arbitrarily interconnected network. This jumble of interconnected information sources gives the Web one of its strengths in that there are often several ways to get to a single source of information. If one of the ways fails then there is always another one to follow.

Each page on the Web contains text known as hypertext which has special reserved keywords to represent formatting and displaying functions. A standard language known as HTML (Hypertext Mark-up Language) has been developed for this purpose.

Hypertext pages, when interpreted by a browser program, display an easy-to-use interface containing formatted text, icons, pictorial hot spots, underscored words, and so on. Each page can also contain links to other related pages.

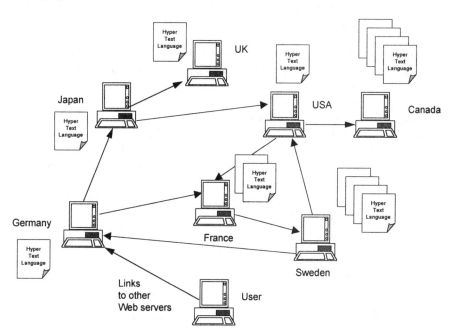

Figure 6.4   Example Web connections

Table 6.1 Advantages and disadvantages of the WWW

	Advantages	Disadvantages
Global information flow	Less control of information by the media, governments and large organisations.	Lack of control on 'criminal' material, such as certain types of pornography, terrorist activity, and s on.
Global transmission	Communication between people and organisations in different countries which should create the Global Village.	Data can easily get lost or state secrets can be easily transmitted ove the world.
Internet connections	Many different types of connections possible, such as dial-up facilities (such as over a modem or with ISDN) or through frame relays. The user only has to pay for the service and the local connection.	Data once on the Internet is easy to tap-into and possibly change.
Global information	Creation of an ever increasing global information database.	Data is relatively easy to tap-into an possibly change.
Multi-media integration	Tailor-made applications with properly designed presentation tools.	Lack of editorial control leads to po quality material which is 'hacked' together.
Increasing WWW usage	Helps to improve its chances of acceptance into the home.	Increased traffic swamps the global information network and slows-dow commercial traffic.
WWW links	Easy to set-up and leads users from one place to the next in a logic manner.	WWW links often fossilise where th link information is out-of-date or doesn't even exist.
Education	Increased usage of remote teaching with full multi-media education	Increase in surface learning and lack of deep research. Also, may lead to an increase in educational time-wasting (too much surfing and to lit learning).

6.3 Typical Web browsers

Web browsers interpret special hypertext pages which consist of the hypertext mark-up language (HTML) and Java script. They then display it in the given format. There are currently four main Web browsers:

- Netscape Navigator – This is the most widely used WWW browser and is available in many different versions on many systems. It runs on PCs (running Windows 3.1, Windows NT or Windows 95), Unix workstations and Macintosh computers. Figure 6.5 shows Netscape Navigator Version 3 for Windows 3.1. Navigator has become the standard WWW browser and has many add-ons and enhancements which have been added by the continual development by Netscape. The basic package also has many compatible software plug-ins which are developed by third party suppliers. These add extra functionality such as video players and sound support.
- NSCA Mosaic – Mosaic was originally the most popular Web browser when the Internet first started. It has now lost its dominance to Microsoft Internet Explorer and Netscape Navigator. NSCA Mosaic was developed by the National Center for Supercomputer Application (NCSA) at the University of Illinois. Figure 6.6 shows a sample window from CompuServe Mosaic.

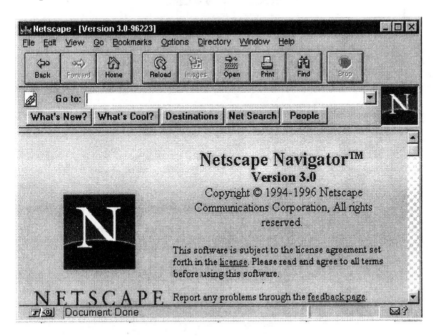

Figure 6.5 Netscape Navigator Version 3.0

- Lynx – Lynx is typically used on Unix-based computers with a modem dial-up connection. It is fast to download pages but does not support many of features supported by Netscape Navigator or Mosaic.
- Microsoft Internet Explorer – This now comes as a standard part of Windows 95/NT and as this will become the most popular computer operating system then so will this browser.

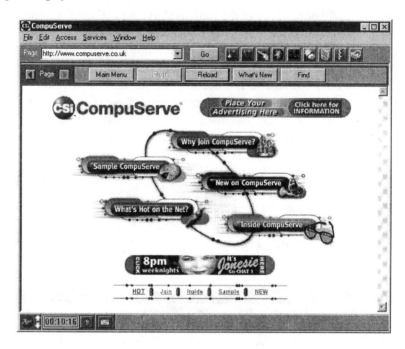

Figure 6.6 CompuServe Mosaic

6.4 Web browser design

The Web browser is a carefully engineered software package which allows the user to efficiently find information on the WWW. Most are similar in their approach and differ in their presentation. Figure 6.7 shows the tool bar for Microsoft Explorer. These are well designed to allow the user to smoothly move through the WWW.

Figure 6.7 Microsoft Explorer tool bar

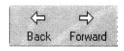

The **Back** and **Forward** options allow the user to transverse backwards and forwards through links. This allows the user to trace back to a previous link and possibly follow it.

The **Stop** option is used by the user to interrupt the current transfer. It is typically used when the user does not want to load the complete page. This often occurs when the browser is loading a graphics image.

The Web browser tries to reduce data transfer by holding recently accessed pages in a memory cache. This cache is typically held on the disk. The **Refresh** forces the browser to re-load the page from the remote location.

Often a user wishes to restart a search and can use the **Home** option to return to it. The home page of the user is set-up by one of the options.

The **Search** option is used to connect to a page which has access to the search programs. Microsoft Explorer typically connects to `http://home.microsoft.com/access/allinone.asp` which displays most of the available search engines. An example screen from Microsoft search facility is given in Figure 6.8. It can be seen that this links to the most commonly used search engines, such as Yahoo, Lycos, Magallan and eXcite.

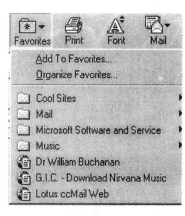

Often a user has a list of favourite Web pages. This can be automatically called from the **Favorites** option. A new favourite can be added with the **Add To Favorites** .. option. These favourites can either be select from the Favorites menu option (such as Lotus ccMail Web) or from within folders (such as Cool Sites and Mail). The favourites are organised using the **Organize Favorites...** option.

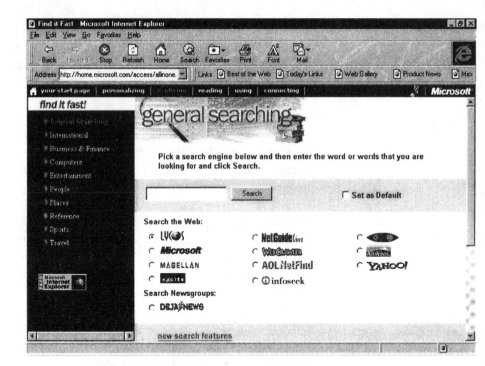

Figure 6.8 Microsoft search facility

Other typically accessed sites can be recalled from Links, such as:

where the options are typically linked to the following:

Best of the Web: `http://home.microsoft.com/access/allinone.asp`
Today's Links: `http://home.microsoft.com/links/link.asp`
Web Gallery: `http://home.microsoft.com/isapi/`
Product news: `http://home.microsoft.com/ie`
Microsoft: `http://home.microsoft.com/`

6.5 Client/server architecture

The WWW is structured with clients and servers, where a client accesses services from the server. These servers can either be local or available through a global network connection. A local connection normally requires the connection over a local area network but a global connection normally requires connection to an Internet provider. These providers are often known as Internet Access Provider (IAP), or sometimes as Internet Connectivity Providers (ICP) or Internet Service Providers (ISP). They basically provide the mechanism to access the Internet and have the required hardware and software to connect from the user to the Internet. This access is typically provided through one of the following:

- Connection to a client computer though a dial-up modem connection (typically at 14.4 kbps or 28.8 kbps).
- Connection to a client computer though a dial-up ISDN connection (typically at 64 kbps or 128 kbps).
- Connection of a client computer to a server computer which connects to the Internet though a frame relay router (typically 56 kbps or 256 kbps).
- Connection to a client computer to a Local Area Network which connects to the Internet though a T-1 1.544 Mbps router.

These connections are illustrated in Figure 6.8. A router automatically routes all traffic to and from the Internet while the dial-up facility of a modem or ISDN link requires a connection to be made over a circuit-switched line (that is, through the Public Telephone Network). Home users and small businesses typically use modem connections (although ISDN connections are becoming more common). Large corporations which require global Internet services tend to use frame routers. Note that an IAP may be a commercial organisation (such as CompuServe or America On-line) or a support organisation (such as giving direct connection to government departments or education institutions). A commercial IAP organisation is likely to provide added services, such as electronic mail, search engines, and so on.

An Internet Presence Provider (IPP) allows organisations to maintain a presence on the Internet without actually having to invest in the Internet hardware. The IPPs typically maintain WWW pages for a given charge (they may also provide sales and support information).

6.6 Internet resources

The Internet expands by the day as the amount of servers and clients which connect to the global network increases and the amount of information contained in the network also increases. The three major services which the Internet provides are:

- The World Wide Web.

- Global electronic mail.
- Information sources.

The main information sources, apart from the WWW, are from FTP, Gopher, WAIS and UseNet servers. These different types of servers will be discussed in the next section.

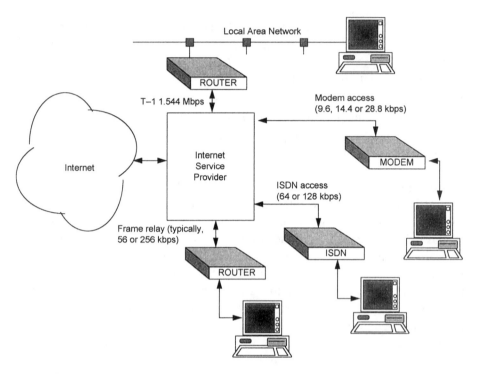

Figure 6.9 Example connection to the Internet

6.7 Universal Resource Locators (URLs)

The URL (uniform resource locator) is the method used to locate a file on the WWW. It basically provides a pointer to any object on a server connected over the Internet. This link could give an FTP access, Hypertext references, and on. It contains:

- The protocol of the file (the scheme).
- The server name (domain).

- The pathname of the file.
- The filename.

Its standard format is:

<scheme>:<scheme-specific-part>

An example is:

```
http://www.toytown.anycor.co/fred/index.html
```

where `http` is the file protocol (HyperText Translation Protocol), `www.toytown.anycor.co` is the server name, `/fred` is the path of the file and the file is named `index.html`. The most common URL formats are:

- `http` – Hypertext Transfer Protocol.
- `ftp` – File Transfer Protocol.
- `gopher` – The Gopher Protocol.
- `mailto` – Electronic mail address.
- `news` – UseNet news.
- `telnet` – Reference to interactive sessions.
- `wais` – Wide Area Information Servers.
- `file` – Host-specific file names.

6.7.1 Electronic Mail Address

The `mailto` scheme defines a link to an Internet email address. An example is:

```
mailto: fred.bloggs@toytown.ac.uk
```

When this URL is selected then an email message will be sent to the email address `fred.bloggs@toytown.ac.uk`. Normally, some form of text editor is called and the user can enter the required email message. Upon successful completion of the message the text message is then sent to the addressee.

6.7.2 File Transfer Protocol (FTP)

The `ftp` URL scheme defines that the files and directories specified are accessed using the FTP protocol. In its simplest form it is defined as:

ftp://<hostname>/<directory-name>/<filename>

The FTP protocol normally requests a user to log into the system. For example, many public domain FTP servers use the login of:

```
anonymous
```

and the password can be anything (but it is normally either the user's full name or Internet email address). Another typical operation is changing directory from a starting directory or the destination file directory. To accommodate this, a more general form is:

ftp://<user>:<password>@<hostname>:<port>/<cd1>/<cd2>/.../<cdn>/<file name>

where the user is defined by <user> and the password by <password> . The host name, <hostname>, is defined after the @ symbol and change directory commands are defined by the cd commands.

6.7.3 Host-specific file names

The file URL defines that the file is local to the computer and is not accessed through a server application. An example, taken from PC, for a file C:\WWW\1.HTM is accessed with the URL:

```
file:///C|/WWW/1.HTM
```

6.7.4 Hypertext Transfer Protocol (HTTP)

HTTP is the protocol which is used to retrieve information connected with hypermedia links. The client and server initially perform a negotiation procedure before the HTTP transfer takes place. This negotiation involves the client sending a list of formats it can support and the server replies with data in the required format. This will be discussed in more detail in the next chapter.

Users generally move from a link on one server to another server. Each time the user moves from one server to another then the client sends an HTTP request to the server. Thus the client does not permanently connect to the server and the server views each transfer as independent from all previous accesses. This is known as a stateless protocol.

6.7.5 Reference to interactive session (TELNET)

The telnet URL allows users to interactively perform a telnet operation, where a user must login to the referred system.

6.7.6 UseNet news

UseNet or NewsGroup servers are part of the increasing use of general discussion news groups which share text-based news items. The news URL scheme defines a link to either a news group or individual articles with a group of UseNet news.

6.7.7 The gopher protocol

Gopher is widely used over the Internet and is basically a distribution system for the retrieval and delivery of documents. Users retrieve documents through a series of hierarchical menus, or through key-word search. Unlike HTML documents it is not based on the hypertext concept.

6.7.8 Wide area information servers (WAIS)

WAIS is a public domain, fully text-based, information retrieval system over the Internet which performs text-based searches. The communications protocol used is based on the ANSI standard Z39.50, which is designed for networking library catalogues.

WAIS services include index generation and search engines. An indexer generates multiple indexes for organisations or individuals who offer services over the Internet. A WAIS search engine searches for particular words or text strings indexes located across multiple Internet attached information servers of various types.

6.8 Universal resource identifier

The Universal Resource Identifier (URI) is defined as a generically designated string of characters which refers to objects on the WWW. A URL is an example of a URI, with a designated access protocol and a specific Internet address.

The usage of URIs is still being specified, but it will basically define the syntax for encoding arbitrary naming or addressing schemes. This should decouple the name of a resource from its location and also from its access method. For example, the file:

```
MYPIC.HTM
```

would be automatically associated with a HTTP protocol.

6.9 Exercises

The following questions are multiple choice. Please select from a–d.

6.9.1   Where was the WWW first conceived:

(a)   UCL
(b)   UMIST
(c)   MIT
(d)   CERN

6.9.2   An MPEG file is what type of file:

(a)   Image
(b)   Motion video
(c)   Sound file
(d)   Generally compressed file

6.9.3   A GIF file is what type of file:

(a)   Image
(b)   Motion video
(c)   Sound file
(d)   Generally compressed file

6.9.4   An ZIP file is what type of file:

(a)   Image
(b)   Motion video
(c)   Sound file
(d)   Generally compressed file

6.9.5   An AU file is what type of file:

(a)   Image
(b)   Motion video
(c)   Sound file
(d)   Generally compressed file

6.9.6   Where is the information on the Web stored:

(a)   Web clients and servers
(b)   Web clients
(c)   Web servers
(d)   Web gateways

6.9.7   Which of the following best describes an Intranet:

(a)   A company specific network using company designed tools
(b)   A local internet which is isolated from the Internet
(c)   A totally incompatible system to the Internet
(d)   A faster version of the Internet

6.10 Tutorial

6.10.1   If possible, search for the following subjects on the Internet:

(a)   Ethernet
(b)   EaStMAN
(c)   Edinburgh
(d)   Napier
(e)   Taxation
(f)   Intel
(g)   FDDI

6.10.2   If possible, access the following WWW servers:

(a)   http://www.microsoft.com
(b)   http://www.intel.com
(c)   http://www.ieee.com
(d)   http://www.winzip.com
(e)   http://www.netscape.com
(f)   http://www.realaudio.com
(g)   http://www.cyrix.com
(h)   http://www.compaq.com
(i)   http://www.psion.com
(j)   http://www.amd.com
(k)   http://www.cnn.com
(l)   http://www.w3.org
(m)   http://www.microsoft.com/ie
(n)   http://www.macromedia.com
(o)   http://www.epson.co.uk
(p)   http://www.euronec.com
(q)   http://www.casio.com
(r)   http://www.hayes.com
(s)   http://www.lotus.com

(t)   http://www.adobe.com
(u)   http://www.corel.com
(v)   http://www.guinness.ie
(w)   http://www.symantec.co.uk
(x)   http://www.fractal.com
(y)   http://www.quarterdeck.com

6.10.3   Discuss the methods that users use to find information on the Web.

6.10.4   The home page for this book can be found at the URL:

http://www.eece.napier.ac.uk/~bill_b/mti.hmtl

Access this page and follow any links it contains.

7 Intranets and HTTP

7.1 Introduction

Chapter 6 discussed the WWW. The foundation protocol of the WWW is the Hypertext Transfer Protocol (HTTP) which can be used in any client-server application involving hypertext. It is used in the WWW for transmitting information using hypertext jumps and can support the transfer of plain text, hypertext, audio, images, or any Internet-compatible information. The most recently defined standard is HTTP 1.1 which has been defined by the IETF standard.

This chapter also discusses the use of Intranet, which allow organisations to connect to the Internet without having the problem of external users from accessing information on their network.

7.2 Intranets

The major disadvantages to organisations using a WWW and Internet connections are:

- The possible usage of the Internet for non-useful applications (by employees).
- The possible connection of non-friendly users from the global connection into the organisation's local network.

For these reasons many organisations have shied away from connection to the global network and have set-up Intranets. These are in-house, tailor-made internets for use within the organisation and provide limited access (if any) to outside services and also limit the external traffic into the Intranet (if any). Possibly an Intranet has access to the global Internet but no access from the Internet to the local Intranet.

Organisations which have a requirement for sharing and distributing electronic information normally have three choices:

- Use a propriety groupware package, such as Lotus Notes.
- Set up an Intranet.
- Set up a connection to the Internet.

Groupware packages normally replicate data locally on a computer whereas Intranets centralise their information on central servers which are then accessed by a single browser package. The stored data normally is open and can be viewed by any compatible WWW browser. Intranet browsers have the great advantage over groupware packages in that they are available for a variety of clients, such as PC, Unix workstations, Macs, and so on. A client browser also provides a single GUI interface which offers easy integration with other applications, such as electronic mail, images, audio, video, animation, and so on.

The main elements of an Intranet are:

- An Intranet server hardware.
- An Intranet server software.
- TCP/IP stack software on the clients and server.
- WWW browsers.
- A firewall.

Typically the Intranet server consists of a PC running the Lynx (PC-based UNIX-like) operating system. The TCP/IP stack is software installed on each computer and allows communications between a client and a server using TCP/IP.

A firewall is the routing computer which isolates the Intranet from the outside world. This will be discussed in the next section.

7.3 Firewalls

A firewall (or security gateway) protects a network against intrusion from outside sources. They tend to differ in their approach but can be characterised by the following:

- Firewalls which block traffic.
- Firewalls which permit traffic.

7.3.1 Packet filters

The packet filter is the simplest form of firewall. It basically keeps a record of allowable source and destination IP addresses and deletes all packets which do not have these addresses. This technique is known as address filtering. The packet filter keeps a separate source and destination table for both directions, that is, into and out of the Intranet. This type of method is useful for companies which have geographically spread sites, as the packet filter can allow incoming traffic from other 'friendly' sites, but block other 'non-friendly' traffic. This is illustrated by Figure 7.1.

Unfortunately this method suffers from the fact that IP addresses can be easily forged. For example, a 'hacker' might determine the list of good source addresses and then add one of these addresses to any packets which are addressed into the Intranet.

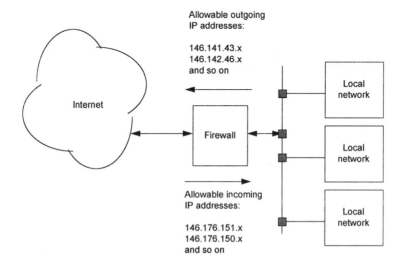

Figure 7.1 Packet filter firewalls

7.3.2 Application level gateway

Application level gateways provide an extra layer of security to connection of an Intranet to the Internet. It has two main components:

- A gateway node.
- Two firewalls which connect on either side of the gateway and only transmit packets which are destined for, or to, the gateway.

Figure 7.2 shows the operation of an application level gateway. In this case, Firewall A discards anything that is not addressed to the gateway node, and discards anything that is not sent by the gateway node. Firewall B, similarly discards anything from the local network that is not addressed to the gateway node, and discards anything that is not sent by the gateway node. Thus to transfer files from the local network into the global network the user must do the following:

- Log onto the gateway node.
- Transfer the file onto the gateway.
- Transfer the file from the gateway onto the global network.

To copy a file from the network an external user must:

- Log onto the gateway node.
- Transfer from the global network onto the gateway.
- Transfer the file from the gateway onto the local network.

A common strategy in organisations is to allow only electronic mail to pass from the Internet to the local network. This specifically disallows file transfer and remote login. Unfortunately electronic mail can be used to transfer files. To overcome this problem the firewall can be designed to specifically disallow very large electronic mail messages, so that it will limit the ability to transfer files. This tends not to a good method as large files can be split-up into small parts and then sent individually.

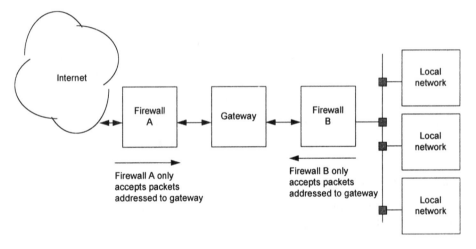

Figure 7.2 Application level gateway

7.3.3 Encrypted tunnels

Packet filters and application level gateways suffer from insecurity which can allow non-friendly users into the local network. Packet filters can be tricked with fake IP addresses and application level gateways can be 'hacked-into' by determining the password of certain users of the gateway and then transferring the files from the network to the firewall, then to the gateway, next to the firewall and out. The best form of protection for this type of attack is to only allow a limited number of people to transfer files onto the gateway.

The best method of protection is to encrypt the data leaving the network and then decrypt it on the remote site. Only friendly sites will have the required encryption key to receive and send data. This has the extra advantage that the data cannot be easily 'tapped-into'.

Only the routers which connect to the Internet require to encrypt and decrypt, as illustrated in Figure 7.3.

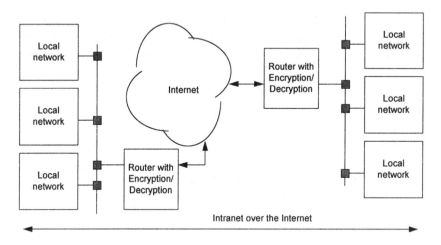

Figure 7.3 Encryption tunnels

7.4 HTTP

HTTP is a stateless protocol where each transaction is independent of any previous transactions. The advantage of being stateless is that it allows the rapid access of WWW pages over a number of widely distributed servers. It uses the TCP protocol to establish a connection between a client and a server for each transaction and then terminates the connection once the transaction completes.

HTTP also supports many different formats of data. Initially a client issues a request to a server which may include a prioritised list of formats that it can handle. This allows new formats to be added easily and also prevents the transmission of unnecessary information.

A client's WWW browser (the user agent) initially establishes a direct connection with destination server which contains the required WWW page. To make this connection the client initiates a TCP connection between the client and the server. After this is established the client then issues an HTTP request, such as the specific command (the method), the URL, and, possibly, extra information such as request parameters, client information. Then when the server receives the request it attempts to perform the requested action. It then returns an HTTP response which includes status information, a success/error code, and extra information itself. After this is received by the client the TCP connection is closed.

7.4.1 Intermediate systems

The previous section discussed the direct connection of a client to a server. On many system organisations do not wish a direct connection to an internal network. Thus HTTP supports other connections which are formed through intermediate systems, such as:

- A proxy.
- A gateway.
- A tunnel.

Each intermediate system is connected by a TCP and acts as a relay for the request to be sent to and returned back to the client. Figure 7.4 shows the setup of the proxies and gateways.

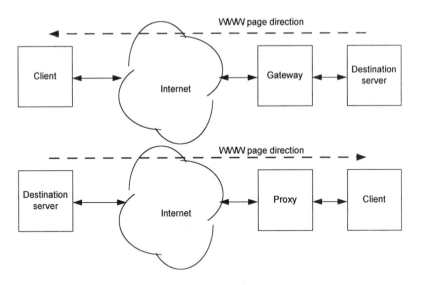

Figure 7.4 Usage of proxies and gateways

Proxy

A proxy connects to a number of clients and acts on behalf of other clients and sends requests from the clients to a server. It thus acts as a client when it communicates with the server, but as a server when communicating with the clients. A proxy is typically used for security purposes where the client and server are separated by a firewall. The proxy connects to the client side of the firewall and the server to the other side of the firewall. Thus the server must authenticate itself to the firewall before a connection can be made with the proxy. Only after this has been authenticated will the proxy pass requests through the firewall.

A proxy can also be used to convert between different versions of HTTP.

Gateway

Gateways are servers that act as if they are the destination server. They are typically used when clients cannot get direct access to the server, and typically for one of the following reasons for security purposes where the gateway acts as a firewall so that the gateway communicates with the Internet and the server only communicates with the Internet through the gateway. The client must then authenticate itself to the proxy, which can then pass the request on to the server.

They can also be used when the destination is a non-HTTP server. Web browsers have built into them the capability to contact servers for protocols other than HTTP, such as FTP and Gopher servers. This capability can also be provided by a gateway. The client makes an HTTP request to a gateway server. The gateway server than contacts the relevant FTP or Gopher server to obtain the desired result. This result is then converted into a form suitable for HTTP and transmitted back to the client.

Tunnel

A tunnel does not perform any operation on the HTTP message and is passed onto the client or server unchanged. This differs from a proxy and gateway which modify the HTTP messages. Tunnels are typically used as firewalls where the firewall authenticates the connection but simply relays the HTTP messages.

7.4.2 Cache

In a computer system a cache is an area of memory that stores information that is likely to be accessed in a fast access memory area. For example a cache controller takes a guess on which information the process is likely to access next. When the processor wishes to access the disk then if the cache controller has guessed right it will load it from the electronic memory rather than loading it from the disk. A WWW cache stores cacheable responses so that there is a reduction in network traffic and an improvement in access times.

7.4.3 HTTP messages

HTTP messages are either request from clients to servers or responses from servers to clients. The message is either a simple-Request, a simple-response, full-request or a full-response. HTTP Version 0.9 defined the simple request/response messages while HTTP Version 1.1 defines full requests/responses.

Simple requests/responses

The simple request is a GET command with the requested URI such as:

```
GET   /info/dept/courses.html
```

The simple response is a block containing the information identified in the URI (called the entity-body).

Full requests/responses

There is very little security or enhanced services built into the simple requests/ responses. HTTP Version 1/1.1 improves on the simple requests/ responses by adding many extra requests and responses, as well as adding extra information about the data supported. Each message header consists of a number of fields which begin on a new line and consists of the field name followed by a colon and the field value. This follows the format of RFC 822 (as shown in Section 5.5.4) and allows for MIME encoding. It is thus similar to MIME-encoded email. A full request starts with a request line command (such as GET, MOVE or DELETE) and is then followed by one or more of the following:

- General-headers which contain general fields which do not apply to the entity being transferred (such as the MIME Version, Date, and so on).
- Request-headers which contain information on the request and the client (for example the client's name, its authorisation, and so on).
- Entity-headers which contain information about the resource identified by the request and entity body information (such as the type of encoding, the language, the title, the time when it was last modified, the type of resource it is, when it expires, and so on).
- Entity-body which contains the body of the message (such as HTML text, an image, a sound file, and so on).

A full response starts with a response status code (such as OK, Moved Temporarily, Accepted, Created, Bad Request, and so on) and is then followed by one or more of the following:

- General-headers, as with requests, contain general fields which do not apply to the entity being transferred (such as the MIME Version, Date, and so on).

- Response-headers which contain information on the response and the server (for example the server's name, its location and the time the client should retry the server).
- Entity-headers, as with request, which contain information about the resource identified by the request and entity body information (such as the type of encoding, the language, the title, the time when it was last modified, the type of resource it is, when it expires, and so on).
- Entity-body, as with requests, which contains the body of the message (such as HTML text, an image, a sound file, and so on).

The following example shows an example request. The first line is always the request method, in this case it is GET. Next there are various headers. The general header field is Content-Type, the request header fields are If-Modified-Since and From. There are no entity parts to the message as the request is to get an image (if the command had been to PUT then there would be an attachment with the request). Notice that the end of the message is delimited by a single blank line as this indicates the end of a request/response. Note that the headers are case sensitive, thus Content-Type with the correct type of letters (and GET is always in uppercase letters).

📖 **Example HTTP request**
```
GET mypic.jpg
Content-Type: Image/jpeg
If-Modified-Since: 06 Mar 1997 12:35:00
From: Fred Bloggs <FREDB@ACOMP.CO.UK>
```

Request messages
The most basic request message is to GET a URI. HTTP/1.1 adds many more requests including:

COPY	DELETE	GET	HEAD	POST
LINK	MOVE	OPTIONS	PATCH	PUT
TRACE	UNLINK	WRAPPED		

As before, the GET method requests a WWW page. The HEAD method requests the server that the client wants to read only the header of the WWW page. If the If-Modified-Since field is included then the server checks the specified date with the date of the URI and if it has not changed since then.

A PUT method requests to store a WWW page and POST appends to a named resource (such as electronic mail). LINK connects two existing resources while the UNLINK breaks the link. A DELETE method removes a WWW page.

The request header fields are mainly used to define the acceptable type of entity that can be received by the client, they include:

```
Accept               Accept-Charset      Accept-Encoding
Authorization        From                Host
If-Modified-Since    If-Modified-Since
Proxy-Authorization
Range                Referer             Unless
User-Agent
```

The `Accept` field is used to list all the media types and ranges that are acceptable to the client. An `Accept-charset` field defines a list of characters set acceptable to the server and `Accept-encoding` is a list of acceptable content encodings (such as the compression or encryption technique). The `Accept-language` field defines a set of preferred natural languages.

The `Authorization` field has a value which authenticates the client to the server. A `From` field defines the e-mail address of the user who is using the client (for example, `From: fred.blogg@anytown.uk`) and the `Host` field specifies name of the host of the resource being requested.

A useful field is the `If-Modified-Since` which is used with the `GET` method. It defines a date and time parameter and specifies that the resource should not be sent if it has not been modified since the specified date and time. This is useful when a client has a local copy of the resource in a local cache and rather than transmitting the unchanged resource it can use its own local copy.

The `Proxy-authorization` field is used by the client to identify itself to a proxy when the proxy requires authorization. A `Range` field is used with the `GET` message to get only a part of the resource.

The `Referer` field defines the URI of the resource from which the `Request-URI` was obtained and enables the server to generate list of back-links. An `Unless` field is used to make a comparison which is based on any Entity-Header field value rather than a date/time value (as with `GET` and `If-Modified-Since`).

The `User-agent` field contains information about the user agent originating this request.

Response messages

In HTTP/0.9 the response from the server was either the entity or no response. HTTP/1.1 includes many other responses, these responses can be grouped into 5 main groupings:

- Client error – `Bad Request`, `Conflict`, `Forbidden`, `Gone`, `Payment required`, `Not Found`, `Method Not Allowed`, `None Acceptable`,

Proxy Authentication Required, Request Timeout, Length Required, Unauthorized and Unless True.

- Informational – Continue and Switching Protocol.
- Redirection – Moved Permanently, Moved Temporarily, Multiple Choices, See Other, Not Modified and User Proxy.
- Server error – Bad Gateway, Internal Server Error, Not Implemented, Service Unavailable and Gateway Timeout.
- Successful – Accepted, Created, OK, Non-Authoritative Information. The OK field is used when the request succeeds and includes the appropriate response information.

The response header fields are:

```
Location            Proxy-Authenticate        Public
Retry-After         Server                    WWW-Authenticate
```

The Location field defines the location of the resource identified by the Request-URI. A Proxy-authenticate field contains the status code of the Proxy Authentication Required response.

The Public field defines non-standard methods supported by this server. A Retry-after field contains values which define the amount of time that a service will be unavailable (and is thus sent with the Service Unavailable response).

The WWW-authenticate field contains the status code for the Unauthorized response.

General header fields
General header fields are used within either requests or responses, they include:

```
Cache-Control    Connection      Date        Forwarded
Keep-Alive       MIME-Version    Pragma      Upgrade
```

The Cache-Control field gives information on the caching mechanism and stops the cache controller from modifying the request/response. A Connection field specifies the header-fields names that apply to the current TCP connection.

The Date field specifies the date and time at which the message originated, this is obviously useful when examining the received message as it gives an indication of the amount of time the message took to arrive at its destination. Gateways and proxies use the Forwarded field to indicate intermediate steps between the client and server. When a gateway or proxy reads the message it can attach a Forwarded field with its own URI (this can help in tracing the route of a message).

The `Keep-Alive` field specifies that the requester wants a persistent connection. It may indicate the maximum amount of time that the sender will wait for the next request before closing the connection. It can also be used to specify the maximum number of additional requests on the current persistent connection.

The `MIME-Version` field indicates the MIME version (such as `MIME-Version: 1.0`). A `Pragma` field contains extra information for specific applications.

In a request the `Upgrade` field specifies the additional protocols that the client supports and wishes to use, while in a response it indicates the protocol to be used.

Entity header fields
Depending on the type of request or response an entity header can be contained, they include:

Allow	Content-Encoding	Content-Language
Content-Length	Content-MD5	Content-Range
Content-Type	Content-Version	Derived-From
Expires	Last-Modified	Link
Title	Transfer-encoding	URI-Header
extension-header		

The `Allow` field defines the supported methods supported by the resource identified in the Request-URI. A `Content-encoding` field indicates content encoding, such as ZIP compression, that have been applied to the resource (`Content-encoding: zip`).

The `Content-language` field identifies natural language(s) of the intended audience for the enclosed entity (for example `Content-language: German`) and the `Content-length` field define the number of bytes that the entity has.

The `Content-range` designates a portion of the identified resource that is included in this response, while `Content-type` indicates the media type of the entity body (such as `content-type=text/html`, `content-type=text/plain`, `content-type=image/gif` or `content-type=image/jpeg`). The version of the entity is defined in the `Content-version` field.

The `Expires` defines the date and time that the entity is considered stale. A `Last-modified` field is the date and time that the resource was last modified.

The `Link` field defines other links and the `Title` field defines the title for the entity. A Transfer-encoding field indicates the transformation type that is applied so that the entity can be transmitted.

The following questions are multiple choice. Please select from a–d.

7.5.1 Which of the following best describes an Intranet:

    (a) A company specific network using company designed tools
    (b) A local internet which is isolated from the Internet
    (c) A totally incompatible system to the Internet
    (d) A faster version of the Internet

7.5.2 The main function of a firewall is:

    (a) To disallow unwanted users into the network and allow wanted traffic
    (b) To allow users access to the Internet
    (c) To allow faster transfer of data between the Intranet and the Internet
    (d) Convert one type of network to connect to another type

7.5.3 Which of the following best describes a proxy:

    (a) It connects to a number of clients and acts on behalf of other clients and sends requests from the clients to a server
    (b) A server that acts as if it is the destination server
    (c) It passes messages to the client or server without modifying it
    (d) It stores responses

7.5.4 Which of the following best describes a gateway:

    (a) It connects to a number of clients and acts on behalf of other clients and sends requests from the clients to a server
    (b) A server that acts as if it is the destination server
    (c) It passes messages to the client or server without modifying it
    (d) It stores responses

7.5.5 Which of the following best describes a tunnel:

    (a) It connects to a number of clients and acts on behalf of other clients and sends requests from the clients to a server
    (b) A server that acts as if it is the destination server
    (c) It passes messages to the client or server without modifying it
    (d) It stores responses

7.6 Tutorial

7.6.1   Explain how proxies and gateways are used to provide security.

7.6.2   Discuss the limitation of simple requests and responses with HTTP.

7.6.3   Discuss request messages and the fields that are set.

7.6.4   Discuss response messages and the fields that are set.

8 HTML (Introduction)

8.1 Introduction

HTML is a standard hypertext language for the WWW and has several different versions. Most WWW browsers support HTML 2 and most of the new versions of the browsers support HTML 3. WWW pages are created and edited with a text editor, a word processor or, as is becoming more common, within the WWW browser.

HTML tags contain special formatting commands and are contained within a less than (<) and a greater than (>) symbol (which are also known as angled brackets). Most tags have an opening and closing version, for example, to highlight bold text the bold opening tag is <B> and the closing tag is </B>. Table 8.1 outlines a few examples.

Table 8.1 Example HTML tags

Open tag	Closing tag	Description
<HTML>	</HTML>	Start and end of HTML
<HEAD>	</HEAD>	Defines the HTML header
<BODY>	</BODY>	Defines the main body of the HTML
<TITLE>	</TITLE>	Defines the title of the WWW page
<I>	</I>	Italic text
<B>	</B>	Bold text
<U>	</U>	Underlined text
<BLINK>	</BLINK>	Make text blink
<EM>	</EM>	Emphasise text
<FONT SIZE=+1>	</FONT>	Increase font size by one increment
<FONT SIZE=-1>	</FONT>	Reduce font size by one increment
<CENTER>	</CENTER>	Centre text
<H1>	</H1>	Section header, level 1
<H2>	</H2>	Section header, level 2
<H3>	</H3>	Section header, level 3
<P>		Create a new paragraph
 		Create a line break
<!-->	-->	Comments
<SUPER>	</SUPER>	Superscript
_		Subscript

HTML script 1 gives an example script and Figure 8.1 shows the output from the WWW browser. The first line is always <HTML> and the last line is </HTML>. After this line the HTML header is defined between <HEAD> and </HEAD>. The title of the window in this case is My first HTML page. The main HTML text is then defined between <BODY> and </BODY>.

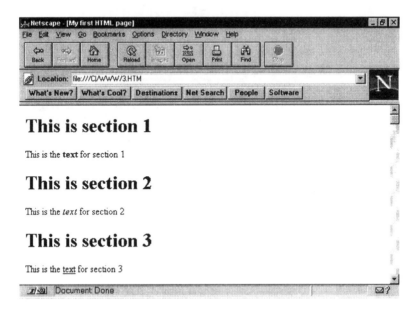

Figure 8.1 Example window from example HTML script

📖 HTML script 8.1

```
<HTML>
<HEAD>
<TITLE>My first HTML page</TITLE>
</HEAD>
<BODY>
<H1> This is section 1</H1>
This is the <b>text</b> for section 1
<H1> This is section 2</H1>
This is the <i>text</i> for section 2
<H1> This is section 3</H1>
This is the <u>text</u> for section 3
<p>
This is the end of the text
</BODY>
</HTML>
```

The WWW browser fits text into the window size and does not interpret line breaks in the HTML source. To force a new line the
 (line break) or a new paragraph (<P>) is used. The example also shows bold, italic and underlined text.

8.2 Links

The topology of the WWW is set-up using links where pages link to other related pages. A reference takes the form:

<A HREF="*url*"> *Reference Name* </A>

where *url* defines the URL for the file, *Reference Name* is the name of the reference and </A> defines the end of the reference name. HTML script 8.2 shows an example of the uses of references and Figure 8.2 shows a sample browser page. The background colour is set using the <BODY BGCOLOR="#FFFFFF"> which set the background colour to white. In this case the default text colour is black and the link is coloured blue.

📖 HTML script 8.2

```
<HTML>

<HEAD>
<TITLE>Fred's page</TITLE>
</HEAD>
<BODY BGCOLOR="#FFFFFF">

<H1>Fred's Home Page</H1>
If you want to access information on
this book <A HREF="adcbook.html">click here</A>.

<P>
A reference to the <A REF="http:www.iee.com/">IEE</A>
</BODY>
</HTML>
```

8.2.1 Other links

Links can be set-up to send e-mail and newsgroups. For example:

```
<A HREF="news:sport.tennis"> Newsgroups for tennis</A>
```

to link to a tennis newsgroup and

```
<A HREF="mailto:f.bloggs@fredco.co.uk">Send a
message to me</A>
```

to send a mail message to the e-mail address: f.bloggs@ fredco.co.uk.

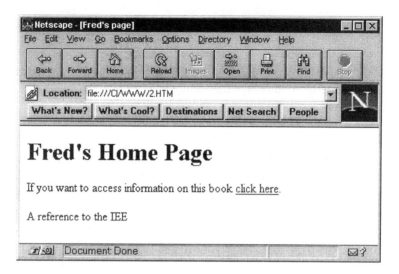

Figure 8.2 Example window from example HTML script 2

8.3 Lists

HTML allows ordered and unordered lists. Lists can be declared anywhere in the body of the HTML.

8.3.1 Ordered lists

The start of an ordered list is defined with `<OL>` and the end of the list by `</OL>`. Each part of the list is defined after the `<LI>` tag. Unordered lists are defined between the `<UL>` and `</UL>` tags. HTML script 8.3 gives examples of an ordered and an unordered list. Figure 8.3 shows the output from the browser.

📖 HTML script 8.3

```
<HTML>
<HEAD>
<TITLE>Fred's page</TITLE>
</HEAD>
<BODY BGCOLOR="#FFFFFF">
<H1>List 1</H1>
<OL>
<LI>Part 1
<LI>Part 2
<LI>Part 3
</OL>
<H1>List 2</H1>
```

```
<UL>
<LI>Section 1
<LI>Section 2
<LI>Section 3
</UL>
</BODY>
</HTML>
```

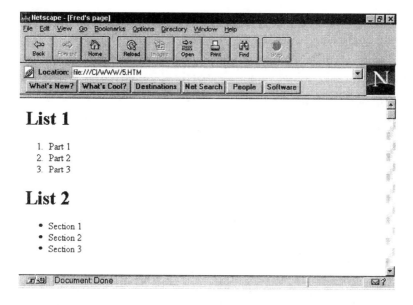

Figure 8.3 WWW browser with an ordered and unordered lists

Some browsers allow the type of numbered list to be defined with the $<$OL
TYPE=$x>$, where x can either be:

- A for capital letters (such as a, b, c, and so on).
- a for small letters (such as a, b, c, and so on).
- I for capital roman letters (such as I, II, III, and so on).
- i for small roman letters (such as i, ii, iii, and so on).
- I for numbers (which is the default).

```
<OL Type=I>
<LI> List 1
<LI> List 2
<LI> List 3
</OL>
<OL Type=A>
<LI> List 1
<LI> List 2
<LI> List 3
</OL>
```

would be displayed as:

I.   List 1
II.   List 2
III. List 3
A.   List 1
B.   List 2
C.   List 3

The starting number of the list can be defined using the <LI VALUE=*n*> where *n* defines the initial value of the defined item list.

8.3.2 Unordered lists

Unordered lists are used to list a series of items in no particular order. They are defined between the <UL> and </UL> tags. Some browsers allow the type of bullet point to be defined with the <LI TYPE=*shape*>, where *shape* can either be:

- *disc* for round solid bullets (which is the default for first level lists).
- *round* for round hollow bullets (which is the default for second level lists).
- *square* for square bullets (which is the default for third).

HTML script 8.4 gives an example of an unnumbered list and Figure 8.4 shows the WWW page output for this script. It can be seen from this that the default bullets for level 1 lists are discs, for level 2 they are round and for level 3 they are square.

📖 HTML script 8.4

```
<HTML>
<HEAD>
<TITLE>Example list</TITLE>
</HEAD>
<H1> Introduction </H1>
<UL>
<LI> OSI Model
<LI> Networks
   <UL>
   <LI> Ethernet
      <UL>
      <LI> MAC addresses
      </UL>
   <LI> Token Ring
   <LI> FDDI
   </UL>
<LI> Conclusion
</UL>
```

```
<H1> Wide Area Networks </H1>
<UL>
<LI> Standards
<LI> Examples
   <UL>
   <LI> EastMan
   </UL>
<LI> Conclusion
</UL>
</BODY>
</HTML>
```

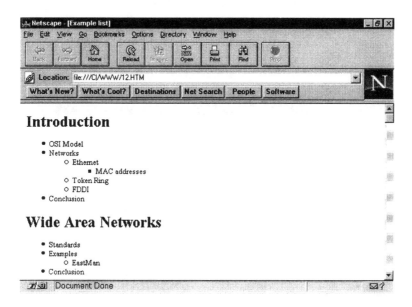

Figure 8.4   WWW page with an unnumbered list

8.3.3 Definition lists

HTML uses the <DL> and </DL> tags for definition lists. These are normally used when building glossaries. Each entry in the definition is defined by the <DT> tag and the text associated with the item is defined after the <DD> tag. The end of the list is defined by </DL>. HTML script 8.5 shows an example with a definition list and Figure 8.5 gives a sample output. Note that it uses the <EM> tag to emphasise the definition subject.

📖 HTML script 8.5
```
<HTML>
<HEAD>
<TITLE>Example list</TITLE>
</HEAD>
<H1> Glossary </H1>
```

```
<DL>
<DT> <EM> Address Resolution Protocol (ARP) </EM>
<DD> A TCP/IP process which maps an IP address to an
Ethernet address.
<DT> <EM> American National Standards Institute
(ANSI) </EM>
<DD> ANSI is a non-profit organization which is made
up of expert committees that publish standards for
national industries.
<DT> <EM> American Standard Code for Information
Interchange (ASCII) </EM>
<DD> An ANSI-defined character alphabet which has
since been adopted as a standard international
alphabet for the interchange of characters.
</DL>
</BODY>
</HTML>
```

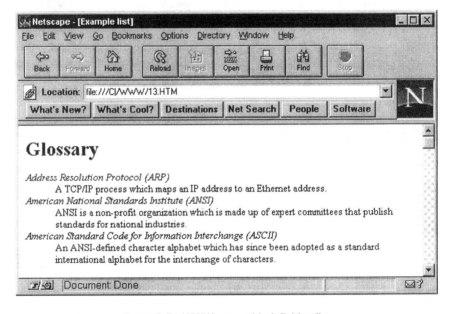

Figure 8.5 WWW page with definition list

8.4 Colours

Colours in HTML are defined in the RGB (red/green/blue) strength. The
format is #rrggbb, where rr is the hexadecimal equivalent for the red
component, gg the hexadecimal equivalent for the green component and bb
the hexadecimal equivalent for the blue component. Table 8.2 lists some of

the codes for certain colours.

Individual hexadecimal numbers use base 16 and range from 0 to F (in decimal this ranges from 0 to 15). A two digit hexadecimal number ranges from 00 to FF (in decimal this ranges from 0 to 255). Table 8.3 outlines hexadecimal equivalents.

HTML uses percentage strengths for the colours. For example FF represents full strength (100%) and 00 represent no strength (0%). Thus, white is made from FF (red), FF (green) and FF (blue) and black is made from 00 (red), 00 (green) and 00 (blue). Grey is made from equal weighting of each of the colours, such as 43, 43, 43 for dark grey (#434343) and D4, D4 and D4 for light grey (#D4D4D4). Thus, pure red with be #FF0000, pure green will be #00FF00 and pure blue with be #0000FF.

Table 8.2 Hexadecimal colours

Colour	Code	Colour	Code
White	#FFFFFF	Dark red	#C91F16
Light red	#DC640D	Orange	#F1A60A
Yellow	#FCE503	Light green	#BED20F
Dark green	#088343	Light blue	#009DBE
Dark blue	#0D3981	Purple	#3A0B59
Pink	#F3D7E3	Nearly black	#434343
Dark grey	#777777	Grey	#A7A7A7
Light grey	#D4D4D4	Black	#000000

Each colour is represented by 8 bits thus the colour is defined by 24 bits. This gives a total of 16 777 216 colours (2^{24} different colours). Note that some video displays will not have enough memory to display 16.777 million colours in the certain mode so that colours may differ depending on the WWW browser and the graphics adapter.

The colours of the background, text and the link can be defined with the BODY tag. An example with a background colour of white, a text colour of orange and a link colour of dark red is:

```
<BODY BGCOLOR="#FFFFFF" TEXT="#F1A60A"  LINK="#C91F16">
```

and for a background colour of red, a text colour of green and a link colour of blue:

```
<BODY BGCOLOR="#FF0000" TEXT="#00FF00"  LINK="#0000FF">
```

When a link has been visited its colour changes. This colour itself can be changed with the VLINK. For example to set-up a visited link colour of yellow:

```
<BODY VLINK="#FCE503" "TEXT=#00FF00"  "LINK=#0000FF">
```

Note that the default link colours are:

Link: #0000FF   (Blue)
Visited link: #FF00FF   (Purple)

Table 8.3 Hexadecimal to decimal conversions

Hex.	Dec.	Hex.	Dec.	Hex.	Dec.	Hex.	Dec.
0	0	1	1	2	2	3	3
4	4	5	5	6	6	7	7
8	8	9	9	A	10	B	11
C	12	D	13	E	14	F	15

8.5 Background images

Image (such as GIF and JPEG) can be used as a background to a WWW page. For this purpose the option BACKGROUND="*src.gif*" is added to the <BODY> tag. An HTML script with a background of CLOUDS.GIF is given in HTML script 8.6. A sample output from a browser is shown in Figure 8.6.

📖 HTML script 8.6

```
<HTML>
<HEAD>

<TITLE>Fred's page</TITLE>

</HEAD>

<BODY BACKGROUND="clouds.gif">

<H1>Fred's Home Page</H1>
If you want to access information on
this book <A HREF="gbook.html">click here</A>.

<P>
A reference to the <A
HREF="http://www.iee.com/">IEE</A>

</BODY>
</HTML>
```

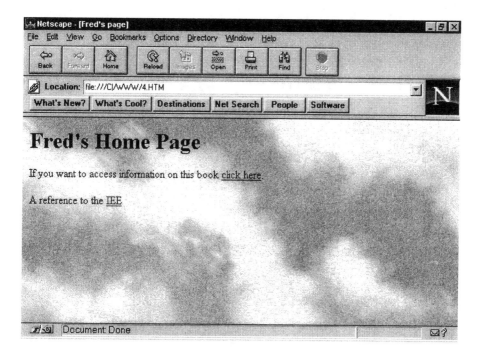

Figure 8.6   WWW page with CLOUD.GIF as a background

8.6 Displaying images

WWW pages can support graphics images within a page. The most common sources of images are either JPEG or GIF files as these types of images normally have a high degree of compression. GIF images, as was previously mentioned, only supports 256 colours from a pallet of 16.7 million colours, whereas JPEG supports more than 256 colours.

8.6.1 Inserting an image

Images can be displayed within a page with the <IMG SRC="*src.gif*"> which inserts the graphic *src.gif*. HTML script 8.7 contains three images: myson.gif, me.gif and myson2.gif. These are aligned either to the left or the right using the ALIGN option within the <IMG SRC> tag. The first image (myson.gif) is aligned to the right, while the second image (me.gif) is aligned to the left. Figure 8.7 shows a sample output from this script. Note that images are left aligned by default.

☐ HTML script 8.7

```
<HTML>
<HEAD>
<TITLE>My first home page</TITLE>
</HEAD>
<BODY BGCOLOR="#ffffff">
<IMG SRC ="myson.gif" ALIGN=RIGHT>
<H1> Picture gallery </H1>
<P>
<P>
Here are a few pictures of me and my family. To the
right is a picture of my youngest son showing his
best smile. Below to the left is a picture of me at
Christmas and to the right is a picture of me and my
son also taken at Christmas.
<P>
<P>
<IMG SRC ="me.gif" ALIGN=LEFT>
<IMG SRC ="myson2.gif" ALIGN=RIGHT>
</BODY>
</HTML>
```

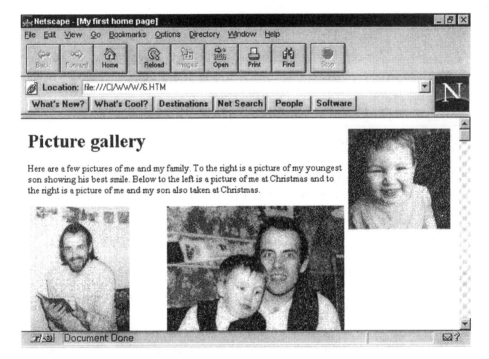

Figure 8.7 WWW page with three images

8.6.2 Alternative text

Often users choose not to view images in a page and select an option on the viewer which stops the viewer from displaying any graphic images. If this is the case then the HTML page can contain substitute text which is shown instead of the image. For example:

```
<IMG SRC ="myson.gif" ALT="Picture of my son"
ALIGN=RIGHT>
<IMG SRC ="me.gif" ALT="Picture of me ALIGN=LEFT>
<IMG SRC ="myson2.gif" ALT="Another picture of my
son" ALIGN=RIGHT>
```

8.6.3 Other options

Other image options can be added, such as:

- HSPACE=x VSPACE=y defines the amount of space that should be left around images. The x value defines the number of pixels in the x-direction and the y value defines the number of pixels in the y-direction.
- WIDTH= x HEIGHT=y defines the scaling in the x- and y-direction, where x and y are the desired pixel width and height, respectively, of the image.
- ALIGN=*direction* defines the alignment of the image. This can be used to align an image with text. Valid options for aligning with text are *texttop, top, middle, absmiddle, bottom, baseline* or *absbottom*. HTML script 8.8 shows an example of image alignment with the image a.gif (which is just the letter 'A' as a graphic) and Figure 8.8 shows a sample output. It can be seen that *texttop* aligns the image with highest part of the text on the line, *top* alights the image with the highest element in the line, *middle* aligns with the middle of the image with the baseline, *absmiddle* alights the middle of the image with the middle of the largest item, *bottom* aligns bottom of the image with the bottom of the text and *absbottom* aligns bottom of the image with the bottom of the largest item.

📖 HTML script 8.8

```
<HTML>
<HEAD>

<TITLE>My first home page</TITLE>
</HEAD>
<BODY BGCOLOR="#ffffff">
<IMG SRC ="a.gif" ALIGN=texttop>pple<P>
<IMG SRC ="a.gif" ALIGN=top>pple<P>
<IMG SRC ="a.gif" ALIGN=middle>pple<P>
<IMG SRC ="a.gif" ALIGN=bottom>pple<P>
<IMG SRC ="a.gif" ALIGN=baseline>pple<P>
<IMG SRC ="a.gif" ALIGN=absbottom>pple

</BODY>
</HTML>
```

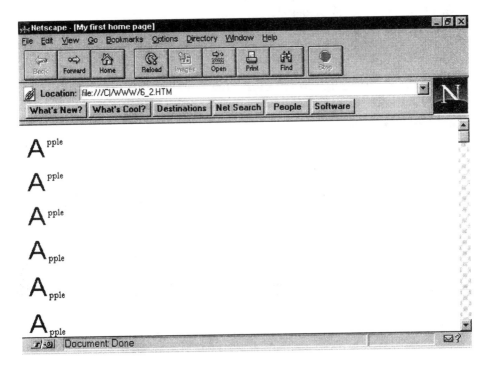

Figure 8.8 WWW page showing image alignment

8.7 Horizontal lines

A horizontal line can be added with the <HR> tag. Most browsers allow extra parameters, such as:

SIZE= *n* – which defines that the height of the rule is *n* pixels.
WIDTH=*w* – which defines that the width of the rule is *w* pixels or as a percentage.
ALIGN=*direction* – where direction refers to the alignment of the rule. Valid options for *direction* are *left, right* or *center*.
NOSHADE – which defines that the line should be solid with no shading.

HTML script 8.9 gives some example horizontal lines and Figure 8.9 show an example output.

HTML script 8.9

```
<HTML>
<HEAD>
<TITLE>My first home page</TITLE>
</HEAD>
<BODY BGCOLOR="#ffffff">
<IMG SRC ="a.gif">pple<P>
<HR>
<IMG SRC ="a.gif">pple<P>
<HR WIDTH=50% ALIGN=CENTER>
<IMG SRC ="a.gif">pple<P>
<HR SIZE=10 NOSHADE>
</BODY>
</HTML>
```

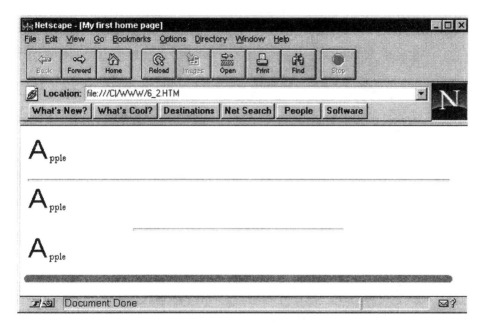

Figure 8.9 WWW page showing horizontal lines

8.8 Exercises

8.8.1 Which HTML tag identifies bold text:

    (a)   `<I>`

    (b)   `<B>`

    (c)   `<P>`

    (d)   `<U>`

8.8.2   Which HTML tag identifies underlined text:

    (a)   `<I>`
    (b)   `<B>`
    (c)   `<P>`
    (d)   `<U>`

8.8.3   Which HTML tag identifies bold text:

    (a)   `<I>`
    (b)   `<B>`
    (c)   `<P>`
    (d)   `<U>`

8.8.4   Which HTML tag identifies italic text:

    (a)   `<I>`
    (b)   `<B>`
    (c)   `<P>`
    (d)   `<U>`

8.8.5   The HTML text for:

```
THESE ARE THE PEOPLE:
FRED
BERT
```

is:

    (a)   `THESE ARE THE PEOPLE:<P>FRED<P>BERT`
    (b)   `THESE ARE THE PEOPLE:<P> FRED<P>BERT`
    (c)   `THESE ARE THE PEOPLE:<P> FRED<P> BERT`
    (d)   `THESE ARE THE PEOPLE:`
           `FRED`
           `BERT`

8.8.6   The HTML text for THIS IS AN **EXAMPLE** TEXT is:

    (a)   `THIS IS AN <B>EXAMPLE TEXT`
    (b)   `THIS IS AN <B>EXAMPLE</B>TEXT`
    (c)   `THIS IS AN <B>EXAMPLE</B> TEXT`
    (d)   `THIS IS AN <B>EXAMPLE TEXT</B>`

8.8.7   The HTML text for **THIS IS** AN **EXAMPLE** TEXT is:

(a)   `<U><B>THIS IS</U> AN EXAMPLE</B> TEXT`
(b)   `<U>THIS IS</U><B> AN EXAMPLE</B> TEXT`
(c)   `<B>THIS IS</U> AN EXAMPLE</B> TEXT`
(d)   `<U><B>THIS IS AN EXAMPLE</B></U> TEXT`

8.8.8   The HTML hexademical colour for pure blue is:

(a)   "FF0000"
(b)   "00FF00"
(c)   "0000FF"
(d)   "FFFFFF"

8.8.9   The HTML hexademical colour for pure red is:

(a)   "FF0000"
(b)   "00FF00"
(c)   "0000FF"
(d)   "FFFFFF"

8.8.10   The HTML hexademical colour for black is:

(a)   "000000"
(b)   "555555"
(c)   "0000FF"
(d)   "FFFFFF"

8.8.11   The HTML hexademical colour for white is:

(a)   "000000"
(b)   "00FF00"
(c)   "0000FF"
(d)   "FFFFFF"

8.8.12   Which of the following HTML hexadecimal colours has the strongest red component:

(a)   "0056F2"
(b)   "103232"
(c)   "A84311"
(d)   "642211"

8.8.13 Which of the following HTML hexadecimal colours has the weakest blue component:

    (a)   "0056F2"
    (b)   "103232"
    (c)   "A84311"
    (d)   "642261"

8.9 Tutorial

8.9.1 The home page for this book can be found at the URL:

```
http://www.eece.napier.ac.uk/~bill_b/mti.hmtl
```

Access this page and follow any links it contains.

8.9.2 If possible, create a WWW page with the following blinking text:

```
This is some blinking text
```

8.9.3 The last part of the server name normally gives an indication of the country that the server is located (for example `www.fredco.co.uk` is located in the UK). Determine which countries use the following country names:

(a) de	(b) nl	(c) it	(d) se	(e) dk	(f) sg
(g) ca	(h) ch	(i) tr	(j) jp	(k) au	

Determine some other country identifier names.

8.9.4 Determine the HTML colour represent for the following:

    (a)   red
    (b)   green
    (c)   blue
    (d)   white
    (e)   black

8.9.5 Determine the HTML for the background, text and link colour:

(a) ```
<BODY BKCOLOR="#00FF00" "TEXT=#FF0000"
                  "LINK=#0000FF">
```
(b) ```
<BODY BKCOLOR="#DC640D" "TEXT=#777777"
                  "LINK=#009DBE">
```

8.9.6   Determine the error in the following HTML script:

📖 HTML script 8.10
```
<HTML>
<HEAD>
<TITLE>Fred's page</TITLE>
</HEAD>
<BODY BGCOLOR="#FFFFFF">
<H1>List 1</H1>
<OL>
<LI>Part 1
<LI>Part 2
<LI>Part 3
<H1>List 2</H1>
<UL>
<LI>Section 1
<LI>Section 2
<LI>Section 3
</UL>
</BODY>
</HTML>
```

9 HTML (Tables, Forms and Helpers)

9.1 Introduction

Chapter 8 introduced HTML, this chapter discusses some of HTML's more advanced features. HTML differs from compiled languages, such as C and Pascal, in that the HTML text file is interpreted by an interpreter (the browser) while languages such as C and Pascal must be precompiled before they can be run. HTML thus does not contain any precompiled, machine specific code and it thus can be interpreted by any type of compatiable browser on any operating system. The main disadvantage of interpreted files is that the interpreter does less error checking as it must produce fast results.

The basic pages on the WWW are likely to evolve around HTML and while HTML can be produced manually with a text editor, it is likely that, in the coming years, that there will be an increase in the amount of graphically-based tools which will automatically produce HTML files. Although these tools are graphics-based they still produce standard HTML text files. Thus a knowledge of HTML is important as it defines the basic specification for the presentation of WWW pages.

9.2 Anchors

An anchor allows users to jump from a reference in a WWW page to an anchor point with the page. The standard format is:

<A NAME= "*anchor name*">

where *anchor name* is the name of the section which is referenced. The </A> tag defines the end of an anchor name. A link is specified by:

<A HREF="#*anchor name*">

followed by the </A> tag. HTML script 9.1 shows a sample script with four anchors and Figure 9.1 shows a sample output. When the user selects one of the references, the browser automatically jumps to that anchor. Figure 9.2 shows the output screen when the user selects the #Token reference. Anchors are typically used when an HTML page is long or when a backwards or forwards reference occurs (such as a reference within a published paper).

HTML script 9.1

```
<HTML><HEAD><TITLE>Sample page</TITLE></HEAD>
<BODY BGCOLOR="#FFFFFF">
<H2>Select which network technology you wish
information:</H2>
<P><A HREF="#Ethernet">Ethernet</A></P>
<P><A HREF="#Token">Token Ring</A></P>
<P><A HREF="#FDDI">FDDI</A></P>
<P><A HREF="#ATM">ATM</A></P>

<H2><A NAME="Ethernet">Ethernet</A></H2>
Ethernet is a popular LAN which works at 10Mbps.

<H2><A NAME="Token">Token Ring</A></H2>
Token ring is a ring based network which operates
at 4 or 16Mbps.

<H2><A NAME="FDDI">FDDI</A></H2>
FDDI is a popular LAN technology which uses a ring of
fibre optic cable and operates at 100Mbps.

<H2><A NAME="ATM">ATM</A></H2>
ATM is a ring based network which operates at
155Mbps.
</BODY></HTML>
```

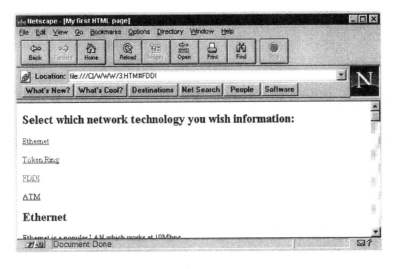

Figure 9.1 Example window with references

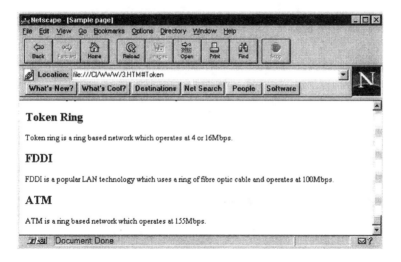

Figure 9.2 Example window with references

Tables are one of the best methods to display complex information in a simple way. Unfortunately, in HTML, they are relatively complicated to set-up. The start of a table is defined with the `<TABLE>` tag and the end of a table by `</TABLE>`. A row is defined between the `<TR>` and `</TR>`, while a table header is defined between `<TH>` and `</TH>`. A regular table entry is defined between `<TD>` and `</TD>`. HTML script 9.2 shows an example of a table with links to other HTML pages. The BORDER=*n* option has been added to the `<TABLE>` tag to define the thickness of the table border (in pixels). In this case the border size has a thickness of 10 pixels.

📖 HTML script 9.2

```
<HTML><HEAD><TITLE> Fred Bloggs</TITLE></HEAD>
<BODY TEXT="#000000" BGCOLOR="#FFFFFF">
<H1>Fred Bloggs Home Page</H1>
I'm Fred Bloggs. Below is a tables of links.
<HR><P>
<TABLE BORDER=10>
<TR>
   <TD><B>General</B></TD>
   <TD><A HREF="res.html">Research</TD>
   <TD><A HREF="cv.html">CV</TD>
   <TD><A HREF="paper.html">Papers Published</TD>
</TR>
<TR>
   <TD><B>HTML Tutorials</B></TD>
```

```
<TD><A HREF="intro.html">Tutorial 1</TD>
<TD><A HREF="inter.html">Tutorial 2</TD>
<TD><A HREF="adv.html">Tutorial 3</TD>
</TR>
<TR>
<TD><B>Java Tutorials</B></TD>
<TD><A HREF="java1.html">Tutorial 1</TD>
<TD><A HREF="java2.html">Tutorial 2</TD>
<TD><A HREF="java3.html">Tutorial 3</TD>
</TR>
</TABLE>
</BODY></HTML>
```

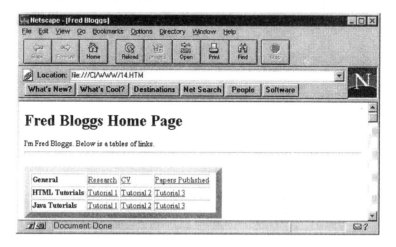

Figure 9.3   Example window from example Java script

Other options in the <TABLE> tag are:

- WIDTH=*x*, HEIGHT=*y* – defines the size of the table with respect to the full window size. The parameters *x* and *y* are either absolute values in pixels for the height and width of the table or are percentages of the full window size.
- CELLSPACING=*n* – defines the number of pixels desired between each cell where *n* is the number of pixels (note that the default cell spacing is 2 pixels).

An individual cell can be modified by adding options to the <TH> or <TD> tag. These include:

- WIDTH=*x*, HEIGHT=*y* – defines the size of the table with respect to the table size. The parameters *x* and *y* are either absolute values in pixels for the height and width of the table or are percentages of the table size.
- COLSPAN=*n* – defines the number of columns the cell should span.

- ROWSPAN=*n* – defines the number of rows the cell should span.
- ALIGN=*direction* – defines how the cell's contents are aligned horizontally. Valid options are *left*, *center* or *right*.
- VALIGN=*direction* – defines how the cell's contents are aligned vertically. Valid options are *top*, *middle* or *baseline*.
- NOWRAP – informs the browser to keep the text on a single line (that is, with no line breaks).

HTML script 9.3 shows an example use of some of the options in the <TABLE> and <TD> options. In this case the text within each row is center aligned. On the second row the second and third cells are merged using the COLSPAN=2 option. The first cell of the second and third rows have also been merged using the ROWSPAN=2 option. Figure 9.4 shows an example output. The table width has been increased to 90% of the full window, with a width of 50%.

📖 HTML script 9.3

```
<HTML><HEAD><TITLE> Fred Bloggs</TITLE></HEAD>
<BODY TEXT="#000000" BGCOLOR="#FFFFFF">
<H1>Fred Bloggs Home Page</H1>
I'm Fred Bloggs. Below is a table of links.
<HR>
<P>
<TABLE BORDER=10 WIDTH=90% LENGTH=50%>
<TR>
   <TD><B>General</B></TD>
   <TD><A HREF="res.html">Research</TD>
   <TD><A HREF="cv.html">CV</TD>
   <TD><A HREF="paper.html">Papers Published</TD>
   <TD></TD>
</TR>
<TR>
   <TD ROWSPAN=2><B>HTML/Java Tutorials</B></TD>
   <TD><A HREF="intro.html">Tutorial 1</TD>
   <TD COLSPAN=2><A HREF="inter.html">Tutorial 2</TD>
</TR>
<TR>
   <TD><A HREF="java1.html">Tutorial 1</TD>
   <TD><A HREF="java2.html">Tutorial 2</TD>
   <TD><A HREF="java3.html">Tutorial 3</TD>
</TR>
</TABLE>
</BODY>
</HTML>
```

9.4 CGI scripts

CGI (Common Gateway Interface) scripts are normally written in either C or Perl and are compiled to produce an executable program. They can also come precomiled or in the form of a batch file. Perl has the advantage in that it is a script that can be easily run on any computer, while a precompiled C program requires to be precompiled for the server computer.

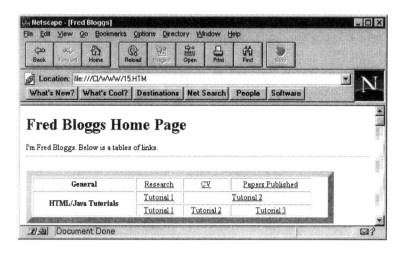

Figure 9.4 Example window from example Java script

CGI scripts allow the user to interact with the server and store and request data. They are often used in conjunction with forms and allow an HTML document to analyse, parse and store information received from a form. On most UNIX-type systems the default directory for CGI scripts is cgi-bin.

9.5 Forms

Forms are excellent methods of gathering data and can be used in conjunction with CGI scripts to collect data for future use.

A form is identified between the <FORM> and </FORM> tags. The method used to get the data from the form is defined with the METHOD="POST". The ACTION option defines the URL script to be run when the form is submitted. Data input is specified by the <INPUT TYPE> tag. HTML script 9.4 form has the following parts:

- <form action="/cgi-bin/AnyForm2" method="POST"> – which defines the start of a form and when the "submit" option is selected the cgi script `/cgi-bin/AnyForm2` will be automatically run.

- `<input type="submit" value="Send Feedback">` – which causes the program defined in the action option in the `<form>` tag to be run. The button on the form will contain the text "`Send Feedback`", see Figure 9.5 for a sample output screen.

- `<input type="reset" value="Reset Form">` – which resets the data in the form. The button on the form will contain the text "`Reset Form`", see Figure 9.5 for a sample output screen.

- `<input type="hidden" name="AnyFormTo" value= "f.bloggs @toytown.ac.uk">` – which passes a value of `f.bloggs@toytown.ac.uk` which has the parameter name of "`AnyFormTo`". The program `AnyForm2` takes this parameter and automatically sends it to the email address defined in the value (that is, `f.bloggs @toytown.ac.uk`).

- `<input type="hidden" name="AnyFormSubject" value="Feedback form">` – which passes a value of Feedback form which has the parameter name of "`AnyFormSubject`". The program `AnyForm2` takes this parameter and adds the text "`Feedback form`" in the text sent to the email recipient (in this case, `f.bloggs @toytown.ac.uk`).

- `Surname <input name="Surname">` – which defines a text input and assigns this input to the parameter name `Surname`.

- `<textarea name="Address" rows=2 cols=40> </textarea>` – which defines a text input area which has two rows and has a width of 40 characters. The thumb bars appear at the right hand side of the form if the text area exceeds more than 2 rows, see Figure 9.5.

📖 HTML script 9.4

```
<HTML>
<HEAD>
<TITLE>Example form</TITLE>
</HEAD>
<H1><CENTER>Example form</CENTER></H1><P>
<form action="/cgi-bin/AnyForm2" method="POST">

<input type="hidden" name="AnyFormTo"
value="f.bloggs@toytown.ac.uk">
<input type="hidden" name="AnyFormSubject"
value="Feedback form">

Surname <input name="Surname"> First Name/Names
<input name="First Name"><P>

Address (including country)<P>
```

```
<textarea name="Address" rows=2
cols=40></textarea><P>

Business Phone <input name="Business Phone">Place of
study (or company) <input name="Study"><P>
E-mail    <input name="E-mail">  Fax Number <input
name="Fax Number"><P>

<input type="submit" value="Send Feedback"> <input
type="reset" value="Reset Form">
</Form>
</HTML>
```

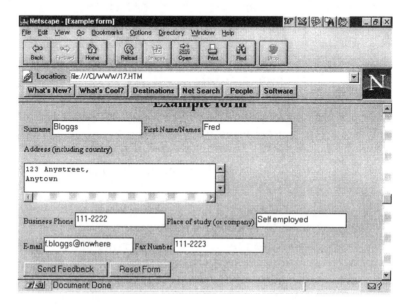

Figure 9.5 Example window showing an example form

In this case the recipient (`f.bloggs@toytown.ac.uk`) will receive an email with the contents:

```
Anyform Subject=Example form
Surname=Bloggs
First name=Fred
Address=123 Anystreet, Anytown
Business Phone=111-222
Place of study (or company)=Self employed
Email= f.bloggs@nowhere
Fax Number=111-2223
```

The extra options to the `<input>` tag are `size="`*n*`"`, where *n* is the width of the input box in characters, and `maxlength="`*m*`"`, where *m* is the maximum number of characters that can be entered, in characters. For example:

```
<input type="text  size="15" maxlength="10">
```

defines that the input type is text, the width of the box is 15 characters and the maximum length of input is 10 characters.

9.5.1 Input types

The type options to the `<input>` tag are defined in Table 9.1. HTML script 9.5 gives a few examples of input types and Figure 9.6 shows a sample output.

Table 9.1 Input type options

TYPE=	*Description*	*Options*
"text"	The input is normal text	NAME="*nm*" where *nm* is the name that will be sent to the server when the text is entered. SIZE="*n*" where *n* is the desired box width in characters. SIZE="*m*" where *m* is the maximum number of input characters.
"password"	The input is a password which will be displayed with *'s. For example if the user inputs a 4-letter password then only **** will be displayed.	SIZE="*n*" where *n* is the desired box width in characters. SIZE="*m*" where *m* is the maximum number of input characters.
"radio"	The input takes the form of a radio button (such as ⊙ or ○). They are used to allow the user to select a single option from a list of options.	NAME="*radname*" where *radname* defines the name of the button. VALUE="*val*" where *val* is the data that will be sent to the server when the button is selected. CHECKED is used to specify that the button is initially set.
"checkbox"	The input takes the form of a checkbox (such as ☒ or ☐). They are used to allow the user to select several options from a list of options.	NAME="*chkname*" where *chkname* defines the common name for all the checkbox options. VALUE="*defval*" where *defval* defines the name of the option. CHECKED is used to specify that the button is initially set.

☐ HTML script 9.5

```
<HTML><HEAD><TITLE>Example form</TITLE> </HEAD>
<FORM METHOD="Post" >
<H2>Enter type of network:</H2><P>
<INPUT TYPE="radio" NAME="network" VALUE="ethernet"
CHECKED>Ethernet <INPUT TYPE="radio" NAME="network"
VALUE="token">
Token Ring <INPUT TYPE="radio" NAME="network"
VALUE="fddi" >
FDDI <INPUT TYPE="radio" NAME="network" VALUE="atm" >
ATM
<H2>Enter usage:</H2><P>
<INPUT TYPE="checkbox" NAME="usage" VALUE="multi"
>Multimedia
<INPUT TYPE="checkbox" NAME="usage" VALUE="word"
>Word Processing
<INPUT TYPE="checkbox" NAME="usage" VALUE="spread"
>Spread Sheets
<P>Enter Password<INPUT TYPE="password" NAME="passwd"
SIZE="10">
</FORM></HTML>
```

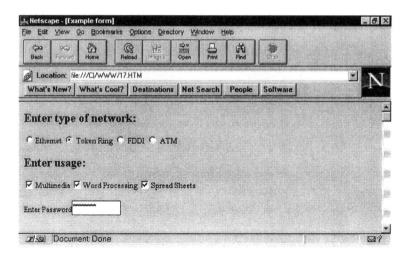

Figure 9.6 Example window with different input options

9.5.2 Menus

Menus are a convenient method of selecting from multiple options. The
<SELECT> tag is used to define start of a list of menu options and the
</SELECT> tag defines the end. Menu elements are then defined with the
<OPTION> tag. The options defined within the <SELECT> are:

- NAME="*name*" – which defines that *name* is the variable name of the menu. This is used when the data is collected by the server.

- SIZE=*"n"* – which defines the number of options which are displayed in the menu.

HTML script 9.6 shows an example of a menu. The additional options to the <OPTION> tag are:

- SELECTED – which defines the default selected option.
- VALUE=*"val"* – where *val* defines the name of the data when it is collected by the server.

📖 HTML script 9.6

```
<HTML><HEAD><TITLE>Example form</TITLE> </HEAD>
<FORM METHOD="Post" >
Enter type of network:
<select Name="network" size="1">
<option>Ethernet
<option SELECTED>Token Ring
<option>FDDI
<option>ATM
</select></FORM></HTML>
```

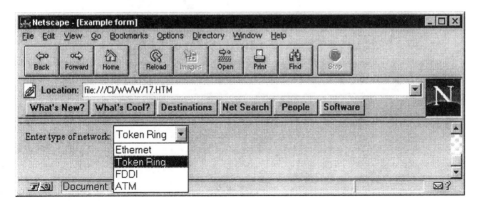

Figure 9.7 Example window showing an example form

9.6 Multimedia

If the browser cannot handle the specified file type then it may call on other application helpers to process the file. This allows other 'third-party' programs to integrate into the browser. Figure 9.8 shows an example of the configuration of the helper programs. The options in this case are:

- View in browser.
- Save to disk.
- Unknown: prompt user.
- Launch an application (such as an audio playback program or MPEG viewer).

For certain applications the user can select as to whether the browser processes the file or another application program processes it. Helper programs make upgrades in helper applications relatively simple and also allows new file types to be added with an application helper. Typically when a program is installed which can be used with a browser it will prompt the user as to whether to automatically update the helper application list so that it can handle the given file type(s).

Each file type is defined by the file extension, such as .ps for postscript files, .exe for a binary executable file, and so on. These file extensions have been standardised in MIME (Multipurpose Internet Mail Extensions) specfication. Table 9.2 shows some typical file extensions.

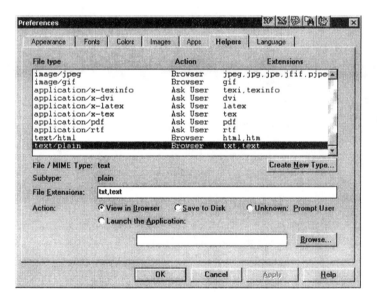

Figure 9.8   Example window showing an example form

Table 9.2 Input type options

Mime type	Extension	Typical action
application/octet-stream	exe, bin	Save
application/postscript	ps, ai, eps	Ask user
application/x-compress	Z	Compress program
application/x-gzip	gz	GZIP compress program
application/x-javascript	js, mocha	Ask user
application/x-msvideo	avi	Audio player
application/x-perl	pl	Save
application/x-tar	tar	Save
application/x-zip-compressed	zip	ZIP program
audio/basic	au, snd	Audio player
image/gif	gif	Browser
image/jpeg	jpeg, jpg, jpe	Browser
image/tiff	tif, tiff	Graphics viewer
image/x-MS-bmp	bmp	Graphics viewer
text/html	htm, html	Browser
text/plain	text, txt	Browser
video/mpeg	mpeg, mpg, mpe, mpv, vbs, mpegv	Video player
video/quicktime	qt, mov, moov	Video player

9.7 Exercise

9.7.1 An anchor is used to:

    (a)   To create non-moveable graphic images
    (b)   Used to stop text from being moved
    (c)   Link to another HTML page
    (d)   Move to a reference with an HTML page

9.7.2 A radio button input is one in which:

    (a)   The user can select one from a list of options
    (b)   The user can select any number of options from a list of options
    (c)   The user must select all of the options
    (d)   The user must deselect all the options

9.7.3 A checkbox input is one in which:

    (a)   The user can select one from a list of options

(b)   The user can select any number of options from a list of options

(c)   The user must select all of the options

(d)   The user must deselect all the options

9.8 Tutorial

9.8.1   Constuct a WWW page with anchor points for the following:

Select the network you wish to find out about:

Ethernet
Token ring
FDDI

Ethernet

Ethernet is the most widely used networking technology used in LAN (Local Area Network). In itself it cannot make a network and needs some other protocol such as TCP/IP or SPX/IPX to allow nodes to communicate. Unfortunately, Ethernet in its standard form does not cope well with heavy traffic. It has many advantages, though, including:

- Networks are easy to plan and cheap to install.
- Network components are cheap and well supported.
- It is well-proven technology which is fairly robust and reliable.
- Simple to add and delete computers on the network.
- Supported by most software and hardware systems.

Token Ring

Token ring networks were developed by several manufacturers, the most prevalent being the IBM Token Ring. Token ring networks cope well with high network traffic loadings. They were at one time extremely popular but their popularity has since been overtaken by Ethernet. Token Ring networks have, in the past, suffered from network management problems and poor network fault tolerance. Token ring networks are well suited to situations which have large amounts of traffic and also works well with most traffic loadings. It is not suited to large networks or networks with physically remote stations. Its main advantage is that it copes better with high traffic rates than Ethernet, but requires a great deal of maintenance especially when faults occur or when new equipment is added to or removed from the network. Much of these problems have now been overcome by MAUs (multi-station access units), which are similar to the hubs using Ethernet.

FDDI

A token-passing mechanism allows orderly access to a network. Apart from Token Ring the most commonly used token-passing network is the Fiber Distributed Data Interchange (FDDI) standard. This operates at a 100 Mbps and, to overcome the problems of line breaks, has two concentric token rings. Fiber optic cables have a much higher specification over copper cables and allow extremely long interconnection lengths. The maximum circumference of the ring is 100 km (62 miles), with a maximum 2 km between stations (in FDDI stations are also known as stations). It is thus an excellent mechanism for connecting interconnecting networks over a city or a campus. Up to 500 stations can connect to each ring with a maximum of 1000 stations for the complete network. Each station connected to the FDDI highway can be a normal station or a bridge to a conventional local area network, such as Ethernet or token ring.

9.8.2 Construct a WWW glossary page with the following terms:

Address	A unique label for the location of data or the identity of a communications device.
Address Resolution Protocol (ARP)	A TCP/IP process which maps an IP address to an Ethernet address.
American National Standards Institute (ANSI)	ANSI is a non-profit organisation which is made up of expert committees that publish standards for national industries.
American Standard Code for Information Interchange (ASCII)	An ANSI-defined character alphabet which has since been adopted as a standard international alphabet for the interchange of characters.
Amplitude modulation (AM)	Information is contained in the amplitude of a carrier.
Amplitude-Shift Keying (ASK)	Uses two, or more, amplitudes to represent binary digits. Typically used to transmit binary data over speech-limited channels.

	Application layer	The highest layer of the OSI model.

Application layer   The highest layer of the OSI model.

Asynchronous transmission   Transmission where individual characters are sent one-by-one. Normally each character is delimited by a start and stop bit. With asynchronous communication the transmitter and receiver only have to be roughly synchronised.

9.8.3   Construct a WWW page which can be used to enter a person's CV (note use a form). The basic fields should be:

Name:
Address:
Email address:
Telephone number:
Experience:
Interests:
Any other information:

9.8.4   Write an HTML script which displays the following timetable.

	9-11	11-1	1-3	3-5
Monday	Data Comms		Networking	
Tuesday	Software Systems		Networking	Data Comms
Wednesday	Networking	FREE	Java	FREE
Thursday	Software Systems	C++	Networking	FREE
Friday	FREE		Networking	

9.8.5   Design your own home page with a basic user home page (index.html) which contains links to a basic CV page (for example, it could be named cv.html) and a page which lists your main interests (myinter.html). Design one of the home pages with a list of links and another with a table of links. If possible incorporate graphics files into the pages.

10 JavaScript

10.1 Introduction

Computer systems contain a microprocessor which controls the operation of the computer. The microprocessor only understands binary information and operates on a series of binary commands known as machine code. It is extremely difficult to write large programs in machine code, so that high-level languages are used instead. A low-level language is one which is similar to machine code and normally involves the usage of keyword macros to replace machine code instructions. High-level languages have a syntax that is almost like written English and thus make programs easy to read and to modify. In most programs the actual operation of the hardware is invisible to the programmer. A compiler changes the high-level language into machine code. Typical high-level languages include C/C++, BASIC, COBOL, FORTRAN and Pascal; an example of a low-level language is 80486 Assembly Language.

Java is a high-level language which has been developed specifically for the WWW and is well suited to networked applications. It was originally developed by Sun Microsystems and is based on C++ (but with less of the difficulties of C++). Most new versions of Web browsers now support its usage. Java's main attributes are:

- It runs either as a stand-alone program or it can run within the Web browser. When run within the browser the Java program is known as an applet.
- Java is a portable language and applets can run on any type of microprocessor type (such as a PC based on Intel 80486 or Pentium, or a Motorola-based computer).
- Java applets are hardware and operating system independent. For example the program itself does not have to interface directly to the hardware such as a video adapter, or mouse. Typical high-level languages, such as C/C++ and Pascal, produce machine-dependent machine code, and can thus only be executed on a specific computer or operating systems.
- Java allows for a client/server approach where the applet can run on the remote computer which thus reduces the loading on the local computer (typically the remote computer will be a powerful multitasking computer with enhanced computer architecture).

- A Java compiler creates stand-alone programs or applets. Many new versions of browsers have an integrated Java compiler.

Figure 10.1 shows the main functional differences between a high-level language, a Java applet and JavaScript. JavaScript is interpreted by the browser, whereas a Java applet is compiled to a virtual machine code which can be run on any computer system. The high-level language produces machine-specific code.

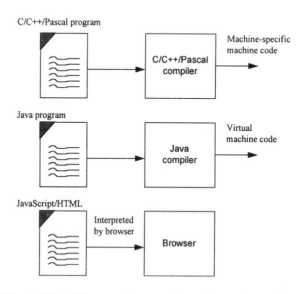

Figure 10.1 Differences between C + + /Java and JavaScript

A normal C++ program allows access to hard-disk drives. This would be a problem on the Web as unsolicited users ('hackers') or novice users could cause damage on the Web server. To overcome this Java does not have any mechanism for file input/output (I/O). It can read standard file types (such as GIF and JPG) but can not store changes to the Web server. A Java developers kit is available, free of charge, from http://java.sun.com.

The following is an example HTML script and highlighted JavaScript. Figure 10.2 gives the browser output.

📖 JavaScript 1

```
<HTML> <HEAD><TITLE>My Java</TITLE></HEAD>
<BODY>
<SCRIPT language="javascript">
document.writeln("This is my first JavaScript");
for (i=0;i<10;i++)
  document.write("<center><font size=+1><b>Loop</b> ",i);
</SCRIPT></BODY></HTML>
```

156　*Mastering the Internet*

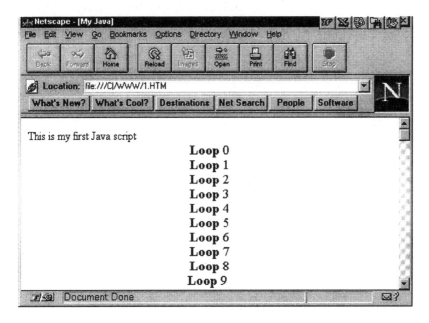

Figure 10.2 Example window from example JavaScript

10.2 JavaScript

Programming languages can either be compiled to produce an executable program or they can be interpreted while the user runs the program. Java is a program language which needs to be compiled before it is used. It thus cannot be used unless the user has the required Java compiler. JavaScript, on the other hand, is a language which is interpreted by the browser. It is similar in many ways to Java but allows the user to embed Java-like code into an HTML page. JavaScript supports a small number of data types representing numeric, Boolean, and string values and is supported by most modern WWW browsers, such as Microsoft Internet Explorer and Netscape.

HTML is useful when pages are short and do not contain expressions, loops or decisions. JavaScript allows most of the functionality of a high-level language for developing client and server Internet applications. It can be used to respond to user events such as mouse clicks, form input, and page navigation.

A major advantage that JavaScript has over HTML is that it supports the use of functions without any special declarative requirements. It is also simpler to use than Java because it has easier syntax, specialised built-in functionality, and minimal requirements for object creation.

Important concepts in Java and JavaScript are objects. Objects are basically containers for values. The main differences between JavaScript and Java are:

- JavaScript is interpreted by the client, while Java is compiled on the server before it is executed.
- JavaScript is embedded into HTML pages, while Java Applets are distinct from HTML and accessed from HTML pages.
- JavaScript has loose typing for variables (that is, a variables data type does not have to be declared), while Java has strong typing (that is, a variables data type must always be declared before it is used).
- JavaScript has dynamic binding where object references are checked at run-time. Java has static binding where object references must exist at compile-time.

10.3 JavaScript values, variables and literals

JavaScript values, variable and literals are similar to the C programming language. Their syntax is discussed in this section.

10.3.1 Values

The four different types of values in JavaScript are:

- Numeric value, such as 12 or 91.5432.
- Boolean values which are either TRUE or FALSE.
- Strings types, such as "Fred Bloggs".
- A special keyword for a NULL value .

Numeric values differ from those in most programming languages in that there is no explicit distinction between a real value (such as 91.5432) and an integer (such as, 12).

10.3.2 Data type conversion

JavaScript differs from Java in that variables do not need to have their data type defined when they are declared (loosely typed). Data types are then automatically converted during the execution of the program. Thus a variable could be declared with a numeric value as:

```
var value

    value = 19
```

and then in the same script it could be assigned a string value, such as:

```
value = "Enter your name >>"
```

The conversion between numeric values and strings in JavaScript is easy, as numeric values are automatically converted to an equivalent string. For example:

```
<HTML><HEAD><TITLE>My Java</TITLE></HEAD>
<BODY BGCOLOR="#ffffff">
<SCRIPT language="javascript">
var x,y,str

        x=13
        y=10
        str= x + " added to " + y + " is " + x+y
        document.writeln(str)

        z=x+y
        str= x + " added to " + y + " is " + z
        document.writeln(str)
</SCRIPT>
</BODY></HTML>
```

Sample run 10.1 gives the output from this script. It can be seen that x and y have been converted to a string value (in this case, "13" and "10") and that x+y in the string conversion statement has been converted to "1310". If a mathematical operation is carried out (z=x+y) then z will contain 23 after the statement is executed.

Sample run 10.1
```
13 added to 10 is 1310   13 added to 10 is 23
```

JavaScript provides several special functions for manipulating string and numeric values:

- The eval (*string*) function which converts a string to a numerical value.
- The parseInt (*string [,radix]*) function which converts a string into an integer of the specified radix (number base). The default radix is base-10.
- The parseFloat (*string*) function which converts a string into an floating-point value.

10.3.3 Variables

Variables are symbolic names for values within the script. A JavaScript identifier must either start with a letter or an underscore ("_"), followed by letters, an underscore or any digit (0-9). Like C, JavaScript is case sensitive so that variables with the same character sequence but with different cases for one or more characters are different. The following are different variable names:

```
i=5
I=10

valueA=3.543
VALUEA=10.543
```

10.3.4 Variable scope

A variable can be declared by either simply assigning it a value or by using the var keyword. For example the following declares to variables Value1 and Value2:

```
var  Value1;
     Value2=23;
```

A variable declared within a function is taken as a local variable and can only be used within that function. A variable declared outside a function is a global variable and can be used anywhere in the script. A variable which is declared locally which is already declared as global variable needs to be declared with the var keyword, otherwise the use of the keyword is optional.

10.3.5 Literals

Literal values have fixed values within the script. Various reserved forms can be used to identify special types, such as hexadecimal values, exponent format, and so on. With an integer the following are used:

- If the value is preceded by a 0x then the value is a hexadecimal value (that is, base 16). Examples of hexadecimal values are 0x1FFF, 0xCB.
- If the value is preceded by a 0 then the value is an octal value (that is, base 8). Examples of octal values are 0777, 010.
- If it is not preceded by either a 0x or a 0 then it is a decimal integer.

Floating-point values

Floating-point values are typically represented as a real value (such as 1.342) or in exponent format. Some exponent format values are:

```
Value            Exponent format
0.000001         1e-6
1342000000       1.342e9
```

Boolean

The true and false literals are used with Boolean operations.

Strings

In C a string is represented with double quotes (*"str"*) whereas JavaScript accepts a string within double (") or single (') quotation marks. Examples of strings are:

```
"A string"
'Another string'
```

C uses an escape character sequence to represent special characters with string. This character sequence always begins with a '\' character. For example, if the escape sequence '\n' appears in the string then this sequence is interpreted as a new-line sequence. Valid escape sequences are:

Character	Meaning	Character	Meaning
\b	backspace	\f	form feed
\n	new line	\r	carriage return
\t	tab	\\	backslash character
\"	prints a " character		

10.4 Expressions and operators

The expression and operators used in Java and JavaScript are based on C and C++. This section outlines the main expressions and operators used in JavaScript.

10.4.1 Expressions

As with C, expression are any valid set of literals, variables, operators, and expressions that evaluate to a single value. There are basically two types of expression, one which assigns a value to a variable and the other which simply gives a single value. A simple assignment is:

```
value = 21
```

which assigns the value of 21 to value (note that the result of the expression is 21).

The result from a JavaScript expression can either be:

- A numeric value.

- A string.
- A logical value (true or false).

10.5 JavaScript operators

Both Java and JavaScript have a rich set of operators, of which there are four main types:

- Arithmetic.
- Logical.
- Bitwise.
- Relational.

10.5.1 Arithmetic

Arithmetic operators operate on numerical values. The basic arithmetic operations are add (+), subtract (-), multiply (*), divide (/) and modulus division (%). Modulus division gives the remainder of an integer division. The following gives the basic syntax of two operands with an arithmetic operator.

operand operator operand

The assignment operator (=) is used when a variable 'takes on the value' of an operation. Other short-handed operators are used with it, including add equals (+=), minus equals (-=), multiplied equals (*=), divide equals (/=) and modulus equals (%=). The following examples illustrate their uses.

Statement	Equivalent
x+=3.0	x=x+3.0
voltage/=sqrt(2)	voltage=voltage/sqrt(2)
bit_mask *=2	bit_mask=bit_mask*2

In many applications it is necessary to increment or decrement a variable by 1. For this purpose Java has two special operators; ++ for increment and -- for decrement. These can either precede or follow the variable. If they precede, then a pre-increment/decrement is conducted, whereas if they follow it, a post-increment/decrement is conducted. The following examples show their usage.

Statement	Equivalent
no_values++	no_values=no_values+1
i--	i=i-1

Table 10.1 summarizes the arithmetic operators.

Table 10.1 Arithmetic operators

Operator	Operation	Example
–	subtraction or minus	5 – 4 → 1
+	addition	4 + 2 → 6
*	multiplication	4 * 3 → 12
/	division	4 / 2 → 2
%	modulus	13 % 3 → 1
+=	add equals	x += 2 is equivalent to x=x+2
-=	minus equals	x -= 2 is equivalent to x=x-2
/=	divide equals	x /= y is equivalent to x=x/y
*=	multiplied equals	x *= 32 is equivalent to x=x*32
=	assignment	x = 1
++	increment	Count++ is equivalent to Count=Count+1
--	decrement	Sec-- is equivalent to Sec=Sec-1

10.5.2 Relationship

The relationship operators determine whether the result of a comparison is TRUE or FALSE. These operators are greater than (>), greater than or equal to (>=), less than (<), less than or equal to (<=), equal to (==) and not equal to (! =). Table 10.2 lists the relationship operators.

10.5.3 Logical (TRUE or FALSE)

A logical operation is one in which a decision is made as to whether the operation performed is TRUE or FALSE. If required, several relationship operations can be grouped together to give the required functionality. C assumes that a numerical value of 0 (zero) is FALSE and that any other value is TRUE. Table 10.3 lists the logical operators.

The logical AND operation will yield a TRUE only if all the operands are TRUE. Table 10.4 gives the result of the AND (&&) operator for the operation A && B. The logical OR operation yields a TRUE if any one of the operands is TRUE. Table 10.4 gives the logical results of the OR (| |) operator for the statement A| | B. Table 10.4 also gives the logical result of the NOT (!) operator for the statement ! A.

Table 10.2 Relationship operators

Operator	Function	Example	TRUE Condition
>	greater than	(b>a)	when b is greater than a
>=	greater than or equal	(a>=4)	when a is greater than or equal to 4
<	less than	(c<f)	when c is less than f
<=	less than or equal	(x<=4)	when x is less than or equal to 4
==	equal to	(x==2)	when x is equal to 2
!=	not equal to	(y!=x)	when y is not equal to x

Table 10.3 Logical operators

Operator	Function	Example	TRUE condition
&&	AND	((x==1) && (y<2))	when x is equal to 1 *and* y is less than 2
||	OR	((a!=b) || (a>0))	when a is not equal to b *or* a is greater than 0
!	NOT	(!(a>0))	when a is *not* greater than 0

Table 10.4 Logical operations

A	B	AND (&&)	OR (||)	NOT (!A)
FALSE	FALSE	FALSE	FALSE	TRUE
FALSE	TRUE	FALSE	TRUE	TRUE
TRUE	FALSE	FALSE	TRUE	FALSE
TRUE	TRUE	TRUE	TRUE	FALSE

10.5.4 Bitwise

The bitwise logical operators work conceptually as follows:

- The operands are converted to 32-bit integers, and expressed as series of bits (zeros and ones).
- Each bit in the first operand is paired with the corresponding bit in the second operand: first bit to first bit, second bit to second bit, and so on.
- The operator is applied to each pair of bits, and the result is constructed bitwise.

The bitwise operators are similar to the logical operators but they should not be confused as their operation differs. Bitwise operators operate directly on the individual bits of an operand(s), whereas logical operators determine whether a condition is TRUE or FALSE.

Numerical values are stored as bit patterns in either an unsigned integer format, signed integer (2's complement) or floating-point notation (an exponent and mantissa). Characters are normally stored as ASCII characters.

The basic bitwise operations are AND (&), OR (|), 1s complement or bitwise inversion (~), XOR (^), shift left (<<) and shift right (>>). Table 10.5 gives the results of the AND bitwise operation on two bits `Bit1` and `Bit2`.

The Boolean bitwise instructions operate logically on individual bits. The XOR function yields a 1 when the bits in a given bit position differ, the AND function yields a 1 only when the given bit positions are both 1s. The OR operation gives a 1 when any one of the given bit positions are a 1. For example:

```
        00110011              10101111            00011001
AND     11101110      OR      10111111    XOR     11011111
        00100010              10111111            11000110
```

Table 10.5 Bitwise operations

A	B	AND	OR	EX-OR
0	0	0	0	0
0	1	0	1	1
1	0	0	1	1
1	1	1	1	0

To perform bit shifts, the <<, >> and >>> operators are used. These operators shift the bits in the operand by a given number defined by a value given on the right-hand side of the operation. The left shift operator (<<) shifts the bits of the operand to the left and zeros fill the result on the right. The sign-propagating right shift operator (>>) shifts the bits of the operand to the right and zeros fill the result if the integer is positive; otherwise it will fill with 1s. The zero-filled right shift operator (>>>) shifts the bits of the operand to the right and fills the result with zeros. The standard format is:

```
operand >>   no_of_bit_shift_positions
operand >>>  no_of_bit_shift_positions
operand <<   no_of_bit_shift_positions
```

10.5.5 Precedence

There are several rules for dealing with operators:

- Two operators, apart from the assignment, should never be placed side by side. For example, x * % 3 is invalid.
- Groupings are formed with parentheses; anything within parentheses will be evaluated first. Nested parentheses can also be used to set priorities.

- A priority level or precedence exists for operators. Operators with a higher precedence are evaluated first; if two operators have the same precedence, then the operator on the left-hand side is evaluated first. The priority levels for operators are as follows:

HIGHEST PRIORITY

() [] .	primary
! ~ ++ -- -	unary
* / %	multiply
+ -	additive
<< >> >>>	shift
< > <= >=	relation
== !=	equality
&	
^	bitwise
|	
&&	logical
||	
= += -=	assignment

LOWEST PRIORITY

The assignment operator has the lowest precedence.

10.5.6 Conditional expressions

Conditional expressions can result in one of two values based depending on a condition. The syntax is:

```
(expression) ? value1 : value2
```

If the expression is true then value1 is executed else value2 is executed. For example:

```
(val >= 0) ? sign="postive" : sign="negative"
```

This will assign the string "positive" to sign if the value of val is greater than or equal to 0, else it will assign "negative".

10.5.7 String Operators

The normal comparison, operators, such as <, >, >=, ==, and so on can be used with strings. In addition the concatenation operator (+) can be used to concatenate two string values together. For example,

```
str="This is " + "an example"
```

will result in the string

```
"This is an example"
```

10.6 JavaScript statements

JavaScript statements are similar to C and allow a great deal of control of the execution of a script. The basic categories are:

- Conditional statements, such as if...else.
- Repetitive statements, such as for, while, break and continue.
- Comments, using either the C++ style for single-line comments (//) or standard C multi-line comments (/*...*/).
- Object manipulation statements and operators, such as for...in, new, this, and with.

10.7 Conditional statements

Conditional statements allow a program to make decisions on the route through a program.

10.7.1 if...else

A decision is made with the if statement. It logically determines whether a conditional expression is TRUE or FALSE. For a TRUE, the program executes one block of code; a FALSE causes the execution of another (if any). The keyword else identifies the FALSE block. Braces are used to define the start and end of the block.

Relationship operators (>,<,>=,<=,==,!=) yield a TRUE or FALSE from their operation. Logical statements (&&, ||, !) can then group these together to give the required functionality. If the operation is not a relationship, such as bitwise or an arithmetic operation, then any non-zero value is TRUE and a zero is FALSE.

The following is an example syntax of the if statement. If the statement block has only one statement the braces ({ }) can be excluded.

```
if (expression)
{
   statement block
}
```

The following is an example format with an `else` extension.

```
if (expression)
{
    statement block1
}
else
{
    statement block2
}
```

It is possible to nest `if...else` statements to give a required functionality. In the next example, *statement block1* is executed if `expression1` is TRUE. If it is FALSE then the program checks the next expression. If this is TRUE the program executes *statement block2*, else it checks the next expression, and so on. If all expressions are FALSE then the program executes the final `else` statement block, in this case, *statement block 4*:

```
if (expression1)
{
    statement block1
}
else if (expression2)
{
    statement block2
}
else
{
    statement block4
}
```

10.8 Loops

10.8.1 *for ()*

Many tasks within a program are repetitive, such as prompting for data, counting values, and so on. The `for` loop allows the execution of a block of code for a given control function. The following is an example format; if there is only one statement in the block then the braces can be omitted.

```
for (starting condition; test condition; operation)
{
    statement block
}
```

where:

```
starting condition  -  the starting value for the loop;
test condition       -  if test condition is TRUE the loop will
                        continue execution;
operation            -  the operation conducted at the end of the loop.
```

10.8.2 while()

The while() statement allows a block of code to be executed while a specified condition is TRUE. It checks the condition at the start of the block; if this is TRUE the block is executed, else it will exit the loop. The syntax is:

```
while (condition)
{
    :          :   statement block
    :          :
}
```

If the statement block contains a single statement then the braces may be omitted (although it does no harm to keep them).

10.9 Comments

Comments are author notations that explain what a script does. Comments are ignored by the interpreter. JavaScript supports Java-style comments:

- Comments on a single line are preceded by a double-slash (//).
- Multiline comments can be preceded by /* and followed by */.

For example the following example shows two comments:

```
// This is a single-line comment.
/* This is a multiple-line comment. It can be of any
length, and you can put whatever you want here. */
```

10.10 Functions

JavaScript supports modular design using functions. A function is defined with a JavaScript with the function reserved word and the code within the function is defined within braces. The standard format is:

```
function myfunct(param1, param2 ...)
{
    statements
    return(val)
}
```

where the parameters (param1, param2, and so on) are the values passed into the function. Note that the return value (val) from the function is only required when a value is returned from the function.

JavaScript 2 gives an example with two functions (add() and mult()). In this case the values value1 and value2 are passed into the variables a and b within the add() function, the result is then sent back from the function into value3.

Table 10.6 Example JavaScript

JavaScript	Output
📖 JavaScript 2	

```
<HTML><TITLE>Example</TITLE>
<BODY BGCOLOR="#FFFFFF">

<SCRIPT>
var value1,value2,value3,value4;

value1=15;
value2=10;
value3=add(value1,value2)
value4=mult(value1,value2)
document.write("Added is ",value3)
document.write("<P>Multiplied is ",value4)

function add(a,b)
{
var   c
      c=a+b
      return(c)
}
function mult(a,b)
{
var   c
      c=a*b
      return(c)
}
</SCRIPT></FORM></HTML>
```

10.11 Objects and properties

JavaScript is based on a simple object-oriented paradigm, where objects are a construct with properties that are JavaScript variables. Each object has properties associated with it and can be accessed with the dot notation, such as:

objectName . propertyName

10.12 Document objects

The document object contains information on the currently opened document. HTML expressions can be displayed with the `document.write()` or `document.writeln()` functions. The standard format is:

```
document.write(exprA, [,exprB], ... [,exprN])
```

which displays one or more expressions to the specified window. To display to the current window the `document.write()` is used. If a display to a specified window then the window reference is defined, for example:

```
mywin=window.open("fred.html")
mywin.document.write("Hello")
```

is used to output to the `mywin` window.

The document object can also be used to display HTML properties. The standard HTML format is:

```
<BODY BACKGROUD="bgndimage" BGCOLOR="bcolor"
TEXT="fcolor" LINK="ufcolor" ALINK="actcolor"
VLINK="fcolor" </BODY>
```

These and other properties can be accessed within a JavaScript with:

```
document.alinkColor        document.anchors
document.bgColor           document.fgColor
document.lastModified      document.linkColor
document.title             document.URL
document.vlinkColor
```

Table 10.7 shows an example.

Table 10.7 Example JavaScript

JavaScript	Output
📖 **JavaScript 3**	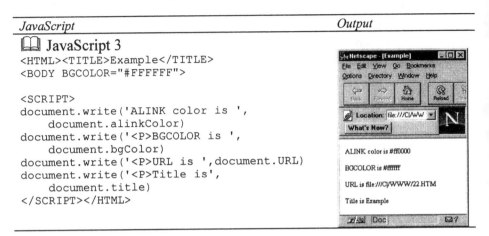

```
<HTML><TITLE>Example</TITLE>
<BODY BGCOLOR="#FFFFFF">

<SCRIPT>
document.write('ALINK color is ',
    document.alinkColor)
document.write('<P>BGCOLOR is ',
    document.bgColor)
document.write('<P>URL is ',document.URL)
document.write('<P>Title is',
    document.title)
</SCRIPT></HTML>
```

10.13 Event handling

JavaScript has event handlers which, on a certain event, causes other events to occur. For example, if a user clicks the mouse button on a certain menu option then the event handler can be made to carry-out a particular action, such as adding two numbers together. Table 10.8 outlines some event handlers.

Table 10.8 Example event handers

Event	Description	Example	Caused by
onBlur	Blur events occur when the select or text field on a form loses focus.	`<INPUT TYPE="text" VALUE="" NAME="userName" onBlur="check(this.value)">`	select, text, textarea
		When the onBlur event occurs the JavaScript code required is executed (in this case the function `check()` is called.	
onChange	The change event occurs when the select or text field loses focus and its value has been modified.	`<INPUT TYPE="button" VALUE="Compute" onClick="Calc(this.form)">`	button, checkbox, radio, link, reset, submit
		When the onChange event occurs the required JavaScript code is executed (in this case the function `Calc()` is called).	
onLoad	The load event occurs when the browser finishes loading a window.	`<BODY onLoad="window.alert("Hello to my excellent page")>`	

onClick	The click event occurs when an object on a form is clicked.	```<INPUT TYPE="button" VALUE="Calculate" onClick="go(this.form)">```	button, checkbox, radio, link, reset, submit
onFocus	The focus event occurs when a field receives input focus by tabbing with the keyboard or clicking with the mouse. Selecting within a field results in a select event and not a focus event.	```<INPUT TYPE="textarea" VALUE="" NAME="valueField" onFocus="valueCheck()">```	select, text, textarea
onMouse Over	A mouseover event occurs each time the mouse pointer moves over an object. Note that a true value must be returned within the event handler.	```<A HREF="http://home.html/" onMouseOver="window.status= 'Select this to go home'; return true"> Go Home</A>```	
onSelect	A select event occurs when a user selects some of the text within a text or textarea field. The onSelect event handler executes JavaScript code when a select event occurs.	```<INPUT TYPE="text" VALUE="" NAME="valueField" onSelect="selectState()">```	
onUnload	An Unload event occurs when the browser quits from a window.	```<BODY onUnload="goodbye()">```	

10.14 Window objects

The window object is the top-level object for documents and can be used to open and close windows.

10.14.1 Window alert

The alert window shows an alert message to the users. It format is:

```
window.alert("Message")
```

or

```
alert("Message");
```

Table 10.9 Example JavaScript

JavaScript	Output

📖 JavaScript 4

```
<HTML><HEAD><TITLE>Example form</TITLE></HEAD>

<BODY BGCOLOR="#ffffff">

<FORM>
Enter name<INPUT TYPE="text" NAME="myname"
    onBlur="testname(myname.value)">
</FORM>

<SCRIPT>
function testname(name)
{
   if (name!="fred") alert("You are not fred");
}
</SCRIPT></HTML>
```

10.14.2 Opening and closing windows

Windows are opened with `window.open()` and closed with `window.close()`. Examples are:

```
fredwin=window.open("fred.html");
```

```
fredwin.close(fredwin);
```

or to open a window it is possible to simply use `open()` and to close the current window the `close()` function is used. The standard format is:

[winVar =][`window`]`.open`(*"url"*, *"winName"*, [*"features"*])

where
winVar is the name of a new window which can be used to refer to a given window.
winName is the window name given to the window;
features is a comma-separated list with any of the following:

toolbar[=yes|no]	location[=yes|no]	directories[=yes|no]
status[=yes|no]	menubar[=yes|no]	scrollbars[=yes|no]
resizable[=yes|no]	width=pixels	height=pixels

10.14.3 Window confirm

The window confirm is used to display a confirm dialogue box with a specified message and the OK and Cancel buttons. If the user selects the OK button then the function returns a TRUE, else it returns a FALSE. Table 10.10 gives an example of the confirm window. In this case when the Exit button is selected then the function `ConfirmExit()` is called. In this function the user is asked to confirm the exit with the confirm window. If the user selects OK then the window is closed (if it is the only window open then the browser quits).

Table 10.10 Example JavaScript with confirm window

JavaScript	Output

``html
<HTML><TITLE>Example</TITLE>
<BODY BGCOLOR="#FFFFFF">
 	
<form name="ExitForm">
<INPUT   TYPE="button"   VALUE="Exit"
onClick="ConfirmExit()">
</FORM>
 	
<SCRIPT>
function ConfirmExit()
{
   if (confirm("Do you want to exit"))
   {
     prompt("Enter your password")
   }
}
</SCRIPT></HTML>
``
	Netscape
	
	JavaScript Confirm:
	Do you want to exit
	
	OK Cancel

10.14.4 Window prompt

The window prompt displays a prompt dialog box which contains a message and an input field. Its standard format is:

```
prompt ("Message") ;
```

10.15 Object manipulation statements and operators

JavaScript has several methods in which objects can be manipulated, these include: the `new` operator, the `this` keyword, the `for...in` statement, and the `with` statement.

10.15.1 this keyword

The `this` keyword is used to refer to the current object. The general format is:

```
this [ .propertyName]
```

JavaScript 5 gives an example of the `this` keyword. In this case `this` is used to pass the property values of the input form. This is then passed to the function `checkval()` when the `onBlur` event occurs.

📖 JavaScript 5

```
<HTML><TITLE>Example</TITLE>
<BODY BGCOLOR="#FFFFFF">

<FORM>
Enter a value<INPUT TYPE = "text" NAME = "inputvalue"
onBlur="checkval(this, 0,10)">

<SCRIPT>
function checkval(val, minval, maxval)
{
   if ((val.value < minval) || (val.value > maxval))
      alert("Invalid value (0-10)")
}

</SCRIPT></FORM>
</HTML>
```

10.15.2 new operator

The new operator is used to define a new user-defined object type or one of the pre-defined object types, such as array, Boolean, date, function and math. JavaScript 6 gives an example which creates an array object with 6 elements and then assigns strings to each of the array. Note that in Java the first element of the array is indexed as 0.

📖 JavaScript 6

```
<HTML><HEAD><TITLE>Java Example</TITLE></HEAD>
<BODY BGCOLOR="#ffffff">
<SCRIPT language="javascript">

no_of_networks=6;
Networks = new Array(no_of_networks);

   Networks[0]="Ethernet"; Networks[1]="Token Ring"
   Networks[2]="FDDI";   Networks[3]="ISDN"
   Networks[4]="RS-232"; Networks[5]="ATM"

   for (i=0;i<no_of_networks;i++)
   {
      document.writeln("Network type "+Networks[i]);
      document.writeln("<P>");
   }

</SCRIPT></BODY></HTML>
```

```
Network type Ethernet
Network type Token Ring
Network type FDDI
Network type ISDN
Network type RS-232
Network type ATM
```

Typically the new operator is used to create new data objects. For example:

```
today = new Date()
Xmasday = new Date("December 25, 1997 00:00:00")
Xmasday = new Date(97,12,25)
```

10.15.3 for...in

The for...in statement is used to iterate a variable through all its properties. In general its format is:

```
for (variable in object)
{
    statements
}
```

10.15.4 with

The with statement defines a specified object for a set of statements. A with statement looks as follows:

```
with (object)
{
    statements
}
```

For example JavaScript 7 contains calls to the Math object for the PI property and cos and sin methods. JavaScript 8 then uses the with statement to define the Match object is the default object.

📖 JavaScript 7
```
<HTML><TITLE>Example</TITLE>
<BODY BGCOLOR="#FFFFFF">
<SCRIPT>
var area,x,y,radius
   radius=20
   area=Math.PI*radius*radius
   x=radius*Math.cos(Math.PI/4)
   y=radius*Math.sin(Math.PI/4)
   document.write("Area is ",area)
   document.write("<P>x is ",x, "<P>y is ",y)
</SCRIPT></FORM></HTML>
```

📖 JavaScript 8

```
<HTML><TITLE>Example</TITLE>
<BODY BGCOLOR="#FFFFFF">

<SCRIPT>
var area,x,y,radius
   radius=10
   with (Math)
   {
      area=PI*radius*radius
      x=radius*cos(PI/4)
      y=radius*sin(PI/4)
      document.write("Area is ",area)
      document.write("<P>x is ",x, "<P>y is ",y)
   }
</SCRIPT></FORM></HTML>
```

10.16 Tutorial

10.16.1 Explain how Java differs from JavaScript.

10.16.2 Explain the main advantages of using Java than a high-level language, such as C++ or Pascal.

10.16.3 Implement the JavaScripts in the text and test their operation.

10.16.4 Write a JavaScript in which the user enters a value and the script calculates the square of that value.

10.16.5 Write a JavaScript in which the user initially enters their name. The script should then test the entered name and if it is not "FRED", "BERT" or "FREDDY" then the browser exits.

11 Java (Introduction)

11.1 Introduction

Java has the great advantage over conventional software languages in that it produces code which is computer hardware independent. This is because the compiled code (called bytecodes) is interpreted by the WWW browser. Unfortunately this leads to slower execution, but as much of the time is spent in graphical user interface programs, to up-date the graphics, then overhead is, as far as the user is concerned, not a great one.

The other advantages that Java has over conventional software languages include:

- It is a more dynamic language than C/C++ and Pascal, and was designed to adapt to an evolving environment. It is extremely easy to add new methods and extra libraries without affecting existing applets. It is also useful in Internet applications as it supports most of the standard image audio and video formats.
- It has networking facilities built-into the language (support for TCP/IP sockets, URLs, IP addresses and datagrams).
- While Java is based on C and C++ it avoids some of the difficult areas of C/C++ code.
- It supports client/server applications where the Java applet runs on the server and the client receives the up-dated graphics information. In the most extreme case the client can simply be a graphics terminal which runs Java applets over a network. The small 'black-box' networked computer is one of the founding principles of Java, and it is hoped in the future that small Java-based computers could replace the complex PC/workstation for general purpose applications, like accessing the Internet or playing network games. This 'black-box' computer concept is illustrated in Figure 11.1.

Most existing Web browsers are enabled for Java applets (such as Internet Explorer 3.0 and Netscape 2.0 and later versions). Figure 11.2 shows how Java applets are created. First the source code is produced with an editor, next a Java compiler compiles the Java source code into bytecode (normally appending the file name with .class). An HTML page is then constructed which has the reference to the applet. After this a Java-enabled browser or applet viewer can then be used to run the applet.

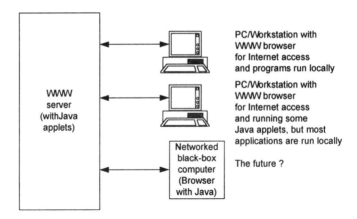

Figure 11.1 Internet accessing

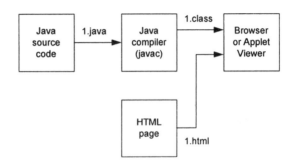

Figure 11.2 Constructing Java applets

The Java Development Kit (JDK) is available, free, from Sun Microsystems at the WWW site http://java.sun.com. This can be used to compile Java applets and standalone programs. There are versions for Windows NT/95, Mac or UNIX-based systems and has many sample applets.

Table 11.1 shows the main files used in the PC version. Figure 11.3 shows the directory structure of the JDK tools. The Java compiler, Java interpreter and applet viewer programs are stored in the bin directory. On the PC, this directory is normally setup in the PATH directory, so that the Java compiler can be called while the user is in another directory. The following is a typical setup (assuming that the home directory is C:\JAVA):

```
PATH=C:\WINDOWS;C:\WINDOWS\COMMAND;C:\JAVA\BIN
CLASSPATH=C:\JAVA\LIB;.;C:\JAVA
```

Table 11.1 JDK programs

File	Description
Javac.exe	Java compiler
Java.exe	Java interpreter
AppletViewer.exe	Applet viewer for testing and running applets
classes.zip	It is needed by the compiler and interpreter
javap.exe	Java class disassembler
javadoc.exe	Java document generator
jbd.exe	Java debugger

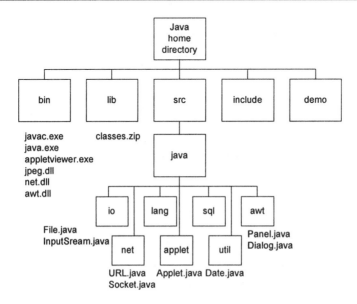

Figure 11.3 Directory structure of JDK

The lib directory contains the classes.zip file which is a zipped-up version of the Java class files. These class files are stored in the directories below the src/java directory. For example, the io classes (such as File.java and InputStream.java) are used for input/output in Java, the awt classes (such as Panel.java and Dialog.java) are used to create and maintain windows. These, and other classes, will be discussed later.

The include directory contains header files for integrating C/C++ programs with Java applets and the demo directory contains some sample Java applets.

11.1.1 Applet tag

An applet is called from within an HTML script with the APPLET tag, such as:

```
<applet code="Test.class" width=200 height=300></applet>
```

which loads an applet called Test.class and sets the applet size to 200 pixels wide and 300 pixels high. Table 11.2 discusses some optional parameters.

11.1.2 Applet viewer

A useful part of the JDK tools is an applet viewer which is used to test applets before they are run within the browse. The applet viewer on the PC version is AppletViewer.exe and the supplied argument is the HTML file that contains the applet tag(s). It then runs all the associated applets in separate windows.

Table 11.2 Other applet HTML parameters

Applet parameters	Description
CODEBASE=*codebaseURL*	Specifies the directory (*codebaseURL*) that contains the applet's code.
CODE=*appletFile*	Specifies the name of the file (*appletFile*) of the compiled applet.
ALT=*alternateText*	Specifies the alternative text that is displayed if the browser cannot run the Java applet.
NAME=*appletInstanceName*	Specifies a name for the applet instance (*appletInstanceName*). This makes it possible for applets on the same page to find each other.
WIDTH= *pixels* HEIGHT=*pixels*	Specifies the initial width and height (in *pixels*) of the applet.
ALIGN=*alignment*	Specifies the *alignment* of the applet. Possible values are: left, right, top, texttop, middle, absmiddle, baseline, bottom and absbottom.
VSPACE=*pixels* HSPACE=*pixels*	Specifies the number of *pixels* above and below the applet (VSPACE) and on each side of the applet (HSPACE).

11.2 Creating an applet

Java applet 11.1 shows a simple Java applet which displays two lines of text and HTML script 11.1 shows how the applet integrates into an HTML script.

Java applet 11.1 (j1.java)

```java
import java.awt.*;
import java.applet.*;

public class j1 extends Applet
{
  public void paint(Graphics g)
  {
    g.drawString("This is my first Java",5,25);
    g.drawString("applet.....",5,45);
  }
}
```

HTML script 11.1 (j1.html)

```html
<HTML>
<TITLE>First Applet</TITLE>
<APPLET CODE=j1.class WIDTH=200 HEIGHT=200>
</APPLET>
</HTML>
```

First the Java applet (j1.java) is created. In this case the edit program is used. The directory listing below shows that the files created are j1.java and j1.html (Note that Windows NT/95 displays the 8.3 filename format on the left hand side of the directory listing and the long filename on the right hand side).

🖥 Sample run 11.1

```
C:\DOCS\notes\INTER\java>edit j1.java

C:\DOCS\notes\INTER\java>dir
 Directory of C:\DOCS\notes\INTER\java
J1~1     JAV          263   07/04/97   13:35 j1.java
J1~1     HTM          105   07/04/97   13:31 j1.html
         2 file(s)             368 bytes
         2 dir(s)      136,085,504 bytes free
```

Next the Java applet is compiled using the javac.exe program. It can be seen from the listing that, if there are no errors, that the compiled file is named j1.class. This can then be used, with the HTML file, to run as an applet.

🖥 Sample run 11.2

```
C:\DOCS\notes\INTER\java>javac j1.java
C:\DOCS\notes\INTER\java>dir
 Directory of C:\DOCS\notes\INTER\java
J1~1     JAV          263   07/04/97   13:35 j1.java
J1~1     HTM          105   07/04/97   13:31 j1.html
J1~1     CLA          440   07/04/97   23:00 j1.class
         3 file(s)             808 bytes
         2 dir(s)      130,826,240 bytes free
C:\DOCS\notes\INTER\java>appletviewer j1.html
```

11.3 Applet basics

Java applet 11.1 recaps the previous Java applet. This section analyses the main parts of this Java applet.

📖 Java applet 11.1 (`j1.java`)

```
import java.awt.*;
import java.applet.*;
public class j1 extends Applet
{
  public void paint(Graphics g)
  {
    g.drawString("This is my first Java",5,25);
    g.drawString("applet.....",5,45);
  }
}
```

11.3.1 Import statements

The `import` statement allows previously written code to be included in the applet. This code is stored in class libraries (or packages), which are compiled Java code. For the JDK tools, the Java source code for these libraries is stored in the `src/java` directory.

Each Java applet created begins with:

```
import java.awt.*;
import java.applet.*;
```

These include the `awt` and `applet` class libraries. The `awt` class provide code that handles windows and graphics operations. The applet in Java script 11.1 uses `awt` code, for example, displays the "This is ..." message within the applet window. Likewise the applet uses the applet code to let the browser run the applet.

The default Java class libraries are stored in the `classes.zip` file in the `lib` directory. This file is in a compressed form and should not be unzipped before it is used. The following is a outline of the file.

```
Searching ZIP: CLASSES.ZIP
Testing: java/
Testing: java/lang/
Testing: java/lang/Object.class
Testing: java/lang/Exception.class
Testing: java/lang/Integer.class
   ::          ::
Testing: java/lang/Win32Process.class
Testing: java/io/
Testing: java/io/FilterOutputStream.class
Testing: java/io/OutputStream.class
   ::          ::
Testing: java/io/StreamTenizer.class
```

```
Testing: java/util/
Testing: java/util/Hashtable.class
Testing: java/util/Enumeration.class
   ::              ::
Testing: java/util/Stack.class
Testing: java/awt/
Testing: java/awt/Toolkit.class
Testing: java/awt/peer/
Testing: java/awt/peer/WindowPeer.class
   ::              ::
Testing: java/awt/peer/DialogPeer.class
Testing: java/awt/Image.class
Testing: java/awt/MenuItem.class
Testing: java/awt/MenuComponent.class
Testing: java/awt/image/
   ::              ::
   ::              ::
Testing: java/awt/ImageMediaEntry.class
Testing: java/awt/AWTException.class
Testing: java/net/
Testing: java/net/URL.class
Testing: java/net/URLStreamHandlerFactory.class
   ::              ::
Testing: java/net/URLEncoder.class
Testing: java/applet/
Testing: java/applet/Applet.class
Testing: java/applet/AppletContext.class
Testing: java/applet/AudioClip.class
Testing: java/applet/AppletStub.class
```

Table 11.3 lists the main class libraries and some sample libraries.

Table 11.3 Class libraries

Class libraries	Description	Example libraries
java.lang.*	Java language	java.lang.Class java.lang.Number java.lang.Process java.lang.String
java.io.*	I/O routines	java.io.InputStream java.io.OutputStream
java.util.*	Utilities	java.util.BitSet java.util.Dictionary
java.awt.*	Windows, menus and graphics	java.awt.Point java.awt.Polygon java.awt.MenuComponent java.awt.MenuBar java.awt.MenuItem
java.net.*	Networking (such as sockets, URL support, ftp, telnet, SMTP and HTTP).	java.net.ServerSocket java.net.Socket java.net.SocketImpl
java.applet.*	Code required to run an applet.	java.applet.AppletContext java.applet.AppletStub java.applet.AudioClip

It can be seen that upgrading the Java compiler is simple as all that is required is to replace the class libraries with new ones. For example if the basic language is upgraded then `java.lang.*` file is simply replaced with a new version. The user can also easily add new class libraries to the standard ones. A complete listing of the classes is given in Appendix X.

11.3.2 Applet class

The start of the applet code is defined in the form:

```
public class j1 extends Applet
```

which informs the Java compiler to create an applet named `j1` that extends the existing Applet class. The `public` keyword at the start of the statement allows the Java browser to run the applet, while if it is omitted the browser cannot access your applet.

The `class` keyword is used to create a class object named `j1` that extends the applet class. After this the applet is defined between the left and right braces (grouping symbols).

11.3.3 Applet functions

Functions allows Java applets to be split into smaller sub-tasks called functions. Theses function have the advantage that:

- They allow code to be reused.
- They allow for top-level design.
- They make applet debugging easier as each function can be tested in isolation to the rest of the applet.

A function has the `public` keyword, followed by the return value (if any) and the name of the function. After this the parameters passed to the function are defined within rounded brackets. Recapping from the previous example:

```
public void paint(Graphics g)
{
    g.drawString("This is my first Java",5,25);
    g.drawString("applet.....",5,45);
}
```

This function has the `public` keyword which allows any user to execute the function. The `void` type defines that there is nothing returned from this function and the name of the function is `paint()`. The parameter passed into the function is g which has the data type of `Graphics`. Within the `paint()` function the `drawString()` function is called. This function is defined in `java.awt.Graphics` class library (this library has been included with the `import java.awt.*` statement). The definition for this function is:

```
public abstract void drawString(String str, int x, int y)
```

which draws a string of characters using the current font and colour. The x,y position is the starting point of the baseline of the string (str).

It should be noted that Java is case sensitive and the names given must be used in the case (that is, uppercase or lowercase) that they are defined as.

11.4 Standalone programs

A Java program can also be run as a stand-alone program. This allows the Java program to be run without a browser and is normally used when testing a Java applet. The method of output to the screen is:

```
System.out.println("message");
```

which prints a message (message) to the display. This type of debugging is messy as these statements need to be manually inserted in the program. It is likely that later versions of the JDK toolkit will contain a run-time debugger which will allow developers to view the execution of the program.

To run a stand-alone program the java.exe program is used and the user adds output statements with the System.out.println() function. Note that there is no output from applet with the System.out.println() function.

Java stand-alone program 11.1 gives a simple example of a stand-alone program. The public static void main(Strings[] args) defines the main function. Sample run 11.3 shows how the Java program is created (with edit) and then compiler (with javac.exe), and then finally run (with java.exe).

📖 Java stand-alone program 11.1 (j2.java)
```
public class j2
{
   public static void main(String[] args)
   {
   int i;
      i=10;

      System.out.println("This is an example of the ");
      System.out.println("output from the standalone");
      System.out.println("program");
      System.out.println("The value of i is " + i);
   }
}
```

```
C:\DOCS\notes\INTER\java>edit j2.java
C:\DOCS\notes\INTER\java>javac j2.java
C:\DOCS\notes\INTER\java>java j2
This is an example of the
output from the standalone
program
The value of i is 10
```

11.5 Java reserved words

Like any programming language, Java has various reserved words which cannot be used as variable names. These are given next:

```
abstract     boolean      break        byte        case          cast
catch        char         class        cons        continue      default
do           double       else         extends     final         finally
float        for          future       generic     goto          if
implements   import       inner        instanceof  in            interface
long         native       new          null        operator      outer
package      private      protected    public      rest          return
short        static       super        switch      synchronized  this
throw        throws       transient    try         var           unsigned
virtual      void         volatile     while
```

11.6 Applet variables

Variables are used to store numeric values and characters. In Java all variables must be declared with their data type before they can be used. The Java data types are similar to C/C++ types, and are stated in Table 11.4.

Table 11.4 Java data types and their range

Type	Storage (bytes)	Range
boolean		True or False
byte	1	−128 to 127
char	2	Alphabetic characters
int	4	−2,147,483,648 to 2,147,483,647
short	2	−32,768 to 32,767
long	4	−2,147,483,648 to 2,147,483,647
float	4	$\pm 3.4 \times 10^{-38}$ to $\pm 3.4 \times 10^{38}$
double	8	$\pm 1.7 \times 10^{-308}$ to $\pm 1.7 \times 10^{308}$

11.6.1 Converting numeric data types

Java is a strongly typed language and various operations follow standard conversions for data types. If the developer wants to convert from one data type to another (such as from an integer to a double) then the data type conversion is used where the converted data type is defined within rounded brackets. For example:

```
double  y,z;
int        x;

   x=(int) (y+z);
```

converts the addition of y and z to an integer.

11.6.2 The paint() object

The paint() object is the object that is called whenever the applet is re-drawn. It will thus be called whenever the applet is run and then it is called whenever the applet is redisplayed.

11.7 Java operators

The table below recaps the Java operators from the previous chapter.

HIGHEST PRIORITY

() [] .	primary
! ~ ++ -- -	unary
* / %	multiply
+ -	additive
<< >> >>>	shift
< > <= >=	relation
== !=	equality
&	bitwise
^	
|	
&&	logical
||	
= += -=	assignment

LOWEST PRIORITY

11.8 Mathematical operations

Java has a basic set of mathematics functions which are defined in the java.lang.Math class library. Table 11.5 outlines these functions. An example of the functions in this library is abs () which can be used to return the absolute value of a double, an int or a long value. Java automatically picks the required format and the return data type will be the type of the value to be operated on.

As the functions are part of the Math class they are preceded with the Math. class method. For example:

```
val2=Math.sqrt(val1);
val3=Math.abs(val2);
z=Math.min(x,y);
```

Java stand-alone program 11.2 shows a few examples of mathematical operations and sample run 11.4 show a sample compilation and run session.

Java has also two predefined mathematical constants, these are:

- Pi is equivalent to 3.14159265358979323846.
- E is equivalent to 2.7182818284590452354.

Table 11.5 Functions defined in java.lang.Math

Function	Description
double abs(double a)	Returns the absolute double value of a.
float abs(float a)	Returns the absolute float value of a.
int abs(int a)	Returns the absolute integer value of a.
long abs(long a)	Returns the absolute long value of a.
double acos(double a)	Returns the arc cosine of a, in the range of 0.0 through Pi.
double asin(double a)	Returns the arc sine of a, in the range of Pi/2 through Pi/2.
double atan(double a)	Returns the arc tangent of a, in the range of –Pi/2 through Pi/2.
double atan2(double a, double b)	Converts rectangular coordinates (a, b) to polar (r, theta).
double ceil(double a)	Returns the 'ceiling' or smallest whole number greater than or equal to a.
double cos(double a)	Returns the trigonometric cosine of an angle.
double exp(double a)	Returns the exponential number e(2.718...) raised to the power of a.
double floor(double a)	Returns the 'floor' or largest whole number less than or equal to a.
double IEEEremainder(double f1, double f2)	Returns the remainder of f1 divided by f2 as defined by IEEE 754.
double log(double a)	Returns the natural logarithm (base e) of a.
double max(double a, double b)	Takes two double values, a and b, and returns the greater number of the two.
double max(float a, float b)	Takes two float values, a and b, and returns the greater number of the two.
int max(int a, int b)	Takes two int values, a and b, and returns the greater number of the two.

`max(long a, long b)`	Takes two long values, a and b, and returns the greater number of the two.
`double min(double a, double b)`	Takes two double values, a and b, and returns the smallest number of the two.
`float min(float a, float b)`	Takes two float values, a and b, and returns the smallest number of the two.
`int min(int a, int b)`	Takes two integer values, a and b, and returns the smallest number of the two.
`long min(long a, long b)`	Takes two long values, a and b, and returns the smallest number of the two.
`double pow(double a, double b)`	Returns the number a raised to the power of b.
`double random()`	Generates a random number between 0.0 and 1.0.
`double rint(double b)`	Converts a double value into an integral value in double format.
`long round(double a)`	Rounds off a double value by first adding 0.5 to it and then returning the largest integer that is less than or equal to this new value.
`int round(float a)`	Rounds off a float value by first adding 0.5 to it and then returning the largest integer that is less than or equal to this new value.
`double sin(double a)`	Returns the trigonometric sine of an angle.
`double sqrt(double a)`	Returns the square root of a.
`double tan(double a)`	Returns the trigonometric tangent of an angle.

📖 Java stand-alone program 11.2 (j3.java)

```
import java.lang.Math;
public class j2
{
    public static void main(String[] args)
    {
    double x,y,z;
    int i;
        i=10;
        y=Math.log(10.0);
        x=Math.pow(3.0,4.0);
        z=Math.random(); // random number from 0 to 1
        System.out.println("Value of i is " + i);
        System.out.println("Value of log(10) is " + y);
        System.out.println("Value of 3^4 is " + x);
        System.out.println("A random number is " + z);
        System.out.println("Square root of 2 is " +
            Math.sqrt(2));
    }
}
```

🖥 Sample run 11.4

```
C:\DOCS\notes\INTER\java>javac j2.java
C:\DOCS\notes\INTER\java>java j2
Value of i is 10
Value of log(10) is 2.30259
Value of 3^4 is 81
A random number is 0.0810851
Square root of 2 is 1.41421
```

11.9 Loops

11.9.1 for()

As with C/C++ and JavaScript the standard format for a for() loop is:

```
for (starting condition;test condition;operation)
{
        statement block
}
```

where:

starting condition – the starting value for the loop;
test condition – if test condition is TRUE the loop will
continue execution;
operation – the operation conducted at the end of the loop.

Java applet 11.3 shows how a for() loop can be used to display the square and cube of the values from 0 to 9. Notice that the final value of i within the for() loop is 9 because the end condition is i<10 (while i is less than 10).

📖 Java applet 11.2 (j4.java)

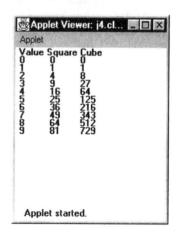

```
import java.awt.*;
import java.applet.*;


public class j4 extends Applet
{
  public void paint(Graphics g)
  {
  int    i;

    g.drawString("Value Square Cube",5,10);
    for (i=0;i<10;i++)
    {
      g.drawString(""+ i,5,20+10*i);
      g.drawString(""+ i*i ,45,20+10*i);
      g.drawString(""+ i*i*i,85,20+10*i);
    }
  }
}
```

📖 HTML script 11.2 (j4.html)

```
<HTML>
<TITLE>First Applet</TITLE>
<APPLET CODE=j4.class WIDTH=200 HEIGHT=200>
</APPLET>
</HTML>
```

11.9.2 `while()`

The `while()` statement allows a block of code to be executed while a specified condition is TRUE. It checks the condition at the start of the block; if this is TRUE the block is executed, else it will exit the loop. The syntax is:

```
while (condition)
{
    :             : statement block
    :             :
}
```

If the statement block contains a single statement then the braces may be omitted (although it does no harm to keep them).

11.10 Conditional statements

Conditional statements allow a program to make decisions on the route through a program.

11.10.1 `if...else`

As with C/C++ and JavaScript the standard format for a `if()` descision is:

```
if (expression)
{
    statement block
}
```

The following is an example format with an `else` extension.

```
if (expression)
{
    statement block1
}
else
{
    statement block2
}
```

Java applet 11.4 uses a `for()` loop and the `if()` statement to test if a value is less than, equal to or greater than 5. The loop is used to repeat the test 10 times.

The `random()` function is used to generate a value between 0 and 1, the returned value is then multiplied by 10 so as to convert to a value between 0 and 10. Then it is converted to an integer using the data type modifier `(int)`. The `if()` statement is then used to test the value.

Java applet 11.3 (j5.java)

```java
import java.awt.*;
import java.applet.*;
import java.lang.Math;

public class j5 extends Applet
{
 public void paint(Graphics g)
 {
  int      i,x;
  double   val;
  for (i=0;i<10;i++)
  {
    val=Math.random();
    x=(int)(val*10.0);
        // Convert value between 0 and 10
    if (x<5)
     g.drawString("Less than 5",5,20+I*10);
    else if (x==5)
     g.drawString("Equal to 5",5,20+i*10);
    else
     g.drawString("Greater than 5",5,20+i*10);
  }
 }
}
```

Applet Viewer: j5.cl...

Applet

Less than 5
Less than 5
Greater than 5
Greater than 5
Greater than 5
Equal to 5
Less than 5
Greater than 5
Less than 5
Less than 5

Applet started.

HTML script 11.3 (j5.html)

```html
<HTML>
<TITLE>First Applet</TITLE>
<APPLET CODE=j5.class WIDTH=200 HEIGHT=200>
</APPLET>
</HTML>
```

11.11 Exercises

11.11.1 The Java compiler converts the Java program into what type of code:

(a)   Object code
(b)   Machine code
(c)   Bytecode
(d)   Executable code

11.11.2 Which software language is Java based on:

(a)   Pascal
(b)   C++
(c)   FORTRAN
(d)   Delphi

11.12.1 Write a Java applet which displays the following table of powers.

Value	Square	Cube	Forth power
1	1	1	1
2	4	8	16
3	9	27	81
4	16	64	256
5	25	125	625
6	36	216	1296

11.12.2 Write a Java applet which displays the following table of square root values from 1 to 15.

Value	Square root
1	1
2	1.414214
3	1.732051
4	2
5	2.236068
6	2.44949
7	2.645751
8	2.828427
9	3
10	3.162278
11	3.316625
12	3.464102
13	3.605551
14	3.741657
15	3.872983

11.12.3 Write a Java applet which display 20 random numbers from between 0 and 20.

11.12.4 Write a Java applet that simulates the rolling of two dice. A smple output is:

Dice 1: 3
Dice 2: 5
Total: 8

12 Java (Extended functions)

12.1 Introduction

Chapter 11 discussed the Java programming language. This chapter investigates event-driven programs, the main events are:

- Initialization and exit functions (`init()`, `start()`, `stop()` and `destroy()`).
- Repainting and resizing (`paint()`).
- Mouse events (`mouseUp()`, `mouseDown()` and `mouseDrag()`).
- Keyboard events (`keyUp()` and `keyDown()`).

12.2 Initialization and exit functions

Java has various reserved functions which are called when various events occur. Table 12.1 shows typical initialization functions and their events, and Figure 12.1 illustrates how they are called.

Table 12.1 Java initialisation and exit functions

Function	Description
`public void init()`	This function is called each time the applet is started. It is typically used to add user-interface components.
`public void start()`	This function is called after the `init()` function is called. It is also called whenever the user returns to the page containing the applet and it thus can be called many times as apposed to the `init()` function which will only be called when the applet is first started. Thus code which is to be executed once only is normally put in the `init()` function and code which must be executed everytime the applet is accessed should be inserted into the `start()` function.

`public void stop()`	This function is called when the user moves away from the page on which the applet resides. It is thus typically used to stop processing while the user is not accessing the applet. Typically it is used to stop animation or audio files, or mathematical processing. The `start()` function normally restarts the processing.
`public void paint(Graphics g)`	This function is called when the applet is first called and whenever the user resizes or moves the windows.
`public void destroy()`	This function is called when the applet is stopped and is normally used to release associated resources, such as freeing memory, closing files, and so on.

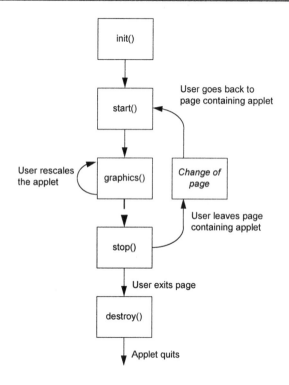

Figure 12.1   Java initialisation and exit functions

Java applet 12.1 gives an example using the `init()` and `start()` functions. In it the variable `i` is declared within the applet and it is set to a value of 5 in the `init()` function. The `start()` function then adds 6 onto this value. After this the `paint()` function is called so that it displays the value of `i` (which should equal 11).

Java applet 12.1 (j6.java)

```java
import java.awt.*;
import java.applet.*;

public class j6 extends Applet
{
int     i;

 public void init()
 {
   i=5;
 }
 public void start()
 {
   i=i+6;
 }
 public void paint(Graphics g)
 {
 g.drawString("The value of i is " + i,5,25);
 }
}
```

```
Applet Viewer: j6.cl...  ▢ ▢ ☒
Applet

The value of i is 11




Applet started.
```

HTML script 12.1 (j6.html)

```html
<HTML>
<TITLE>Applet</TITLE>
<APPLET CODE=j6.class WIDTH=200 HEIGHT=200>
</APPLET>
</HTML>
```

12.3 Mouse events

Most Java applets require some user interaction, normally with the mouse or from the keyboard. A mouse operation causes mouse event. The three basic events which are supported in Java are:

- mouseUp().
- mouseDown().
- mouseDrag().

Java applet 12.2 uses the three mouse events to display the current mouse cursor. Each of the functions must return a true value to identify that the event has been handled successfully (the return type is of data type Boolean thus the return could only be a true or a false). In the example applet, on moving the mouse cursor with the left mouse key pressed down the mouseDrag() function is automatically called. The x and y co-ordinate of the cursor is stored in the x and y variable when the event occurs. This is used in the functions to build a message string (in the case of the drag event the string name is MouseDragMsg).

📖 Java applet 12.2 (j6.java)

```
import java.awt.*;
import java.applet.*;

public class j7 extends Applet
{
String  MouseDownMsg=null;
String  MouseUpMsg=null;
String  MouseDragMsg=null;

  public boolean mouseUp(Event event, int x,
     int y)
  {
    MouseUpMsg = "UP>" +x + "," + y;
    repaint();   // call paint()
    return(true);
  }
  public boolean mouseDown(Event event, int x,
      int y)
  {
    MouseDownMsg = "DOWN>" +x + "," + y;
    repaint();   // call paint()
    return(true);
  }

  public boolean mouseDrag(Event event, int x,
       int y)
  {
    MouseDragMsg = "DRAG>" +x + "," + y;
    repaint();   // call paint()
    return(true);
  }

  public void paint(Graphics g)
  {
    if (MouseUpMsg !=null)
      g.drawString(MouseUpMsg,5,20);
    if (MouseDownMsg !=null)
      g.drawString(MouseDownMsg,5,40);
    if (MouseDragMsg !=null)
      g.drawString(MouseDragMsg,5,60);
  }
}
```

📖 HTML script 12.2 (j7.html)

```
<HTML>
<TITLE>Applet</TITLE>
<APPLET CODE=j7.class WIDTH=200 HEIGHT=200>
</APPLET>
</HTML>
```

12.4 Mouse selection

In many applets the user is prompted to select an object using the mouse. To achieve this the x and y position of the event is tested to determine if the cursor is within the defined area. Java applet 12.3 is a program which allows the user to press the mouse button on the applet screen. The applet then uses the mouse events to determine if the cursor is within a given area of the screen (in this case between 10,10 and 100,100). If the user is within this defined area then the message displayed is HIT, else it is MISS. The graphics function g.drawRect(x1,y1,x2,y2) draws a rectangle from (x1,y1) to (x2,y2).

📖 Java applet 12.3 (j8.java)

```java
import java.awt.*;
import java.applet.*;
public class j8 extends Applet
{
String  Msg=null;
int     x_start,y_start,x_end,y_end;
  public void init()
  {
    x_start=10;   y_start=10;
    x_end=100;    y_end=50;
  }

  public boolean mouseUp(Event event, int x,
      int y)
  {
    if ((x>x_start) && (x<x_end) &&
            (y>y_start) && (y<y_end))
            Msg = "HIT";
    else Msg="MISS";
    repaint();   // call paint()
    return(true);
  }
  public boolean mouseDown(Event event, int x,
      int y)
  {
    if ((x>x_start) && (x<x_end) &&
            (y>y_start) && (y<y_end))
            Msg = "HIT";
    else Msg="MISS";
    repaint();   // call paint()
    return(true);
  }

  public void paint(Graphics g)
  {
    g.drawRect(x_start,y_start,x_end,y_end);
    g.drawString("Hit",30,30);
    if (Msg !=null)
      g.drawString("HIT OR MISS: " + Msg,5,80);
  }
}
```

📖 HTML script 12.3 (j8.html)

```html
<HTML>
<TITLE>Applet</TITLE>
<APPLET CODE=j8.class WIDTH=200 HEIGHT=200>
</APPLET></HTML>
```

12.5 Keyboard input

Java provides for two keyboard events, these are:

- `keyUp()`. Is called when a key has been released.
- `keyDown()`. Is called when a key has been pressed.

The parameters passed into these functions are `event` (which defines the keyboard state) and an integer `Keypressed` which describes the key pressed.

📖 Java applet 12.4 (`j9.java`)

```
import java.awt.*;
import java.applet.*;

public class j9 extends Applet
{
String  Msg=null;

 public boolean keyUp(Event event, int KeyPress)
  {
   Msg="Key pressed="+(char)KeyPress;
   repaint();    // call paint()
   return(true);
  }
  public void paint(Graphics g)
  {
   if (Msg !=null)
         g.drawString(Msg,5,80);
  }
}
```

Applet Viewer:...

Applet

Key pressed=f

Applet started.

📖 HTML script 12.4 (`j9.html`)

```
<HTML>
<TITLE>Applet</TITLE>
<APPLET CODE=j9.class WIDTH=200 HEIGHT=200>
</APPLET>
</HTML>
```

The event contains an identification as to the type of event it is. When one of the function keys is pressed then the variable `event.id` is set to the macro `Event.KEY_ACTION` (as shown in Java applet 12.5). Other keys, such as the Ctrl, Alt and Shift keys set bits in the `event.modifier` variable. The test for the Ctrl key is:

```
if ((event.modifiers & Event.CTRL_MASK)!=0)
    Msg="CONTROL KEY "+KeyPress;
```

This tests the `CTRL_MASK` bit, if it is a 1 then the CTRL key has been pressed. Java applet 12.5 shows its uses.

📖 Java applet 12.5 (j10.java)

```java
import java.awt.*;
import java.applet.*;

public class j10 extends Applet
{
String  Msg=null;

  public boolean keyDown(Event event,
                         int KeyPress)
  {
   if (event.id == Event.KEY_ACTION)
     Msg="FUNCTION KEY "+KeyPress;
   else if ((event.modifiers & Event.SHIFT_MASK)!=0)
     Msg="SHIFT KEY "+KeyPress;
   else if ((event.modifiers & Event.CTRL_MASK)!=0)
     Msg="CONTROL KEY "+KeyPress;
   else if ((event.modifiers & Event.ALT_MASK)!=0)
     Msg="ALT KEY "+KeyPress;
   else Msg=""+(char)KeyPress;
   repaint();   // call paint()
   return(true);
  }
  public void paint(Graphics g)
  {
   if (Msg!=null)
     g.drawString(Msg,5,80);
  }
}
```

```
Applet Viewer: j10....

Applet


CONTROL KEY 2



Applet started.
```

📖 HTML script 12.5 (j10.html)

```
<HTML>
<TITLE>Applet</TITLE>
<APPLET CODE=j10.class WIDTH=200 HEIGHT=200>
</APPLET></HTML>
```

For function keys the KeyPress variable has the following values:

Key	Value	Key	Value	Key	Value	Key	Value	Key	Value
F1	1008	F2	1009	F3	1010	F4	1011	F5	1012
F7	1014	F8	1015	F9	1016	F10	1017	F11	1018

Thus to test for the function keys the following routine can be used:

```java
if (event.id == Event.KEY_ACTION)
   if (KeyPress==1008) Msg="F1";
   else if (KeyPress==1009) Msg="F2";
   else if (KeyPress==1010) Msg="F3";
   else if (KeyPress==1011) Msg="F4";
   else if (KeyPress==1012) Msg="F5";
   else if (KeyPress==1013) Msg="F6";
   else if (KeyPress==1014) Msg="F7";
   else if (KeyPress==1015) Msg="F8";
   else if (KeyPress==1016) Msg="F9";
   else if (KeyPress==1017) Msg="F10";
```

For control keys the KeyPress variable has the following values:

Key	Value	Key	Value	Key	Value	Key	Value
Cntrl-A	1	Cntrl-B	2	Cntrl-C	3	Cntrl-D	4
Cntrl-E	5	Cntrl-F	6	Cntrl-G	7	Cntrl-H	8

Thus to test for the control keys the following routine can be used:

```
if ((event.modifiers & Event.CTRL_MASK)!=0)
    if (KeyPress==1) Msg="Cntrl-A";
    else if (KeyPress==2) Msg="Cntrl-B";
    else if (KeyPress==3) Msg="Cntrl-C";
    else if (KeyPress==4) Msg="Cntrl-D";
```

12.6 Graphics images

Java has excellent support images and sound. For graphics files it has support for GIF and JPEG files, each of which are in a compressed form. The image object is declared with:

```
Image mypic;
```

Next the graphics image is associated with the image object with the getImage() function:

```
mypic=getImage(getCodeBase(),"myson.gif");
```

where the getCodeBase() function returns the applets URL (such as www.eece.napier.ac.uk) and the second argument is the name of the graphics file (in this case, myson.gif).
After this the image can be displayed with:

```
g.drawImage(mypic,x,y,this);
```

where mypic is the name of the image object, the x and y values are the co-ordinates of the upper-left hand corner of the image. The this keyword associates the current object (in this case it is the graphics image) and the current applet. Java applet 12.6 gives an applet which displays an image.

Java applet 12.6 (j11.java)

```java
import java.awt.*;
import java.applet.*;

public class j11 extends Applet
{
Image    mypic;
 public void init()
  {
   mypic=getImage(getCodeBase(),"myson.gif");
  }

 public void paint(Graphics g)
  {
    g.drawImage(mypic,0,0,this);
  }
}
```

HTML script 12.6 (j11.html)

```html
<HTML><TITLE>Applet</TITLE>
<APPLET CODE=j11.class WIDTH=200 HEIGHT=200>
</APPLET></HTML>
```

12.7 Graphics

The `java.awt.Graphics` class contains a great deal of graphics-based functions, these are stated in Table 12.2.

Table 12.2 Java graphics functions

Graphics function	Description
`public abstract void translate(int x,int y)`	Translates the specified parameters into the origin of the graphics context. All subsequent operations on this graphics context will be relative to this origin. Parameters: x - the x coordinate y - the y coordinate
`public abstract Color getColor()`	Gets the current colour.
`public abstract void setColor(Color c)`	Set current drawing colour.
`public abstract Font getFont()`	Gets the current font.
`public abstract void setFont(Font font)`	Set the current font.
`public FontMetrics getFontMetrics()`	Gets the current font metrics.
`public abstract FontMetrics getFontMetrics(Font f)`	Gets the current font metrics for the specified font.

```
public abstract void
   copyArea(int x, int y,
       int width, int height,
       int dx,int dy)
```
Copies an area of the screen where (x,y) is the co-ordinate of the top left-hand corner, width and height are the width and height, and dx is the horizontal distance and dy the vertical distance.

```
public abstract void
drawLine(int x1,int y1,
     int x2,   int y2)
```
Draws a line between the (x1,y1) and (x2,y2).

```
public abstract void
    fillRect(int x, int y,
        int width,int height)
```
Fills the specified rectangle with the current colour.

```
public void
    drawRect(int x,int y,
        int width,  int height)
```
Draws the outline of the specified rectangle using the current colour.

```
public abstract void
    clearRect(int x, int y,
        int width, int height)
```
Clears the specified rectangle by filling it with the current background colour of the current drawing surface.

```
public void draw3DRect(int x,
    int y, int width,
    int height,boolean raised)
```
Draws a highlighted 3-D rectangle where raised is a boolean value that defines whether the rectangle is raised or not.

```
public void fill3DRect(int x,
    int y,int width,
    int height,boolean raised)
```
Paints a highlighted 3-D rectangle using the current colour.

```
public abstract void
    drawOval(int x,int y,
        int width, int height)
```
Draws an oval inside the specified rectangle using the current colour.

```
public abstract void
    fillOval(int x,int y,
        int width, int height)
```
Fills an oval inside the specified rectangle using the current colour.

```
public abstract void
  drawArc(int x, int y,
    int width, int height,
    int startAngle,int arcAngle)
```
Draws an arc bounded by the specified rectangle starting. Zero degrees for startAngle is at the 3-o'clock position and arcAngle specifies the extent of the arc. A positive value for arcAngle indicates a counter-clockwise rotation while a negative value indicates a clockwise rotation. The parameter (x,y) specifies the centre point, and width and height specifies the width and height of a rectangle

```
public abstract void
    fillArc(int x, int y,
    int width, int height,
    int startAngle,
    int arcAngle)
```
Fills an pie-shaped arc using the current colour.

```
public abstract void
    drawPolygon(int xPoints[],
        int yPoints[],int nPoints)
```
Draws a polygon using an array of x and y points (xPoints[ ] and yPoints[ ]). The number of points within the array is specified by nPoints.

```
public abstract void
    fillPolygon(int xPoints[],
        int yPoints[],int nPoints)
```
Fills a polygon with the current colour.

`public abstract void`
`    drawString(String str,`
`        int x, int y)`
	Draws the specified String using the current font and colour.

`public abstract boolean`
`    drawImage(Image img,int x,`
`        int y)`
	Draws the specified image at the specified coordinate (x, y).

`public abstract void dispose()`	Disposes of this graphics context.

12.7.1 Setting the colour

The current drawing colour is set using the `setColor()` function. It is used as follows:

```
g.setColor(Color.yellow);
```

Colours are defined in the `java.awt.Color` class and valid colours are:

```
Color.black        Color.blue         Color.cyan
Color.darkGray     Color.gray         Color.green
Color.lightGray    Color.magenta      Color.orange
Color.pink         Color.red          Color.white
Color.yellow
```

Any other 24-bit colour can be generated with the function Color which has the format:

```
public Color(int r, int g, int b)
```

where r, g and b are values of strength from 0 to 255. For example:
`Color(255,0,0)` gives red;
`Color(255,255,255)` gives white;
`Color(0,128,128)` gives blue/green;
`Color(0,0,0)` gives black.

12.7.2 Drawing lines and circles

Normally to draw a graphics object the user must plan its layout for the dimension within the object. Figure 12.2 shows an example graphic with the required dimensions. The `drawOval()` function uses the top level hand point for the x and y parameters in the function and the width and height define the width and height of the oval shape. Thus the `drawOval()` function can be used to draw circles (if the width is equal to the height) or ovals (if the width is not equal to the height). Java applet 12.7 shows the Java code to draw the object. This applet uses the `setColor()` function to make the circle yellow and the other shapes blue.

12.7.3 Drawing polygons

The drawPolygon() function can be used to draw complex objects where the object is defined as a group of (x,y) coordinates. Java applet 12.8 draws a basic picture of a car and the xpoints array holds the x co-ordinates and ypoints hold the y co-ordinates. Figure 12.3 illustrates the object.

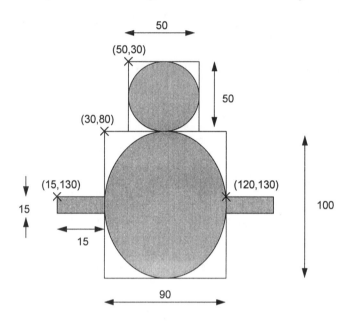

Figure 12.2 Dimensions for graphic

📖 Java applet 12.7 (j11.java)

```
import java.awt.*;
import java.applet.*;
public class j12 extends Applet
{
  public void paint(Graphics g)
  {
    g.setColor(Color.yellow);
    g.fillOval(50,30,50,50);
    g.setColor(Color.blue);
    g.fillOval(30,80,90,100);
    g.fillRect(15,130,15,10);
    g.fillRect(120,130,15,10);
  }
}
```

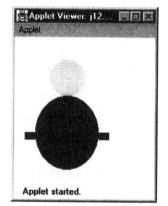

📖 HTML script 12.7 (j11.html)

```
<HTML><TITLE>Applet</TITLE>
<APPLET CODE=j12.class WIDTH=200 HEIGHT=200>
</APPLET></HTML>
```

Java applet 12.8 (j13.java)

```java
import java.awt.*;
import java.applet.*;
public class j13 extends Applet
{
int
xpoints[]={10,30,30,90,100,140,140,110,110,
           90,90,40,40,20,10,10},
  ypoints[]={50,50,30,30,50,50,70,70,60,60,
             70,70,60,60,70,70,50};
  public void paint(Graphics g)
  {
    g.drawPolygon(xpoints,ypoints,17);
  }
}
```

HTML script 12.8 (j13.html)

```html
<HTML><TITLE>Applet</TITLE>
<APPLET CODE=j13.class WIDTH=200 HEIGHT=200>
</APPLET></HTML>
```

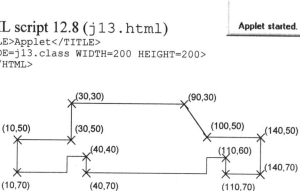

```
xpoints[]={10,30,30,90,100,140,140,110,110,90,
           90,40,40,20,20,10,10},
ypoints[]={50,50,30,30,50,50,70,70,60,60,70,
           70,60,60,70,70,50};
```

Figure 12.3 Co-ordinates of graphic

12.8 Sound

The playing of sound files is similar to displaying graphics files. Java applet 12.9 shows a sample applet which plays an audio file (in this case, test.au). Unfortunately the current version of the Java compiler only supports the AU format, thus WAV files need to be converted into AU format.

The initialization process uses the getAudioClip() function and the audio file is played with the loop() function. This function is contained in the java.applet.AudioClip class, these functions are:

```
public abstract void play()     Plays the audio file and finishes at the end.
public abstract void loop()     Starts playing the clip in a loop.
public abstract void stop()     Stops playing the clip.
```

Java applet 12.9 (j14.java)

```
import java.awt.*;
import java.applet.*;

public class j14 extends Applet
{
AudioClip    audClip;
  public void paint(Graphics g)
  {
    audClip=getAudioClip(getCodeBase(),"hello.au");
    audClip.loop();
  }
}
```

HTML script 12.9 (j14.html)

```
<HTML>
<TITLE>Applet</TITLE>
<APPLET CODE=j14.class WIDTH=200 HEIGHT=200>
</APPLET></HTML>
```

12.9 Dialog-boxes

One of the features of Java is that it supports dialog boxes and check boxes. These are used with event handlers to produce and event-driven options.

12.9.1 Buttons and events

Java applet 12.10 creates three Button objects. These are created with the add() function which displays the button in the applet window.

Java applet 12.10 (j15.java)

```
import java.awt.*;
import java.applet.*;

public class j15 extends Applet
{
  public void init()
  {
    add(new Button("Help"));
    add(new Button("Show"));
    add(new Button("Exit"));
  }
}
```

HTML script 12.10 (j15.html)

```
<HTML><TITLE>Applet</TITLE>
<APPLET CODE=j15.class WIDTH=200 HEIGHT=200>
</APPLET></HTML>
```

Applet 12.10 creates three buttons which do not have any action associated with them. Java applet 12.11 uses the action function which is called when an event occurs. Within this function the event variable is tested to see if one of the buttons caused the event. This is achieved with:

```
if (event.target instanceof Button)
```

If this tests to the true then the Msg string takes on the value of the Object, which holds the name of the button that caused the event.

📖 **Java applet 12.11 (j15.java)**

```
import java.awt.*;
import java.applet.*;

public class j16 extends Applet
{
String  Msg=null;

 public void init()
 {
  add(new Button("Help"));
  add(new Button("Show"));
  add(new Button("Exit"));
 }
 public boolean action(Event event, Object object)
 {
  if (event.target instanceof Button)
  {
    Msg = (String) object;
    repaint();
  }
  return(true);
 }
 public void paint(Graphics g)
 {
  if (Msg!=null)
    g.drawString("Button:" + Msg,30,80);
 }
}
```

📖 **HTML script 12.11 (j15.html)**

```
<HTML>
<TITLE>Applet</TITLE>
<APPLET CODE=j15.class WIDTH=200 HEIGHT=200>
</APPLET></HTML>
```

12.9.2 Checkboxes

Typically checkboxes are used to select from a number of options. Java applet 12.12 shows how an applet can use checkboxes. As before the action function is called when a checkbox changes its state and within the function event.target parameter is tested for the checkbox with:

```
if (event.target instanceof Checkbox)
```

If this is true then the function DetermineCheckState() is called which tests event.target for the checkbox value and its state (true or false).

📖 Java applet 12.12 (j17.java)

```java
import java.awt.*;
import java.applet.*;
public class j17 extends Applet
{
String  Msg=null;

 public void init()
 {
  add(new Checkbox("FAX"));
  add(new Checkbox("Telephone"));
  add(new Checkbox("Email"));
  add(new Checkbox("Post",null,true));
 }
 public void DetermineCheckState(Checkbox Cbox)
 {
  Msg=Cbox.getLabel() + " " + Cbox.getState();
  repaint();
 }
 public boolean action(Event event, Object object)
 {
  if (event.target instanceof Checkbox)
    DetermineCheckState((Checkbox)event.target);
  return(true);
 }
 public void paint(Graphics g)
 {
  if (Msg!=null)
    g.drawString("Check box:" + Msg,30,80);
 }
}
```

Applet Viewer: j17.... ☐☐☒
Applet

☐ FAX   ☑ Telephone

☑ Email   ☑ Post

Check box:Telephone true

Applet started.

📖 HTML script 12.12 (j17.html)

```html
<HTML>
<TITLE>Applet</TITLE>
<APPLET CODE=j17.class WIDTH=200 HEIGHT=200>
</APPLET></HTML>
```

12.9.3 Radio buttons

The standard checkboxes allows any number of options to be selected. A radiobutton only allows one option to be selected at a time. The previous example can be changed as follows:

```java
public void init()
{
    add(new Checkbox("FAX",RadioGroup,false));
    add(new Checkbox("Telephone",RadioGroup,false));
    add(new Checkbox("Email",RadioGroup,false));
    add(new Checkbox("Post",RadioGroup,true));
}
```

This sets the checkbox type to RadioGroup and it can be seen that only one of the checkboxes is initally set (that is, "Post").

12.9.4 Pop-up menu choices

To create a pop-up menu the Choice object is initally created with:

```
Choice mymenu = new Choice();
```

After this the menu options are defined using the addItem method. Java applet 12.13 shows an example usage of a pop-up menu.

📖 **Java applet 12.13 (j15.java)**

```
import java.awt.*;
import java.applet.*;

public class j18 extends Applet
{
String  Msg=null;
Choice  mymenu= new Choice();

   public void init()
   {
     mymenu.addItem("FAX");
     mymenu.addItem("Telephone");
     mymenu.addItem("Email");
     mymenu.addItem("Post");
     add(mymenu);
   }
   public void DetermineCheckState(Choice mymenu)
   {
     Msg=mymenu.getItem(mymenu.getSelectedIndex());
     repaint();
   }
   public boolean action(Event event, Object object)
   {
    if (event.target instanceof Choice)
      DetermineCheckState((Choice)event.target);
    return(true);
   }
   public void paint(Graphics g)
   {
     if (Msg!=null)
       g.drawString("Menu select:" + Msg,30,120);
   }
}
```

📖 **HTML script 12.13 (j15.html)**

```
<HTML>
<TITLE>Applet</TITLE>
<APPLET CODE=j15.class WIDTH=200 HEIGHT=200>
</APPLET></HTML>
```

12.9.5 Text input

Text can be entered into a Java applet using the TextField action. In Java applet 12.14 the TextField(20) defines a 20-character input field.

📖 Java applet 12.14 (j15.java)

```java
import java.awt.*;
import java.applet.*;

public class j19 extends Applet
{
String  Msg=null;

 public void init()
 {
   add(new Label("Enter your name"));
   add(new TextField(20));
 }
 public void DetermineText(TextField mytext)
 {
   Msg=mytext.getText();
   repaint();
 }

 public boolean action(Event event, Object object)
 {
   if (event.target instanceof TextField)
      DetermineText((TextField)event.target);
   return(true);
 }
 public void paint(Graphics g)
 {
   if (Msg!=null)
      g.drawString("Your name is:" + Msg,30,120);
 }
}
```

Applet Viewer: j19... ☐☐☒
Applet

Enter your name

fred bloggs

Your name is:fred bloggs

Applet started.

📖 HTML script 12.14 (j15.html)

```html
<HTML>
<TITLE>Applet</TITLE>
<APPLET CODE=j15.class WIDTH=200 HEIGHT=200>
</APPLET></HTML>
```

12.10 Fonts

Java is well supported with different fonts. The class library
java.awt.Font defines the Font class and the general format for defining
the font is:

Font font = new Font (*font_type, font_attrib, font_size*)

The main font_types are:

"TimesRoman"   "Helvetica"   "Courier"   "Symbol"

This book is written in Times Roman. Helvetica looks good as a header, such
as **Header 1**. Courier produces a monospace font where all of the characters

have the same width. The Java applets in this chapter use the Courier font. Symbol is normally used when special symbols are required. The *font_attrib* can either be BOLD, ITALIC or NORMAL. and the font_size is an integer value which is supported by the compiler. The font size of this text is 11 and most normal text varies between 8 and 12.

Java applet 12.15 shows an example applet using different fonts.

📖 Java applet 12.15 (j20.java)

```java
import java.awt.*;
import java.applet.*;

public class j20 extends Applet
{
Font   TimesRoman= new Font("TimesRoman",Font.BOLD,24);
Font   Courier= new Font("Courier",Font.BOLD,24);
Font   Helvetica= new Font("Helvetica",Font.BOLD,24);
Font   Symbol= new Font("Symbol",Font.BOLD,24);

  public void paint(Graphics g)
  {
    g.setFont(TimesRoman);
    g.drawString("Sample text",10,40);
    g.setFont(Courier);
    g.drawString("Sample text",10,60);
    g.setFont(Helvetica);
    g.drawString("Sample text",10,80);
    g.setFont(Symbol);
    g.drawString("Sample text",10,100);
  }
}
```

📖 HTML script 12.15 (j20.html)

```html
<HTML><TITLE>Applet</TITLE>
<APPLET CODE=j20.class WIDTH=200 HEIGHT=200>
</APPLET></HTML>
```

12.11 Exercises

12.11.1 The Java function which is first called when the applet is run is:

    (a)   `destroy()`
    (b)   `new()`
    (c)   `paint()`
    (d)   `init()`

12.11.2 The Java function which is called every time the display is updated is:

(a)   `draw()`
(b)   `again()`
(c)   `paint()`
(d)   `redo()`

12.12 Tutorial

12.11.1 Explain how the three mouse events occur.

12.11.2 Write a Java applet that contains a target which has areas with different point's values. These point values are 50, 100 and 150. The program should accumulate the score so far. A sample screen is given in Figure 12.4 (refer to Java applet 12.3 for the outline of the program).

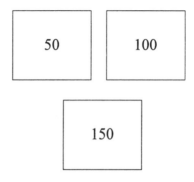

Points: 400

Figure 12.4

12.11.3 Modify the program in 12.11.2 so that a RESET button is displayed. When selected the points value should be reset to zero.

12.11.4 Write a Java applet which displays a square at a starting position (50,50) with a width and length of 50 units. The user should then be able to move the rectangle up, down, left or right using the u key (for up), d key (for down), l key (for left) and r key (for right). The program should continue until the x key is pressed.

12.11.5 Write a Java applet which displays which function key or control key (Cntrl) has been pressed. The program should run continuously until the Cntrl-Z keystroke is pressed.

12.11.6 Write separate Java applets, using simple rectangles and circles, to display the following graphics:

(a) a television (a sample graphic is shown in Figure 12.5)
(b) a face
(c) a house
(d) a robot

Figure 12.5

12.11.7 Locate three GIF or JPEG files. Then write a Java applet which allows the user to choose which one should be displayed. The function key F1 selects the first image, F2 the second and F3 the third. The function key F4 should exit the applet.

12.11.8 Using an applet which displays the text TEST TEXT, determine the approximate colour of the following colour settings:

(a) color(100, 50, 10)
(b) color(200,200,0)
(c) color(10,100,100)
(d) color(200,200,200)
(e) color(10,10,100)

12.11.9 Write an applet using a polygon for the following shapes:

(a) a ship (a sample is shown in Figure 12.6)
(b) a tank
(c) a plane

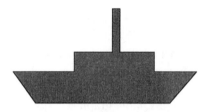

12.11.10 Locate a sound file and write an application which uses it.

12.11.11 Write a Java applet which displays the following:

Sample Applet

Please press the x key to exit

Note that Sample Applet is bold Arial text with a size of 20 and the other text is Courier of size of 14.

12.11.12 Write a Java applet in which the user enters some text. If the user enters EXIT then the program will exit.

13 | Windows NT/95 Networking

13.1 Introduction

Windows NT/95 supports connection to the remote computers over the Internet. Operating systems now use networks to make peer-to-peer connections and also connections to servers for access to file systems and print servers. A peer-to-peer connection is one in which one computer uses the resources of another.

The three most widely used operating systems are MS-DOS, Microsoft Windows and UNIX. Microsoft Windows come in many flavours, the main versions in current use are:

- Microsoft Windows 3.1/3.11 – which is a 16-bit PC-based operating system with limited multi-tasking. It runs from MS-DOS and thus still uses MS-DOS functionality and file system structure. The networking capabilities have been bolted onto the operating system. TCP/IP utilities are available through third party software vendors.
- Microsoft Windows 95 – which is a robust 32-bit multi-tasking operating system with integrated networking. It can run most MS-DOS applications, Microsoft Windows 3.1/3.11 applications and 32-bit applications.
- Microsoft Windows NT – which is a robust 32-bit multi-tasking operating system with integrated networking. Networks are built with NT servers and clients, and, as with Microsoft Windows 95, it can run MS-DOS, Microsoft Windows 3.1/3.11 applications and 32-bit applications.

Microsoft Windows 3.11 for Workgroups was Microsoft's first attempt at a commonly available networked operating system. The operating system has basically Microsoft Windows 3.1 with networking utilities added on top of it. Table 13.1 lists some of their attributes.

Microsoft Windows NT and Windows 95 are completely new operating systems and do not use DOS. They have proved to be an excellent network operating system. Its main advantages are:

- It communicates directly with many different types of networks, protocols and computer architectures.

- It supports TCP/IP for Internet communications.
- It contains standard TCP/IP programs such as TELNET and FTP.
- It contains an integrated Internet browser, Explorer.
- It can operate as a stand-alone or a networked operating system.
- It is relatively simple to set-up and maintain.

Table 13.1 Windows comparisons.

	Windows 3.1	*Windows 95*	*Windows NT*
Pre-emptive multi-tasking		✓	✓
32-bit operating system		✓	✓
Long file names		✓	✓
TCP/IP	✓	✓	✓
32-bit applications		✓	✓
Flat memory model		✓	✓
32-bit disk access	✓	✓	✓
32-bit file access	✓	✓	✓
Centralised configuration storage		✓	✓
OpenGL 3D graphics			✓

13.2 Novell NetWare networking

Novell NetWare is one of the most popular systems for PC LANs and provides file and print server facilities. The protocol used is SPX/IPX, which can also be used by Windows NT to communicate with NetWare networks. The Internet Packet Exchange (IPX) protocol is a network layer protocol for transportation of data between computers on a Novell network. IPX is very fast and has a small connectionless datagram protocol. Sequenced Packet Interchange (SPX) provides a communications protocol which supervises the transmission of the packet and ensures its successful delivery.

13.3 Servers, workstations and clients

Microsoft Windows NT is a 32-bit, pre-emptive, multi-tasking operating system. One of the major advantages it has over UNIX is that it can run PC-based software. A Windows NT network normally consists of a server and a number of clients. The server provides file and print servers as well as powerful networking applications, such as electronic mail applications, access to local and remote peripherals, and so on.

The Windows NT client can either:

- Operate as a stand-alone operating system.
- Connect with a peer-to-peer connection.
- Connect to a Windows NT server.

A peer-to-peer connection is when one computer logs into another computer. Windows NT provides unlimited outbound peer-to-peer connections and typically up to 10 simultaneous inbound connections.

13.4 Workgroups and domains

Windows NT assigns users to workgroups which are a collection of users who are grouped together with a common purpose. This purpose might be to share resources such as file systems or printers and each workgroup has their own unique name. With workgroups each Windows NT workstation interacts with a common group of computers on a peer-to-peer level. Each workstation then manages its own resources and user accounts. Workgroups are useful for small groups where a small number of users require to access resources on other computers

A domain, in Windows NT, is a logical collection of computers sharing a common user accounts database and security policy. Thus each domain must have at least one Windows NT server.

Windows NT is designed to operate with either workgroups or domains. Figure 13.1 illustrates the difference between domains and workgroups.

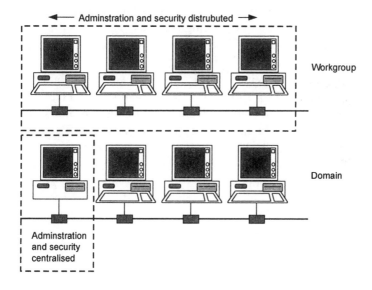

Figure 13.1 Workgroups and domains

Domains have the advantages that:

- Each domain forms a single administrative unit with shared security and user account information. This domain has one database containing user and group information and security policy settings.
- They segment the resources of the network so that users, by default, can view all networks for a particular domain.
- User accounts are automatically validated by the domain controller. This stops invalid users from gaining access to network resources.

13.5 Windows NT/95 networking

Network must use a protocol to transmit data. Typical protocols are:

- IPX/SPX   – used with Novell NetWare which gives access to file and printer services.
- TCP/IP   – used for Internet access and client/server applications.
- SNA DLC   – used mainly by IBM mainframes and minicomputers.
- AppleTalk – used by Macintosh computers.
- NetBEUI   – used in some small LANs (stands for NetBIOS Extended User Interface).

Novell NetWare is installed in many organisations to create local area networks of PCs. It uses IPX/SPX for transmitting data and allows computers to access file servers and network printing services. TCP/IP is the standard protocol used when accessing the Internet and also for client/serve applications (such as remote file transfer and remote login).

A major advantage of Windows NT is that networking is built-into the operating system. Figure 13.3 shows how it is organised in relation to the OSI model. Windows NT has the great advantage in that it is protocol-independent and will work with most standard protocols, such as TCP/IP, IPX/SPX, NetBEUI, DLC and AppleTalk. The default protocol is NetBEUI.

Figure 13.4 shows a sample configuration for Windows NT client for the default network configurations.

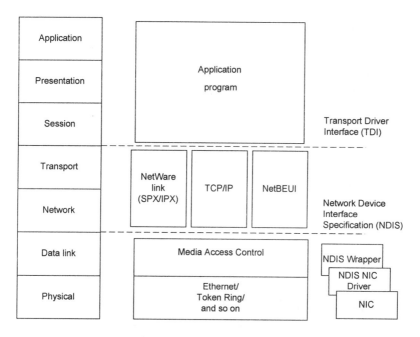

Figure 13.2 Windows NT network interfaces.

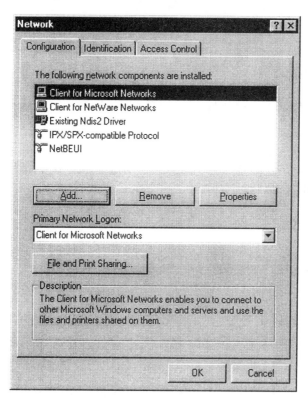

Figure 13.3 Windows NT network interfaces

There are two main boundaries in Windows NT and NDIS and TDI. The Network Device Interface Standard (NDIS) boundary layer interfaces to several network interface adapters (such as Ethernet, Token Ring, RS-232, modems, and so on) with different protocols. It allows for an unlimited number of network interface cards (NICs) and protocols to be connected to be used with the operating system. In Windows NT, a single software module, NDIS.SYS, (the NDIS wrapper) interfaces with the manufacturer-supplied NDIS NIC device driver. The wrapper provides a uniform interface between the protocol drivers (such as TCP/IP or IPX/SPX) and the NDIS device driver. Figure 13.5 shows the set-up of the network adapter.

13.5.1 IPX/SPX

NetWare networks use SPX/IPX and is supported through Windows NT using the NWLlnk protocol stack. This protocol is covered in more detail in the next chapter.

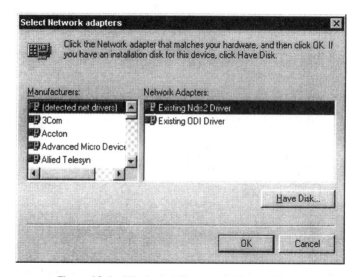

Figure 13.4   Windows NT network adapter drivers

13.5.2 NetBEUI

NetBEUI (NetBIOS extended user interface) has been used with network operating systems, such as Microsoft LAN manager and OS/2 LAN server. In Windows NT, the NetBEUI frame (NBF) protocol stack gives backward compatibility with existing NetBEUI implementation and also provides for enhanced implementation. NetBEUI is the standard technique that NT clients and servers use to intercommunicate.

NBF is similar to TCP/IP and SPX/IPX and is used to establish sessions between a client and a server, and also to provide the reliable transport of the data across the connection-oriented session. Thus NetBEUI tries to provide

224   *Mastering the Internet*

reliable data transfer through error checking and acknowledgement of each successfully received data packet. In the standard form of NetBEUI the packets must be acknowledged after the delivery of each packet. This is wasteful in time. Windows NT uses NBF which improves NetBEUI as it allows several packets to be sent before an acknowledgement is sent (called an adaptive sliding window protocol).

Each NetBEUI is assigned a 1-byte session number and thus allows a maximum of 254 simultaneously-active sessions (as two of the connection numbers are reserved). NBF enhances this by allowing 254 connections to computers with 254 sessions for each connection (thus there is a maximum of 254×254 sessions).

13.5.3 AppleTalk

The AppleTalk protocol allows Windows NT to share a network with Macintosh clients. It can also act as an AppleShare server.

13.5.4 DLC

Data-link control (DLC) is a communications protocol which is used with IBM mainframes. Windows NT interface to a DLC network.

13.6 Setting up TCP/IP networking on Windows NT/95

The default internetworking protocol for Windows NT/95 is NetBEUI. To use any Internet applications (such as FTP, TELNET, WWW browsers, and so) the TCP/IP protocol must be installed. To achieve this the Network icon in the Control Panel is selected, as shown in Figure 13.6. Next the Network Configuration screen is shown.

Windows NT has a DHCP (Dynamic Host Configuration Program) which assigns IP addresses from a pool of addresses. It relieves the system manager from assigning IP addresses to individual workstations and maintaining those addresses. Windows NT also has a name resolution service called WINS (Windows Internet Name Service). This program maps a computer name to an IP address, such as www.napier.ac.uk which is mapped to the IP address 146.176.131.10. This facility is similar to the DNS server which is used on many TCP/IP networks. Note that a Windows NT server can support both WINS and DNS.

Figure 13.5 Windows NT selection of networking configuration

The setting for TCP/IP is set up by selecting Control Panel→Network and then, if it is not already set-up, select Add→Protocol→Microsoft→TCP/IP (as shown in Figure 13.7). After the network adapter is selected (such as NDIS) then select Properties from the TCP/IP option. This then gives the settings for:

- TCP/IP properties – which is used to set the IP address of the host node. In the example in Figure 13.8 the node has an IP address of 146.176.151.130 and the subnet mask is 255.255.255.0.
- DNS configuration – which sets the IP address of the DNS server. In the case in Figure 13.9 there are two DNS servers, these are 146.176.150.62 and 146.176.151.99. The host has a name of pc419 in the domain of eece.napier.ac.uk.
- Gateway – which is used to define the gateway node. In Figure 13.10 the gateway node is defined as 146.176.151.254.
- WINS server – which is used to define a WINS node (which does the function of a DNS server). In Figure 13.11 the WINS node is defined as 146.176.151.50.

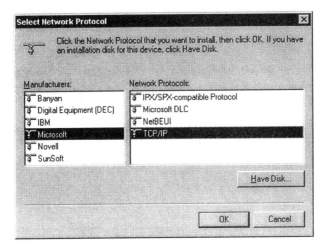

Figure 13.6 Set-up for TCP/IP

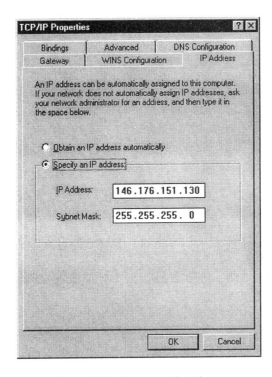

Figure 13.7 Set-up an IP address

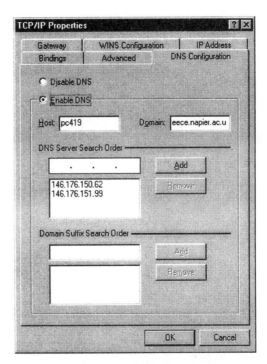

Figure 13.8 Windows NT DNS set-up

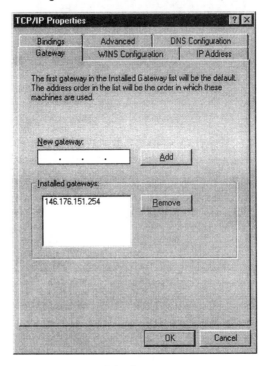

Figure 13.9 Set-up gateway

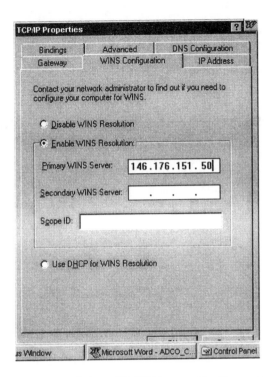

Figure 13.10 Windows NT WINS server IP address set-up

13.7 Windows sockets

Windows sockets (WinSock) are a standard method that allows nodes over a network to communicate with each other using a standard interface. It supports internetworking protocols such as TCP/IP, IPX/SPX, AppleTalk and NetBEUI. WinSock communicates through the TDI interface and uses the WINSOCK.DLL or WINSOCK32.DLL files. These DLLs (dynamic link libraries) contain a number of networking functions which are called in order to communicate with the transport and network layers (such as TCP/IP or SPX/IPX). As it communicates with these layers it is independent of the networking interface (such as Ethernet or FDDI).

13.8 TCP/IP applications

After the TCP/IP protocol has been installed (and all other TCP/IP drivers have been removed) then the system will be ready to run any TCP/IP applications. For example Microsoft NT and 95 are installed with Telnet and ftp. In Windows NT they are run by entering either Telnet or ftp from the Run command, as illustrated in Figure 13.12 and 13.13.

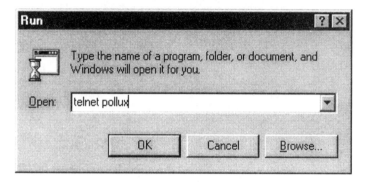

Figure 13.11   Running telnet

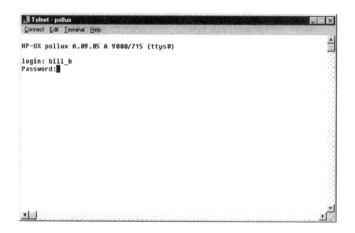

Figure 13.12   Example Telnet program

13.9 Windows NT network drives

Windows NT/95 displays the currently mounted network drives within the My Computer group. Figure 13.22 shows drives which are either local (C:, D: and E:) or mounted using NetWare (F:, G:, and so on). Windows NT/95 also automatically scan the neighing networks to find network servers. An example of this is shown in Figure 13.14 and 13.15. Figure 13.14 shows the current mounted servers (for example, EECE_1) and by selecting the Global Network icon all the other connected Local servers can be shown. Figure 13.15 shows an example network.

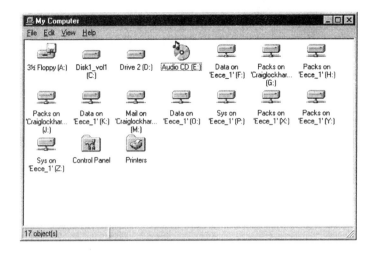

Figure 13.13 Mounted network and local drives

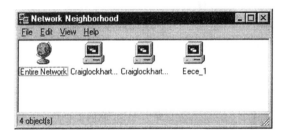

Figure 13.14 Network neighbourhood

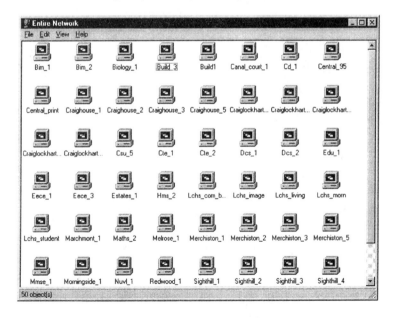

Figure 13.15 Local neighbourhood servers

13.10 Point-to-point protocol (PPP)

PPP is a set of industry standard protocols which allow a remote computer to connect to a remote network using a dial-up connection. Windows NT/95 can connect to a remote network using this protocol and the Dial-Up Networking facility. It is typically used to connect to an Internet provider or to an Organisational network.

To set it up in Windows NT/95 the user first selects the **Dial-Up Network** program from within **My Computer,** as shown in Figure 13.16.

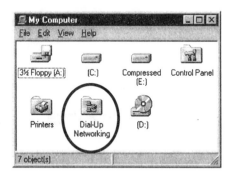

Figure 13.16 Local neighbourhood servers

Next the user selects the name of the connection, as shown in Figure 13.17.

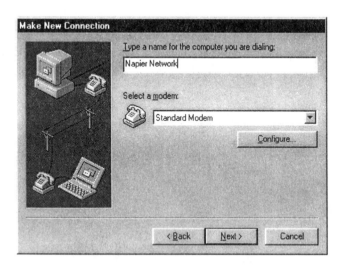

Figure 13.17 Local neighbourhood servers

After this the user enters the telephone number of the remote modem with the local code and country code. Figure 13.18 shows an example set-up (note that the telephone number has been set at 0131-xxx xxxx).

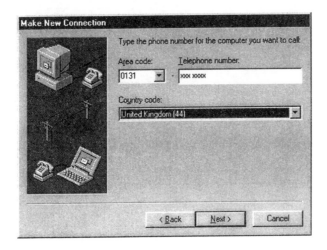

Figure 13.18 Connection settings

After the Next option is selected a connection icon is made, as shown in Figure 13.19.

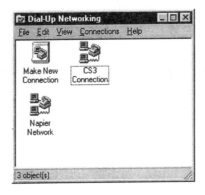

Figure 13.19 Connection settings

Next the server type is set by selecting File→Properties option to give the window shown in Figure 13.20. From this window the Server Type option is selected. This will then show the window shown in Figure 13.21. The type of server should be set to:

```
PPP; Windows 95; Windows NT
```

and the protocol to:

```
TCP/IP
```

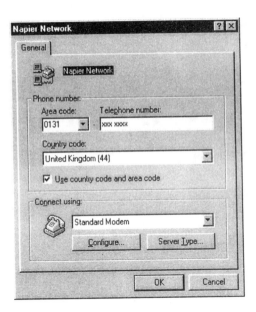

Figure 13.20 Connection settings

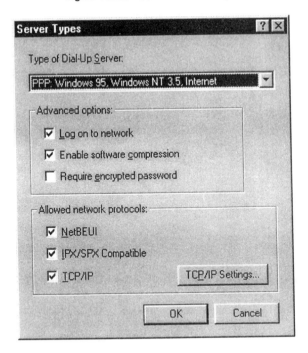

Figure 13.21 Server types

After these have been set then the user can log into the remote network, as shown in Figure 13.22 and 13.23.

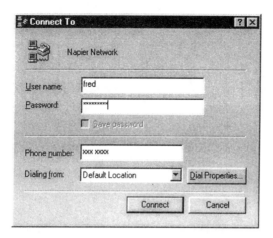

Figure 13.22   Local neighbourhood servers

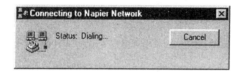

Figure 13.23   Local neighbourhood servers

13.11 Exercises

13.11.1 Which of the following describes Windows NT/95:

    (a)   An 8-bit operating system
    (b)   A 16-bit operating system
    (c)   A 32-bit operating system
    (d)   A 64-bit operating system

13.11.2 By default, which type of protocol does Novell NetWare use:

    (a)   TCP/IP
    (b)   IPX/SPX
    (c)   NetBEUI
    (d)   AppleTalk

13.11.3 By default, which type of protocol does Windows 95/NT use:

    (a)   TCP/IP

> (b) IPX/SPX
> (c) NetBEUI
> (d) AppleTalk

13.11.4 Which standard protocol is used for remote network connections using a modem:

> (a) NFS
> (b) TCP/IP
> (c) NetBEUI
> (d) PPP

13.11.5 Which program is used to dynamically allocate IP addresses:

> (a) DIP
> (b) WINS
> (c) PPP
> (d) DHCP

13.11.6 Which program is used to provide name resolution:

> (a) DIP
> (b) WINS
> (c) PPP
> (d) DHCP

13.12 Tutorial

13.12.1 Explain how TCP/IP communications is set-up on a Windows NT/95 computer.

13.12.2 Explain how PPP communications is set-up on a Windows NT/95 computer.

ASCII Coding

A.1 ASCII character set

ANSI defined a standard alphabet known as ASCII. This has since been adopted by the CCITT as a standard, known as IA5 (International Alphabet No. 5). The following tables define this alphabet in binary, as a decimal, as a hexadecimal value and as a character.

Binary	Decimal	Hex	Character	Binary	Decimal	Hex	Character
00000000	0	00	NUL	00010000	16	10	DLE
00000001	1	01	SOH	00010001	17	11	DC1
00000010	2	02	STX	00010010	18	12	DC2
00000011	3	03	ETX	00010011	19	13	DC3
00000100	4	04	EOT	00010100	20	14	DC4
00000101	5	05	ENQ	00010101	21	15	NAK
00000110	6	06	ACK	00010110	22	16	SYN
00000111	7	07	BEL	00010111	23	17	ETB
00001000	8	08	BS	00011000	24	18	CAN
00001001	9	09	HT	00011001	25	19	EM
00001010	10	0A	LF	00011010	26	1A	SUB
00001011	11	0B	VT	00011011	27	1B	ESC
00001100	12	0C	FF	00011100	28	1C	FS
00001101	13	0D	CR	00011101	29	1D	GS
00001110	14	0E	SO	00011110	30	1E	RS
00001111	15	0F	SI	00011111	31	1F	US

Binary	Decimal	Hex	Character	Binary	Decimal	Hex	Character
00100000	32	20	SPACE	00110000	48	30	0
00100001	33	21	!	00110001	49	31	1
00100010	34	22	"	00110010	50	32	2
00100011	35	23	#	00110011	51	33	3
00100100	36	24	$	00110100	52	34	4
00100101	37	25	%	00110101	53	35	5
00100110	38	26	&	00110110	54	36	6
00100111	39	27	/	00110111	55	37	7
00101000	40	28	(	00111000	56	38	8
00101001	41	29	)	00111001	57	39	9
00101010	42	2A	*	00111010	58	3A	:
00101011	43	2B	+	00111011	59	3B	;
00101100	44	2C	,	00111100	60	3C	<
00101101	45	2D	–	00111101	61	3D	=
00101110	46	2E	.	00111110	62	3E	>
00101111	47	2F	/	00111111	63	3F	?

Binary	Decimal	Hex	Character	Binary	Decimal	Hex	Character
01000000	64	40	@	01010000	80	50	P
01000001	65	41	A	01010001	81	51	Q
01000010	66	42	B	01010010	82	52	R
01000011	67	43	C	01010011	83	53	S
01000100	68	44	D	01010100	84	54	T
01000101	69	45	E	01010101	85	55	U
01000110	70	46	F	01010110	86	56	V
01000111	71	47	G	01010111	87	57	W
01001000	72	48	H	01011000	88	58	X
01001001	73	49	I	01011001	89	59	Y
01001010	74	4A	J	01011010	90	5A	Z
01001011	75	4B	K	01011011	91	5B	[
01001100	76	4C	L	01011100	92	5C	\
01001101	77	4D	M	01011101	93	5D	]
01001110	78	4E	N	01011110	94	5E	'
01001111	79	4F	O	01011111	95	5F	_

Binary	Decimal	Hex	Character	Binary	Decimal	Hex	Character
01100000	96	60		01110000	112	70	p
01100001	97	61	a	01110001	113	71	q
01100010	98	62	b	01110010	114	72	r
01100011	99	63	c	01110011	115	73	s
01100100	100	64	d	01110100	116	74	t
01100101	101	65	e	01110101	117	75	u
01100110	102	66	f	01110110	118	76	v
01100111	103	67	g	01110111	119	77	w
01101000	104	68	h	01111000	120	78	x
01101001	105	69	i	01111001	121	79	y
01101010	106	6A	j	01111010	122	7A	z
01101011	107	6B	k	01111011	123	7B	{
01101100	108	6C	l	01111100	124	7C	:
01101101	109	6D	m	01111101	125	7D	}
01101110	110	6E	n	01111110	126	7E	~
01101111	111	6F	o	01111111	127	7F	DEL

The standard ASCII character set is a 7-bit character and ranges from 0 to 127. This code is rather limited as it does not contain symbols such as Greek letters, lines, and so on. For this purpose the extended ASCII code has been defined. This fits into character number 128 to 255. The following 4 tables define a typical extended ASCII character set.

Binary	Decimal	Hex	Character	Binary	Decimal	Hex	Character
10000000	128	80	Ç	10010000	144	90	É
10000001	129	81	ü	10010001	145	91	æ
10000010	130	82	é	10010010	146	92	Æ
10000011	131	83	â	10010011	147	93	ô
10000100	132	84	ä	10010100	148	94	ö
10000101	133	85	à	10010101	149	95	ò
10000110	134	86	å	10010110	150	96	û
10000111	135	87	ç	10010111	151	97	ù
10001000	136	88	ê	10011000	152	98	ÿ
10001001	137	89	ë	10011001	153	99	Ö
10001010	138	8A	è	10011010	154	9A	Ü
10001011	139	8B	ï	10011011	155	9B	¢
10001100	140	8C	î	10011100	156	9C	£
10001101	141	8D	ì	10011101	157	9D	¥
10001110	142	8E	Ä	10011110	158	9E	₧
10001111	143	8F	Å	10011111	159	9F	ƒ

Binary	Decimal	Hex	Character	Binary	Decimal	Hex	Character
10100000	160	A0	á	10110000	176	B0	░
10100001	161	A1	í	10110001	177	B1	▓
10100010	162	A2	ó	10110010	178	B2	█
10100011	163	A3	ú	10110011	179	B3	│
10100100	164	A4	ñ	10110100	180	B4	┤
10100101	165	A5	Ñ	10110101	181	B5	╡
10100110	166	A6	ª	10110110	182	B6	╢
10100111	167	A7	º	10110111	183	B7	╖
10101000	168	A8	¿	10111000	184	B8	╕
10101001	169	A9	⌐	10111001	185	B9	╣
10101010	170	AA	¬	10111010	186	BA	║
10101011	171	AB	½	10111011	187	BB	╗
10101100	172	AC	¼	10111100	188	BC	╝
10101101	173	AD	¡	10111101	189	BD	╜
10101110	174	AE	«	10111110	190	BE	╛
10101111	175	AF	»	10111111	191	BF	┐

Binary	Decimal	Hex	Character	Binary	Decimal	Hex	Character
11000000	192	C0	└	11010000	208	D0	╨
11000001	193	C1	⊥	11010001	209	D1	╤
11000010	194	C2	┬	11010010	210	D2	╥
11000011	195	C3	├	11010011	211	D3	╙
11000100	196	C4	─	11010100	212	D4	└
11000101	197	C5	┼	11010101	213	D5	╒
11000110	198	C6	╞	11010110	214	D6	╓
11000111	199	C7	╟	11010111	215	D7	╫
11001000	200	C8	╚	11011000	216	D8	╪
11001001	201	C9	╔	11011001	217	D9	┘
11001010	202	CA	╩	11011010	218	DA	┌
11001011	203	CB	╦	11011011	219	DB	█
11001100	204	CC	╠	11011100	220	DC	▄
11001101	205	CD	═	11011101	221	DD	▌
11001110	206	CE	╬	11011110	222	DE	▐
11001111	207	CF	╧	11011111	223	DF	▀

Binary	Decimal	Hex	Character	Binary	Decimal	Hex	Character
11100000	224	E0	α	11110000	240	F0	Ξ
11100001	225	E1	ß	11110001	241	F1	±
11100010	226	E2	Γ	11110010	242	F2	≥
11100011	227	E3	π	11110011	243	F3	≤
11100100	228	E4	Σ	11110100	244	F4	⌠
11100101	229	E5	σ	11110101	245	F5	⌡
11100110	230	E6	µ	11110110	246	F6	÷
11100111	231	E7	τ	11110111	247	F7	≈
11101000	232	E8	Φ	11111000	248	F8	°
11101001	233	E9	Θ	11111001	249	F9	•
11101010	234	EA	Ω	11111010	250	FA	·
11101011	235	EB	δ	11111011	251	FB	√
11101100	236	EC	φ	11111100	252	FC	ⁿ
11101101	237	ED	φ	11111101	253	FD	²
11101110	238	EE	E	11111110	254	FE	■
11101111	239	EF	Λ	11111111	255	FF	□

B | IAB Recommendations

The IAB (Internet Advisor Board) have published many documents on the TCP/IP protocol family. These are known as RFC (Request for Comment) and can be obtained using FTP from the Internet Network Information Center (NIC) at `nic.ddn.mil`, or one of the several other FTP sites. The main RFC documents are:

RFC768	User Datagram Protocol
RFC775	Directory-Oriented FTP Commands
RFC781	Specification of the Internet Protocol Timestamp Option
RFC783	TFTP Protocol
RFC786	User Datagram Protocol(UDP)
RFC791	Internet Protocol(IP)
RFC792	Internet Control Message Protocol(ICMP)
RFC793	Transmission Control Protocol(TCP)
RFC799	Internet Name Domains
RFC813	Window and Acknowledgment in TCP
RFC815	IP Datagram Reassembly Algorithms
RFC821	Simple Mail-Transfer Protocol(SMTP)
RFC821	Simple Main Transfer Protocol
RFC822	Standard for the Format of ARPA Internet Text Messages
RFC822	Standard for the Format of ARPA Internet Text Messages
RFC823	DARPA Internet Gateway
RFC827	Exterior Gateway Protocol (EGP)
RFC877	Standard for the Transmission of IP Datagrams over Public Data Networks
RFC879	TCP Maximum Segment Size and Related Topics
RFC886	Proposed Standard for Message Headers
RFC893	Trailer Encapsulations
RFC894	Standard for the Transmission of IP Datagrams over Ethernet Networks
RFC895	Standard for the Transmission of IP Datagrams over Experimental Ethernet Networks
RFC896	Congestion Control in TCP/IP Internetworks
RFC903	Reverse Address Resolution Protocol
RFC904	Exterior Gateway Protocol Formal Specifications
RFC906	Bootstrap Loading Using TFTP
RFC919	Broadcast Internet Datagram
RFC920	Domain Requirements
RFC932	Subnetwork Addressing Schema
RFC949	FTP Unique-Named Store Command
RFC950	Internet Standard Subnetting Procedure
RFC951	Bootstrap Protocol
RFC959	File Transfer Protocol
RFC974	Mail Routing and the Domain System
RFC974	Mail Routing and the Domain System

RFC980	Protocol Document Order Information
RFC1009	Requirements for Internet Gateways
RFC1011	Official Internet Protocol
RFC1013	X Windows System Protocol
RFC1014	XDR: External Data Representation Standard
RFC1027	Using ARP to Implement Transparent Subnet Gateways
RFC1032	Domain Administrators Guide
RFC1033	Domain Administrators Operation Guide
RFC1034	Domain Names - Concepts and Facilities
RFC1035	Domain Names - Implementation and Specifications
RFC1041	Telnet 3270 Regime Option
RFC1042	Standard for the Transmission of IP Datagrams over IEEE 802 Networks
RFC1043	Telnet Data Entry Terminal Option
RFC1044	Internet Protocol on Network System's HYPERchannel
RFC1053	Telnet X.3 PAD Option
RFC1055	Nonstandard for Transmission of IP Datagrams over Serial Lines
RFC1056	PCMAIL: A Distributed Mail System for Personal Computers
RFC1058	Routing Information Protocol
RFC1068	Background File Transfer Program (BFTP)
RFC1072	TCP Extensions of Long-Delay Paths
RFC1073	Telnet Window Size Option
RFC1074	NSFNET Backbone SPF-based Interior Gateway Protocol
RFC1079	Telnet Terminal Speed Option
RFC1080	Telnet Remote Flow Control Option
RFC1084	BOOTP Vendor Information Extensions
RFC1088	Standard for the Transmission of IP Datagrams over NetBIOS Network
RFC1089	SNMP over Ethernet
RFC1091	Telnet Terminal-Type Option
RFC1094	NFS: Network File System Protocol Specification
RFC1101	DNS Encoding of Network Names and Other Types
RFC1102	Policy Routing in Internet Protocols
RFC1104	Models of Policy-Based Routing
RFC1112	Host Extension for IP Multicasting
RFC1122	Requirement for Internet Hosts - Communication Layers
RFC1123	Requirement for Internet Hosts - Application and Support
RFC1124	Policy Issues in Interconnecting Networks
RFC1125	Policy Requirements for Inter-Administrative Domain Routing
RFC1127	Perspective on the Host Requirements RFC
RFC1129	Internet Time Protocol
RFC1143	Q Method of Implementing Telnet Option Negotiation
RFC1147	FYI on a Network Management Tool Catalog
RFC1149	Standard for the Transmission of IP Datagrams over Avian Carriers
RFC1155	Structure and Identification of Management Information for TCP/IP-Based Internets
RFC1156	Management Information Base for Network Management of TCP/IP-Based Internets
RFC1157	Simple Network Management Protocol (SNMP)
RFC1163	Border Gateway Protocol (BGP)
RFC1164	Application of the Border Gateway Protocol in the Internet
RFC1166	Internet numbers
RFC1171	Point-to-Point Protocol for the Transmission of Multi-Protocol Datagrams
RFC1172	Point-to-Point Protocol Initial Configuration Options
RFC1173	Responsibilities of Host and Network Managers

RFC1175	FYI on Where to Start: A Bibliography of Internetworking Information
RFC1178	Choosing a Name For Your Computer
RFC1179	Line Printer Daemon Protocol
RFC1184	Telnet Linemode Option
RFC1187	Bulk Table Retrieval with the SNMP
RFC1188	Proposed Standard for the Transmission of TP Datagrams over FDDI Networks
RFC1195	Use of OSI IS-IS for Routing in TCP/IP and Dual Environments
RFC1196	Finger User Information Protocol
RFC1198	FYI on the X Windows System
RFC1201	Transmitting IP Traffic over ARCNET Networks
RFC1205	520 Telnet Interface
RFC1208	Glossary of Networking Terms
RFC1209	Transmission of IP Datagrams over the SMDS Service
RFC1212	Concise MIB Definitions
RFC1213	MIB for Network Management of TCP/IP-Based Internets
RFC1214	OSI Internet Management: Management Information Base
RFC1215	Convention for Defining Traps for Use with the SNMP
RFC1219	On the Assignment of Subnet Numbers
RFC1220	Point-to-Point Protocol Extensions for Bridges
RFC1224	Techniques for Managing Asynchronous Generated Alerts
RFC1227	SNMP MUX Protocol and MIB
RFC1228	SNMP-DPI: Simple Network Management Protocol Distributed Program Interface
RFC1229	Extensions to the Generic-interface MIB
RFC1230	IEEE 802.4 Token Bus MIB
RFC1231	IEEE 802.5 Token Ring MIB
RFC1232	Definitions of Managed Objects for the DS1 Interface Type
RFC1233	Definitions of Managed Objects for the DS3 Interface Type
RFC1236	IP to X.121 Address Mapping for DDN IP
RFC1238	CLNS MIB for Use with Connectionless Network Protocol
RFC1239	Reassignment of Experiment MIBs to Standard MIBs
RFC1243	Appletalk Management Information Base
RFC1245	OSPF Protocol Analysis
RFC1246	Experience with the OSPF Protocol
RFC1247	OSPF Version 2
RFC1253	OSPE Version 2: Management Information Base
RFC1254	Gateway Congestion Control Survey
RFC1267	A Border Gateway Protocol (BGP-3)
RFC1271	Remote Network Monitoring Management Information Base
RFC1321	The MD5 Message-Digest Algorithm
RFC1340	Assigned numbers
RFC1341	MIME Mechanism for Specifying and Describing the Format of Internet Message Bodies
RFC1360	IAB Official Protocol Standards
RFC1522	MIME (Multipurpose Internet Mail Extensions) Part Two : Message Header Extensions for Non-ASCII Text
RFC1521	MIME (Multipurpose Internet Mail Extensions) Part One : Mechanisms for Specifying and Describing the Format of Internet Mail Message Bodies)
RFC1583	OSPF Version 2
RFC1630	Universal Resource Identifiers in WWW
RFC1738	Uniform Resource Identifiers (URL)
RFC1752	The Recommendation for the IP Next-Generation Protocol
RFC1771	A Border Gateway Protocol 4 (BGP-4)
RFC1808	Relative Uniform Resource Identifiers

RFC1809	Using the Flow Label in IPv6
RFC1825	Security Architecture for the Internet Protocol
RFC1826	IP Authentication Header
RFC1827	IP Encapsulating Security Payload(ESP)
RFC1828	IP Authentication Using Keyed MD5
RFC1829	The ESP DES-CBC Transform
RFC1883	Internet Protocol, Version 6 Specification
RFC1884	IP Version 6 Addressing Architecture
RFC1885	Internet Control Message Protocol (ICMPv6) for the Internet Protocol Version-6 (IPv6) Specification
RFC1886	DNS Extensions to Support IP Version 6
RFC1887	An Architecture for IPv6 Unicast Address Allocation
RFC1901	Introduction to Community-Based SNMPv2
RFC1902	Structure of Management Information for SNMPv2
RFC1903	Textual Conventions for SNMPv2
RFC1904	Conformance Statements for SNMPv2
RFC1905	Protocol Operations for SNMPv2
RFC1906	Transport Mappings for SNMPv2
RFC1907	Management Information base for SNMPv2
RFC1908	Coexistence Between Version 1 and Version 2 of the Internet-Standard Network Management Framework

C | Java Classes

java/
java/lang/
java/lang/Object.class
java/lang/Exception.class
java/lang/Integer.class
java/lang/NumberFormatException.class
java/lang/Throwable.class
java/lang/Class.class
java/lang/IllegalAccessException.class
java/lang/StringBuffer.class
java/lang/ClassNotFoundException.class
java/lang/IllegalArgumentException.class
java/lang/Number.class
java/lang/InterruptedException.class
java/lang/String.class
java/lang/RuntimeException.class
java/lang/InternalError.class
java/lang/Long.class
java/lang/Character.class
java/lang/CloneNotSupportedException.class
java/lang/InstantiationException.class
java/lang/VirtualMachineError.class
java/lang/Double.class
java/lang/Error.class
java/lang/NullPointerException.class
java/lang/Cloneable.class
java/lang/System.class
java/lang/ClassLoader.class
java/lang/Math.class
java/lang/Float.class
java/lang/Runtime.class
java/lang/StringIndexOutOfBoundsException.class
java/lang/IndexOutOfBoundsException.class
java/lang/SecurityException.class
java/lang/LinkageError.class
java/lang/Runnable.class
java/lang/Process.class
java/lang/SecurityManager.class
java/lang/Thread.class
java/lang/UnsatisfiedLinkError.class
java/lang/IncompatibleClassChangeError.class
java/lang/NoSuchMethodError.class
java/lang/IllegalThreadStateException.class
java/lang/ThreadGroup.class
java/lang/ThreadDeath.class
java/lang/ArrayIndexOutOfBoundsException.class
java/lang/Boolean.class
java/lang/Compiler.class
java/lang/NoSuchMethodException.class
java/lang/ArithmeticException.class

java/lang/ArrayStoreException.class
java/lang/ClassCastException.class
java/lang/NegativeArraySizeException.class
java/lang/IllegalMonitorStateException.class
java/lang/ClassCircularityError.class
java/lang/ClassFormatError.class
java/lang/AbstractMethodError.class
java/lang/IllegalAccessError.class
java/lang/InstantiationError.class
java/lang/NoSuchFieldError.class
java/lang/NoClassDefFoundError.class
java/lang/VerifyError.class
java/lang/OutOfMemoryError.class
java/lang/StackOverflowError.class
java/lang/UnknownError.class
java/lang/Win32Process.class
java/io/
java/io/FilterOutputStream.class
java/io/OutputStream.class
java/io/IOException.class
java/io/PrintStream.class
java/io/FileInputStream.class
java/io/InterruptedIOException.class
java/io/File.class
java/io/InputStream.class
java/io/BufferedInputStream.class
java/io/FileOutputStream.class
java/io/FileNotFoundException.class
java/io/BufferedOutputStream.class
java/io/FileDescriptor.class
java/io/FilenameFilter.class
java/io/FilterInputStream.class
java/io/PipedInputStream.class
java/io/PipedOutputStream.class
java/io/EOFException.class
java/io/UTFDataFormatException.class
java/io/DataInput.class
java/io/DataOutput.class
java/io/DataInputStream.class
java/io/PushbackInputStream.class
java/io/ByteArrayInputStream.class
java/io/SequenceInputStream.class
java/io/StringBufferInputStream.class
java/io/LineNumberInputStream.class
java/io/DataOutputStream.class
java/io/ByteArrayOutputStream.class
java/io/RandomAccessFile.class
java/io/StreamTokenizer.class
java/util/
java/util/Hashtable.class

java/util/Enumeration.class
java/util/HashtableEnumerator.class
java/util/Properties.class
java/util/HashtableEntry.class
java/util/Dictionary.class
java/util/Date.class
java/util/NoSuchElementException.class
java/util/StringTokenizer.class
java/util/Random.class
java/util/VectorEnumerator.class
java/util/Vector.class
java/util/BitSet.class
java/util/EmptyStackException.class
java/util/Observable.class
java/util/Observer.class
java/util/ObserverList.class
java/util/Stack.class
java/awt/
java/awt/Toolkit.class
java/awt/peer/
java/awt/peer/WindowPeer.class
java/awt/peer/TextFieldPeer.class
java/awt/peer/ContainerPeer.class
java/awt/peer/PanelPeer.class
java/awt/peer/CanvasPeer.class
java/awt/peer/FramePeer.class
java/awt/peer/ChoicePeer.class
java/awt/peer/CheckboxMenuItemPeer.class
java/awt/peer/TextAreaPeer.class
java/awt/peer/FileDialogPeer.class
java/awt/peer/TextComponentPeer.class
java/awt/peer/ScrollbarPeer.class
java/awt/peer/ButtonPeer.class
java/awt/peer/ComponentPeer.class
java/awt/peer/MenuComponentPeer.class
java/awt/peer/MenuItemPeer.class
java/awt/peer/CheckboxPeer.class
java/awt/peer/MenuPeer.class
java/awt/peer/ListPeer.class
java/awt/peer/MenuBarPeer.class
java/awt/peer/LabelPeer.class
java/awt/peer/DialogPeer.class
java/awt/Image.class
java/awt/MenuItem.class
java/awt/MenuComponent.class
java/awt/image/
java/awt/image/ImageProducer.class
java/awt/image/ColorModel.class
java/awt/image/DirectColorModel.class
java/awt/image/ImageConsumer.class
java/awt/image/ImageObserver.class
java/awt/image/CropImageFilter.class
java/awt/image/ImageFilter.class
java/awt/image/FilteredImageSource.class
java/awt/image/IndexColorModel.class
java/awt/image/MemoryImageSource.class
java/awt/image/PixelGrabber.class
java/awt/image/RGBImageFilter.class
java/awt/FontMetrics.class

java/awt/Checkbox.class
java/awt/CheckboxGroup.class
java/awt/MenuContainer.class
java/awt/Menu.class
java/awt/Insets.class
java/awt/MenuBar.class
java/awt/List.class
java/awt/Label.class
java/awt/Component.class
java/awt/TextField.class
java/awt/TextComponent.class
java/awt/Dialog.class
java/awt/Font.class
java/awt/Window.class
java/awt/FocusManager.class
java/awt/Panel.class
java/awt/Container.class
java/awt/Graphics.class
java/awt/CheckboxMenuItem.class
java/awt/Canvas.class
java/awt/Frame.class
java/awt/Choice.class
java/awt/Event.class
java/awt/TextArea.class
java/awt/AWTError.class
java/awt/Polygon.class
java/awt/FlowLayout.class
java/awt/Point.class
java/awt/FileDialog.class
java/awt/Scrollbar.class
java/awt/Dimension.class
java/awt/Color.class
java/awt/Button.class
java/awt/LayoutManager.class
java/awt/Rectangle.class
java/awt/BorderLayout.class
java/awt/GridLayout.class
java/awt/GridBagConstraints.class
java/awt/GridBagLayout.class
java/awt/GridBagLayoutInfo.class
java/awt/CardLayout.class
java/awt/MediaTracker.class
java/awt/MediaEntry.class
java/awt/ImageMediaEntry.class
java/awt/AWTException.class
java/net/
java/net/URL.class
java/net/URLStreamHandlerFactory.class
java/net/InetAddress.class
java/net/UnknownContentHandler.class
java/net/UnknownHostException.class
java/net/URLStreamHandler.class
java/net/URLConnection.class
java/net/MalformedURLException.class
java/net/ContentHandlerFactory.class
java/net/ContentHandler.class
java/net/UnknownServiceException.class
java/net/ServerSocket.class
java/net/PlainSocketImpl.class

java/net/SocketImpl.class
java/net/ProtocolException.class
java/net/SocketException.class
java/net/SocketInputStream.class
java/net/Socket.class
java/net/SocketImplFactory.class
java/net/SocketOutputStream.class
java/net/DatagramPacket.class
java/net/DatagramSocket.class
java/net/URLEncoder.class
java/applet/
java/applet/Applet.class
java/applet/AppletContext.class
java/applet/AudioClip.class
java/applet/AppletStub.class
sun/
sun/tools/
sun/tools/debug/
sun/tools/debug/BreakpointQueue.class
sun/tools/debug/DebuggerCallback.class
sun/tools/debug/RemoteThread.class
sun/tools/debug/StackFrame.class
sun/tools/debug/RemoteAgent.class
sun/tools/debug/AgentConstants.class
sun/tools/debug/AgentIn.class
sun/tools/debug/RemoteObject.class
sun/tools/debug/RemoteStackVariable.class
sun/tools/debug/RemoteValue.class
sun/tools/debug/RemoteClass.class
sun/tools/debug/Agent.class
sun/tools/debug/RemoteBoolean.class
sun/tools/debug/RemoteChar.class
sun/tools/debug/RemoteString.class
sun/tools/debug/NoSessionException.class
sun/tools/debug/Field.class
sun/tools/debug/NoSuchLineNumberException.class
sun/tools/debug/RemoteShort.class
sun/tools/debug/RemoteThreadGroup.class
sun/tools/debug/RemoteInt.class
sun/tools/debug/ResponseStream.class
sun/tools/debug/RemoteDouble.class
sun/tools/debug/LocalVariable.class
sun/tools/debug/BreakpointSet.class
sun/tools/debug/RemoteStackFrame.class
sun/tools/debug/MainThread.class
sun/tools/debug/BreakpointHandler.class
sun/tools/debug/AgentOutputStream.class
sun/tools/debug/RemoteLong.class
sun/tools/debug/RemoteFloat.class
sun/tools/debug/RemoteArray.class
sun/tools/debug/InvalidPCException.class
sun/tools/debug/LineNumber.class
sun/tools/debug/RemoteField.class
sun/tools/debug/NoSuchFieldException.class
sun/tools/debug/RemoteByte.class
sun/tools/debug/EmptyApp.class
sun/tools/debug/RemoteDebugger.class
sun/tools/java/
sun/tools/java/RuntimeConstants.class

sun/tools/java/Constants.class
sun/tools/java/Environment.class
sun/tools/java/ClassPath.class
sun/tools/java/ClassDeclaration.class
sun/tools/java/FieldDefinition.class
sun/tools/java/Type.class
sun/tools/java/ClassNotFound.class
sun/tools/java/ClassType.class
sun/tools/java/ClassDefinition.class
sun/tools/java/Parser.class
sun/tools/java/ClassPathEntry.class
sun/tools/java/CompilerError.class
sun/tools/java/Identifier.class
sun/tools/java/Package.class
sun/tools/java/ClassFile.class
sun/tools/java/Imports.class
sun/tools/java/ArrayType.class
sun/tools/java/AmbiguousField.class
sun/tools/java/MethodType.class
sun/tools/java/Scanner.class
sun/tools/java/SyntaxError.class
sun/tools/java/BinaryClass.class
sun/tools/java/BinaryField.class
sun/tools/java/AmbiguousClass.class
sun/tools/java/BinaryConstantPool.class
sun/tools/java/ScannerInputStream.class
sun/tools/java/BinaryAttribute.class
sun/tools/java/BinaryCode.class
sun/tools/java/BinaryExceptionHandler.class
sun/tools/javac/
sun/tools/javac/Main.class
sun/tools/javac/SourceClass.class
sun/tools/javac/CompilerField.class
sun/tools/javac/SourceField.class
sun/tools/javac/BatchEnvironment.class
sun/tools/javac/ErrorConsumer.class
sun/tools/javac/ErrorMessage.class
sun/tools/javac/BatchParser.class
sun/tools/zip/
sun/tools/zip/ZipFile.class
sun/tools/zip/ZipEntry.class
sun/tools/zip/ZipFileInputStream.class
sun/tools/zip/ZipConstants.class
sun/tools/zip/ZipFormatException.class
sun/tools/zip/ZipReaderInputStream.class
sun/tools/zip/ZipReader.class
sun/tools/tree/
sun/tools/tree/ConstantExpression.class
sun/tools/tree/LocalField.class
sun/tools/tree/Expression.class
sun/tools/tree/IncDecExpression.class
sun/tools/tree/SuperExpression.class
sun/tools/tree/NaryExpression.class
sun/tools/tree/StringExpression.class
sun/tools/tree/UnaryExpression.class
sun/tools/tree/Context.class
sun/tools/tree/ExpressionStatement.class
sun/tools/tree/ConditionVars.class
sun/tools/tree/Node.class

sun/tools/tree/CharExpression.class
sun/tools/tree/CaseStatement.class
sun/tools/tree/LessExpression.class
sun/tools/tree/IntegerExpression.class
sun/tools/tree/SubtractExpression.class
sun/tools/tree/ArrayAccessExpression.class
sun/tools/tree/TryStatement.class
sun/tools/tree/BinaryEqualityExpression.class
sun/tools/tree/Statement.class
sun/tools/tree/AssignSubtractExpression.class
sun/tools/tree/FinallyStatement.class
sun/tools/tree/ForStatement.class
sun/tools/tree/DivRemExpression.class
sun/tools/tree/BinaryExpression.class
sun/tools/tree/ShiftRightExpression.class
sun/tools/tree/AssignMultiplyExpression.class
sun/tools/tree/BooleanExpression.class
sun/tools/tree/BinaryArithmeticExpression.class
sun/tools/tree/ThrowStatement.class
sun/tools/tree/AssignDivideExpression.class
sun/tools/tree/AssignShiftLeftExpression.class
sun/tools/tree/NewArrayExpression.class
sun/tools/tree/AndExpression.class
sun/tools/tree/AssignBitOrExpression.class
sun/tools/tree/BreakStatement.class
sun/tools/tree/SynchronizedStatement.class
sun/tools/tree/PreDecExpression.class
sun/tools/tree/CompoundStatement.class
sun/tools/tree/DoubleExpression.class
sun/tools/tree/ConvertExpression.class
sun/tools/tree/NullExpression.class
sun/tools/tree/LessOrEqualExpression.class
sun/tools/tree/IdentifierExpression.class
sun/tools/tree/ReturnStatement.class
sun/tools/tree/BitNotExpression.class
sun/tools/tree/LongExpression.class
sun/tools/tree/VarDeclarationStatement.class
sun/tools/tree/MethodExpression.class
sun/tools/tree/ThisExpression.class
sun/tools/tree/BitOrExpression.class
sun/tools/tree/PositiveExpression.class
sun/tools/tree/IfStatement.class
sun/tools/tree/FloatExpression.class
sun/tools/tree/NotEqualExpression.class
sun/tools/tree/InstanceOfExpression.class
sun/tools/tree/NotExpression.class
sun/tools/tree/BitAndExpression.class
sun/tools/tree/DivideExpression.class
sun/tools/tree/ShortExpression.class
sun/tools/tree/RemainderExpression.class
sun/tools/tree/NewInstanceExpression.class
sun/tools/tree/SwitchStatement.class
sun/tools/tree/AddExpression.class
sun/tools/tree/AssignOpExpression.class
sun/tools/tree/EqualExpression.class
sun/tools/tree/PostIncExpression.class
sun/tools/tree/GreaterExpression.class
sun/tools/tree/PostDecExpression.class
sun/tools/tree/AssignExpression.class

sun/tools/tree/WhileStatement.class
sun/tools/tree/ContinueStatement.class
sun/tools/tree/ConditionalExpression.class
sun/tools/tree/AssignAddExpression.class
sun/tools/tree/BinaryBitExpression.class
sun/tools/tree/CastExpression.class
sun/tools/tree/AssignBitXorExpression.class
sun/tools/tree/ArrayExpression.class
sun/tools/tree/InlineMethodExpression.class
sun/tools/tree/InlineNewInstanceExpression.class
sun/tools/tree/CodeContext.class
sun/tools/tree/AssignShiftRightExpression.class
sun/tools/tree/UnsignedShiftRightExpression.class
sun/tools/tree/AssignBitAndExpression.class
sun/tools/tree/ShiftLeftExpression.class
sun/tools/tree/CatchStatement.class
sun/tools/tree/IntExpression.class
sun/tools/tree/TypeExpression.class
sun/tools/tree/CommaExpression.class
sun/tools/tree/
      AssignUnsignedShiftRightExpression.class
sun/tools/tree/ExprExpression.class
sun/tools/tree/AssignRemainderExpression.class
sun/tools/tree/ByteExpression.class
sun/tools/tree/BinaryAssignExpression.class
sun/tools/tree/DoStatement.class
sun/tools/tree/DeclarationStatement.class
sun/tools/tree/MultiplyExpression.class
sun/tools/tree/InlineReturnStatement.class
sun/tools/tree/BitXorExpression.class
sun/tools/tree/BinaryCompareExpression.class
sun/tools/tree/BinaryShiftExpression.class
sun/tools/tree/CheckContext.class
sun/tools/tree/PreIncExpression.class
sun/tools/tree/GreaterOrEqualExpression.class
sun/tools/tree/FieldExpression.class
sun/tools/tree/OrExpression.class
sun/tools/tree/BinaryLogicalExpression.class
sun/tools/tree/NegativeExpression.class
sun/tools/tree/LengthExpression.class
sun/tools/asm/
sun/tools/asm/Assembler.class
sun/tools/asm/Instruction.class
sun/tools/asm/LocalVariable.class
sun/tools/asm/ArrayData.class
sun/tools/asm/LocalVariableTable.class
sun/tools/asm/SwitchDataEnumeration.class
sun/tools/asm/ConstantPool.class
sun/tools/asm/ConstantPoolData.class
sun/tools/asm/NameAndTypeConstantData.class
sun/tools/asm/NumberConstantData.class
sun/tools/asm/FieldConstantData.class
sun/tools/asm/TryData.class
sun/tools/asm/Label.class
sun/tools/asm/SwitchData.class
sun/tools/asm/CatchData.class
sun/tools/asm/StringExpressionConstantData.class
sun/tools/asm/NameAndTypeData.class
sun/tools/asm/StringConstantData.class

sun/tools/asm/ClassConstantData.class
sun/tools/ttydebug/
sun/tools/ttydebug/TTY.class
sun/tools/javadoc/
sun/tools/javadoc/Main.class
sun/tools/javadoc/DocumentationGenerator.class
sun/tools/javadoc/
      HTMLDocumentationGenerator.class
sun/tools/javadoc/
      MIFDocumentationGenerator.class
sun/tools/javadoc/MIFPrintStream.class
sun/net/
sun/net/MulticastSocket.class
sun/net/URLCanonicalizer.class
sun/net/NetworkClient.class
sun/net/NetworkServer.class
sun/net/ProgressData.class
sun/net/ProgressEntry.class
sun/net/TelnetInputStream.class
sun/net/TelnetProtocolException.class
sun/net/TelnetOutputStream.class
sun/net/TransferProtocolClient.class
sun/net/ftp/
sun/net/ftp/FtpInputStream.class
sun/net/ftp/FtpClient.class
sun/net/ftp/FtpLoginException.class
sun/net/ftp/FtpProtocolException.class
sun/net/ftp/IftpClient.class
sun/net/nntp/
sun/net/nntp/NewsgroupInfo.class
sun/net/nntp/NntpClient.class
sun/net/nntp/UnknownNewsgroupException.class
sun/net/nntp/NntpProtocolException.class
sun/net/nntp/NntpInputStream.class
sun/net/smtp/
sun/net/smtp/SmtpPrintStream.class
sun/net/smtp/SmtpClient.class
sun/net/smtp/SmtpProtocolException.class
sun/net/www/
sun/net/www/auth/
sun/net/www/auth/Authenticator.class
sun/net/www/auth/basic.class
sun/net/www/content/
sun/net/www/content/text/
sun/net/www/content/text/Generic.class
sun/net/www/content/text/plain.class
sun/net/www/content/image/
sun/net/www/content/image/gif.class
sun/net/www/content/image/jpeg.class
sun/net/www/content/image/x_xbitmap.class
sun/net/www/content/image/x_xpixmap.class
sun/net/www/FormatException.class
sun/net/www/MessageHeader.class
sun/net/www/MeteredStream.class
sun/net/www/ProgressReport.class
sun/net/www/MimeEntry.class
sun/net/www/MimeLauncher.class
sun/net/www/MimeTable.class
sun/net/www/URLConnection.class

sun/net/www/UnknownContentException.class
sun/net/www/UnknownContentHandler.class
sun/net/www/protocol/
sun/net/www/protocol/file/
sun/net/www/protocol/file/Handler.class
sun/net/www/protocol/file/FileURLConnection.class
sun/net/www/protocol/http/
sun/net/www/protocol/http/Handler.class
sun/net/www/protocol/http/HttpURLConnection.class
sun/net/www/protocol/http/
      HttpPostBufferStream.class
sun/net/www/protocol/doc/
sun/net/www/protocol/doc/Handler.class
sun/net/www/protocol/verbatim/
sun/net/www/protocol/verbatim/Handler.class
sun/net/www/protocol/verbatim/
      VerbatimConnection.class
sun/net/www/protocol/gopher/
sun/net/www/protocol/gopher/GopherClient.class
sun/net/www/protocol/gopher/
      GopherInputStream.class
sun/net/www/http/
sun/net/www/http/
      UnauthorizedHttpRequestException.class
sun/net/www/http/HttpClient.class
sun/net/www/http/AuthenticationInfo.class
sun/awt/
sun/awt/HorizBagLayout.class
sun/awt/VerticalBagLayout.class
sun/awt/VariableGridLayout.class
sun/awt/FocusingTextField.class
sun/awt/win32/
sun/awt/win32/MToolkit.class
sun/awt/win32/MMenuBarPeer.class
sun/awt/win32/MButtonPeer.class
sun/awt/win32/Win32Image.class
sun/awt/win32/MScrollbarPeer.class
sun/awt/win32/MDialogPeer.class
sun/awt/win32/MCheckboxMenuItemPeer.class
sun/awt/win32/Win32Graphics.class
sun/awt/win32/MListPeer.class
sun/awt/win32/MWindowPeer.class
sun/awt/win32/MMenuItemPeer.class
sun/awt/win32/ModalThread.class
sun/awt/win32/MCanvasPeer.class
sun/awt/win32/MFileDialogPeer.class
sun/awt/win32/MTextAreaPeer.class
sun/awt/win32/MPanelPeer.class
sun/awt/win32/MComponentPeer.class
sun/awt/win32/MCheckboxPeer.class
sun/awt/win32/MLabelPeer.class
sun/awt/win32/Win32FontMetrics.class
sun/awt/win32/MFramePeer.class
sun/awt/win32/MMenuPeer.class
sun/awt/win32/MChoicePeer.class
sun/awt/win32/MTextFieldPeer.class
sun/awt/win32/Win32PrintJob.class
sun/awt/image/
sun/awt/image/URLImageSource.class

sun/awt/image/ImageWatched.class
sun/awt/image/InputStreamImageSource.class
sun/awt/image/ConsumerQueue.class
sun/awt/image/ImageDecoder.class
sun/awt/image/ImageRepresentation.class
sun/awt/image/ImageInfoGrabber.class
sun/awt/image/XbmImageDecoder.class
sun/awt/image/GifImageDecoder.class
sun/awt/image/ImageFetcher.class
sun/awt/image/PixelStore.class
sun/awt/image/JPEGImageDecoder.class
sun/awt/image/PixelStore8.class
sun/awt/image/ImageFetchable.class
sun/awt/image/OffScreenImageSource.class
sun/awt/image/PixelStore32.class
sun/awt/image/ImageFormatException.class
sun/awt/image/FileImageSource.class
sun/awt/image/Image.class
sun/awt/UpdateClient.class
sun/awt/ScreenUpdaterEntry.class
sun/awt/ScreenUpdater.class
sun/misc/
sun/misc/Ref.class
sun/misc/MessageUtils.class
sun/misc/Cache.class
sun/misc/CacheEntry.class
sun/misc/CacheEnumerator.class
sun/misc/CEFormatException.class
sun/misc/CEStreamExhausted.class
sun/misc/CRC16.class
sun/misc/CharacterDecoder.class
sun/misc/BASE64Decoder.class
sun/misc/UCDecoder.class
sun/misc/UUDecoder.class
sun/misc/CharacterEncoder.class
sun/misc/BASE64Encoder.class
sun/misc/HexDumpEncoder.class
sun/misc/UCEncoder.class
sun/misc/UUEncoder.class
sun/misc/Timeable.class
sun/misc/TimerTickThread.class
sun/misc/Timer.class
sun/misc/TimerThread.class
sun/misc/ConditionLock.class
sun/misc/Lock.class
sun/audio/
sun/audio/AudioDataStream.class
sun/audio/AudioData.class
sun/audio/AudioDevice.class
sun/audio/AudioPlayer.class
sun/audio/AudioStream.class
sun/audio/NativeAudioStream.class
sun/audio/InvalidAudioFormatException.class
sun/audio/AudioTranslatorStream.class
sun/audio/AudioStreamSequence.class
sun/audio/ContinuousAudioDataStream.class
sun/applet/
sun/applet/StdAppletViewerFactory.class
sun/applet/TextFrame.class

sun/applet/AppletViewerFactory.class
sun/applet/AppletViewer.class
sun/applet/AppletCopyright.class
sun/applet/AppletAudioClip.class
sun/applet/AppletSecurity.class
sun/applet/AppletThreadGroup.class
sun/applet/AppletClassLoader.class
sun/applet/AppletPanel.class
sun/applet/AppletViewerPanel.class
sun/applet/AppletProps.class
sun/applet/AppletSecurityException.class
sun/applet/AppletZipClassLoader.class

Common Abbreviations

AC	access control
ACK	acknowledge
ANSI	American National Standards Institute
ASCII	American Standards Code for Information Interchange
ATM	asynchronous transfer mode
BCC	blind carbon copy
BCD	binary coded decimal
BIOS	basic input/output system
B-ISDN	broadband ISDN
BMP	bitmapped
BNC	British Naval Connector
BPS	bits per second
CAN	concentrated area network
CCITT	International Telegraph and Telephone Consultative Committee
CD-ROM	compact disk - read-only memory
CGI	common gateway interface
CGM	computer graphics metafile
CIF	common interface format
CMOS	complementary MOS
CPU	central processing unit
CRC	cyclic redundancy check
CRT	cathode ray tube
CSMA	carrier sense multiple access
CSMA/CD	CSMA with collision detection
DA	destination address
DAC	digital-to-analogue converter
DARPA	Defense Advanced Research Projects Agency
DBF	NetBEUI frame
DC	direct current
DHCP	dynamic host configuration program
DLC	data-link control
DLL	dynamic link library
DNS	domain name server
DOS	disk operating system
DRAM	dynamic RAM
EaStMAN	Edinburgh/Stirling MAN
EBCDIC	Extended Binary-Coded Decimal Interchange Code
EIA	Electrical Industries Association
ENQ	enquiry

EOT	end of transmission
ETB	end of transmitted block
ETX	end of text
FC	frame control
FCS	frame check sequence
FDDI	fibre distributed data interface
FDX	full duplex
FTP	file transfer protocol
GIF	graphics interface format
GUI	graphical user interface
HDLC	high-level data link control
HDX	half duplex
HTML	hypertext mark-up language
HTTP	hypertext transfer protocol
Hz	Hertz
IA5	international alphabet no. 5
IAB	internet advisory board
IAP	internet access provider
ICMP	Internet Control Message Protocol
ICP	internet connectivity provider
IEEE	Institute of Electrical and Electronic Engineers
IP	internet protocol
IPP	internet presence provider
IPX	internet packet exchange
ISDN	integrated services digital network
ISO	International Standards Organisation
ISP	internet service provider
ITU	International Telecommunications Union
JANET	joint academic network
JISC	Joint Information Systems Committee
JPEG	Joint Photographic Expert Group
LAN	local area network
LLC	logical link control
MAC	media access control
MAN	metropolitan area network
MIME	multi-purpose internet mail extension
MODEM	modulation/demodulator
NAK	negative acknowledge
NDIS	network device interface standard
NETBEUI	NetBIOS extended user interface
NIC	network interface card
NRZI	non-return to zero with inversion
NCSA	National Center for Supercomputer Applications
OSI	open systems interconnection
PC	personal computer
PING	packet internet gopher
PPP	point-to-point protocol

PSTN	public-switched telephone network
REJ	reject
RFC	request for comment
RGB	red, green and blue
RTF	rich text format
SHEFC	Scottish Higher Education Funding Council
SMDS	switched multi-bit data stream
SMTP	simple message transport protocol
SPX	sequenced packet exchange
STP	shielded twisted-pair
TCP	transmission control protocol
TDM	time-division multiplexing
TIF	tagged input file
URI	universal resource identifier
URL	uniform resource locator
UTP	unshielded twisted-pair
WAN	wide area network
WIMPs	windows, icons, menus and pointers
WINS	windows internet name service
WINSOCK	windows sockets
WWW	World Wide Web

Index

MHS, 66
Microprocessor, 155
Microsoft, 59, 66, 67, 93–96, 157, 219,
220, 224, 226, 230
Microsoft LAN, 224
Microsoft Windows, 219, 220
Military, 44
MIME, 54, 64, 67, 75, 76, 78–83, 85, 112,
115, 116, 150
base64, 82
boundary name, 78, 85
content-transfer-encoding, 81
content-type, 78
example, 78, 79, 80, 81
version, 76, 112
MIT, 102
Modem connection, 3, 97
Modems, 3, 224
Motion video, 64, 102
Motorola, 155
MOV, 88
MPEG, 79–81, 88, 102, 150
MS Mail, 67
Multimedia, 148, 149
Multiplexing, 51
Multiplexing/demultiplexing, 51
Multiplication, 163
Multitasking, 155

—N—

Napier, 59, 78
EECE department, 44, 54, 57, 58, 61,
77, 104, 136, 204, 226
NCSA, 87, 93
NDIS, 224, 226
NetBEUI, 222, 224, 225, 229, 236
Netscape, 93, 94, 157, 179
Netstat, 58
Network, 5, 9, 16, 19, 27, 42, 66, 97, 152,
176, 177, 222, 224, 225, 226, 231, 232
Network addresses, 43
Network Information Centre, 42
Network layer, 12, 14, 30, 33, 51, 220,
229
Network management, 27, 152
Network topologies, 9
Network traffic, 22, 111, 152
Network transport protocol, 66
NFS, 57, 236
NIC, 42, 224
Novell NetWare, 220, 222, 235
NSCA, 93

Nslookup, 57, 61
NT, 93, 94, 180, 183, 219–236
NTE, 4
N-type, 23, 24, 25, 31

—O—

Operating system, 14, 94, 106, 139, 155,
219–224, 235
Ordered, 79, 122, 123
Organization, 126
OS/2, 224
OSI, 4, 5, 6, 12, 16, 20, 30, 33, 34, 51, 66,
124, 154

—P—

Packet, 5, 12–14, 36, 50, 55, 58, 59, 60,
106, 220, 225
Packet filters, 106, 108
Paragraph, 120
Parallel, 79
Pascal, 139, 155, 178, 179
PC, 56, 58, 65, 67, 100, 106, 155, 179,
180, 182, 219, 220
Pentium, 155
Phone, 43
Physical, 5, 16, 30
Physical layer, 5, 6, 12
Ping, 34, 37, 47, 54, 55, 61
Pixels, 131, 132, 141, 142, 174, 182
PKZIP, 85
Plain text, 105
Polygons, 208
Port number, 51–53
Postal service, 2, 63
Postscript, 88
Precedence, 165, 166, 189
Presentation, 5, 6, 51, 92, 94, 139
Presentation layer, 5, 6
Print servers, 219
Printable, 81
Priority, 27, 36, 50, 166
Proxy, 110, 111, 114, 115, 117
PS, 88
PSTN, 3
Public switched telecommunications net-
work, *see* PSTN
Public telephone, 3, 15, 34, 43
Public telephone network, 15, 97

—R—

Real-time, 27, 65, 83
Red, 126, 127, 135, 136, 207
Redundancy, 21, 22
Relationship operator, 163
Repeater, 12, 31
Repeaters, 12
Resolution, 236
RFC 821, 66, 68, 74, 84
RFC 822, 66, 72, 73, 74, 76, 77, 79, 84, 112
RG-50, 23, 25
RGB, 126
Ring network, 9–11, 16, 27, 33, 152
RIP, 14
RJ-45, 13, 24, 25, 31
Routers, 12, 14
Routing protocols
    OSPF, 14
    BGP, 14
    EGP, 14
    RIP, 14
RS-232, 176, 177, 224

—S—

Sampling, 79
Sampling rate, 79
Search, 34, 89, 90, 95, 96, 97, 101, 103
Section header, 119
Segment, 12, 23–27, 33, 39, 52–55, 222
Sequence number, 38, 52, 53
Serial, 56
Server, 57, 73, 115, 233, 234
Server name, 99, 136
Servers, 27, 43, 57, 70, 87, 88, 91, 96, 98, 100, 101, 103, 106, 109, 111, 112, 219, 222, 226, 230–232, 235
Session layer, 6
SMA, 24, 30, 31
SMDS, 59
SMTP, 52, 54, 64, 66–75, 83–86, 185
    example transmission, 73
SMTP responses, 71
SMTP transfer, 71, 86
SMTP.MIME, 67
SNA DLC, 222
SNMP, 52
Socket number, 51, 52
Sony, 43
Sound, 63, 88, 93, 112, 113, 204, 209, 218
Source, 11, 13, 14, 19, 21, 35, 36, 38, 49, 51, 52, 53, 64, 65, 80, 88–91, 107, 120, 184
Source address, 107
Speech, 3, 27, 63, 64, 83
SPX, 15, 152, 220, 222, 224, 229, 236
SPX/IPX, 15, 152, 220, 224, 229
ST connector, 24
Standards, 4, 21, 125, 126, 153
Star network, 9, 10, 16
Start delimiter, 21
Stateless protocol, 100, 109
Statement block, 168, 169, 192, 193
Statements, 162
Static, 158, 187, 188, 191
Statments
    logical, 167
Stop bit, 154
Subnet, 33, 41–45, 226
Subnet masks, 42
Sun Microsystems, 155, 180
Synchronized, 188

—T—

Tables, 58, 141
TCP, 1, 6, 15, 19, 33, 34, 36, 38, 39, 47–55, 57, 60, 61, 64, 68, 69, 70, 72, 106, 109, 110, 115, 126, 152, 153, 179, 219, 220, 222, 224–227, 229, 230, 236
    header format, 52, 53
    Protocol Data Unit, 52
TCP/IP, 1, 15, 19, 33, 34, 36, 38, 39, 47–49, 53, 54, 55, 57, 60, 61, 64, 68, 106, 126, 152, 153, 179, 219, 220, 222, 224–227, 229, 230, 236
    Class A, 42
    Class B, 40, 42
    Class C, 40, 42
    ports and sockets, 49, 52
TCP/IP gateway, 34, 39
TCP/IP implementation, 38
TCP/IP internets, 38
TCP/IP version number, 36
TD, 141–143
TDI, 224, 229
Telephone, 3, 7, 15, 34, 43, 47, 63, 64, 232
Telephone number, 43, 232
Television, 217
Telnet, 34, 48, 49, 52, 54, 57, 61, 99, 100, 185, 220, 225, 230
Text, 88, 213
Text blink, 119